REVERSING
THE ODDS

REVERSING THE ODDS

Improving Outcomes for Babies in the Child Welfare System

by

Sheryl Dicker, J.D.
Department of Pediatrics
The Children's Hospital at Montefiore Medical Center
Albert Einstein College of Medicine
Bronx, New York

·P A U L·H·
BROOKES
PUBLISHING CO.®

Baltimore • London • Sydney

Paul H. Brookes Publishing Co.
Post Office Box 10624
Baltimore, Maryland 21285-0624
USA

www.brookespublishing.com

Typeset by Spearhead Global, Inc., Bear, Delaware.
Manufactured in the United States of America by
Versa Press, Inc., East Peoria, Illinois.

The individuals described in this book are composites, pseudonyms, or fictional accounts based on actual experiences. Individuals' names have been changed and identifying details have been altered to protect confidentiality.

Library of Congress Cataloging-in-Publication Data

Dicker, Sheryl.
    Reversing the odds : improving outcomes for babies in the child welfare
system / by Sheryl Dicker.
        p.   cm.
    Includes bibliographical references and index.
    ISBN-13: 978-1-55766-961-2 (pbk.)
    ISBN-10: 1-55766-961-9 (pbk.)
    1. Child welfare—United States.   2. Child development—United States.   3. Social service—
United States.   4. Early childhood education—United States.   5. Children—Services for—
United States.   I. Title.

    HV741.D53 2009
    362.7083'20973—dc22   2009010895

British Library Cataloguing in Publication data are available from the British Library.

2013   2012   2011   2010   2009

10   9   8   7   6   5   4   3   1

Contents

IV   Conclusion

About the Author

Sheryl Dicker, J.D., has worked for more than three decades on behalf of children challenged by poverty and disability. During those years, she was a legal services attorney and manager, a foundation project director, a state official, and a member of the faculty at a medical school. In those capacities, she drafted legislation, regulations, and court rules; litigated class action lawsuits; wrote dozens of publications; developed projects to improve the lives of poor children; served on national and state commissions, and taught thousands of professionals about the rights of children confronted by the child welfare and disability systems, including pediatricians, judges, and attorneys.

After working as a law student on emerging disability cases, Ms. Dicker began her career as a legal services lawyer in Philadelphia. Those first professional experiences paved the way for her career addressing concerns related to disability, poverty, and child welfare. She would later serve as a managing attorney of the American Bar Association Commission on the Mentally Disabled's Pennsylvania Advocacy Project as well as the founder and director of the Arkansas Developmental Disabilities Law Project. In 1983, Ms. Dicker was appointed by then Gov. Bill Clinton as General Counsel of the Arkansas Department of Human Services. President Clinton appointed her to the President's Committee on Mental Retardation (PCMR) in 1999.

In 1991, Ms. Dicker began her 16-year tenure as the executive director of the New York Permanent Judicial Commission on Justice for Children, the nation's first children's commission based in the judiciary. New York's Chief Judge Judith Kaye chairs the Commission, and its membership is composed of judges, lawyers, pediatricians, psychologists, advocates, and policy experts. Under Ms. Dicker's stewardship, the Commission achieved major reforms including passing New York's Early Intervention laws, establishing the nation's first statewide system of children's centers in the courts, spearheading implementation of the federal Court Improvement Project to improve child welfare proceedings, and developing three projects (health, education, and infants) to ensure the healthy development of children in foster care.

In 2003, Ms. Dicker was selected as a Harris Mid-Career Leader for the 21st Century, ZERO-TO-THREE Fellow. Ms. Dicker served as a senior advisor at the National Center on Children in Poverty. In 2008, she joined the faculty of the department of pediatrics at The Children's Hospital at Montefiore Medical Center, Albert Einstein College of Medicine, Bronx, New York.

Ms. Dicker has written extensively about children in the child welfare and disability systems. In addition to dozens of publications on the health and developmental needs of children in foster care, she is also the editor of *Stepping Stones: Successful Advocacy for Children* (Foundation for Child Development, 1990).

Foreword

This book signals a warning for all who care about America's youngest children. It focuses on more than 250,000 babies—infants and toddlers under age 3—who have been abused or neglected. More than 100,000 of these babies will find themselves in the foster care system, often lacking a loving, consistent caregiver who is vital for early literacy and bright futures. These are not at-risk children; they are children who have already been harmed. The majority of these babies were born low birth weight or premature and have already been exposed to violence and toxic substances such as drugs or alcohol. Many of these babies have chronic medical problems or developmental delays. If those early life problems—not just risks—are left unaddressed, these children are likely to drop out of school, become teen parents or homeless, or become enmeshed in the criminal justice system.

This book explores the challenge of reversing those odds by ensuring the healthy development of these youngest children in the child welfare system. It is a hopeful, not a discouraging, work. It is an advocacy book, explaining how to create reform. Not only does this book summarize the scientific research on the importance of early relationships, early literacy, effective health care, and early intervention services, it provides an explanation of the laws that can implement this research. It even includes the first review of the newest law passed by Congress concerning children in the child welfare system, Fostering Connections to Success and Increasing Adoptions Act of 2008 (PL 110-351). Half of this book is devoted to case studies of real efforts that illustrate how to use the research and the law to improve the lives of very young children in the child welfare system. These step-by-step stories will enable others to apply this book's lessons, particularly its major lesson of the importance of collaboration between those working inside and outside of government.

Unique among books concerned with young children found in child welfare systems, this volume highlights the importance of the courts. For many, the critical role of our nation's juvenile and family courts in the lives of these children will be new information. Tapping the power of the judicial system is an important tool because courts make critical decisions concerning children in the child welfare system. Using this tool can identify and ensure receipt of important early education and other services for these children.

From personal experience, I know that readers could not find a better guide for the challenges posed by this book than Sheryl Dicker. Sheryl and I first met 30 years ago when she provided legal assistance to my family, helping secure placement in a general education kindergarten class for our son, rather than in a separate school solely for children considered "orthopedically handicapped." After my son's placement, Sheryl and I worked together to better ensure that all children with physical disabilities had access to regular public schools in Little Rock, Arkansas. Sheryl and I also were colleagues in the administration of Governor Bill Clinton, focusing on issues ranging from child welfare to developmental disabilities. When I entered the White House to direct President Clinton's domestic policy council, Sheryl and I met often to study and debate matters related to the child welfare, disability, early childhood, and court systems. And when I became President of Reading Is Fundamental, Sheryl and I worked together to bring literacy programs into the courts.

This book will be an important addition to the libraries of educators, health care providers, child welfare professionals, judges, advocates, and parents. By applying its lessons, all of us can open the door to improving the chances of all of America's children—including those in the child welfare system—to lead full lives as readers and contributors to society.

Carol H. Rasco
President
Reading Is Fundamental (RIF)
Washington, DC

REFERENCES

Fostering Connections to Success and Increasing Adoptions Act of 2008 (PL 110-351), 42 U.S.C. Sec. 104 §§ *et seq.*

Acknowledgments

This book would not have been written without the foresight of Jessica Allan, former Senior Acquisitions Editor at Paul H. Brookes Publishing Co. For more than 5 years, Jessica arranged to meet me almost every time I spoke at a national conference in an effort to persuade me to write a book. Slowly, Jessica shepherded me through the outline and book proposal. Fortunately, the acceptance process occurred before she left Brookes. Her successor, Sarah Shepke, has continued to be a supportive and incisive editor, fully committed to this project. Leslie Eckard, Senior Production Editor, also has greatly enhanced this volume by her skilled copyediting and consistent support. I thank them all for their enormous help.

I am also grateful to the many talents of Davida Marion, who assisted in the research and editing of this book. Davida's persistence and creative skills helped to shape this volume and I expect to read her innovative books in the future. Two others had an invisible but strong influence on this book. Elysa Gordon was my writing partner for almost a decade, but due to personal circumstances, she was unable to co-author this book. Nevertheless, her insights permeate this volume. In addition, Chief Judge Judith Kaye of New York, Chair of the New York Permanent Judicial Commission on Justice for Children, afforded me an opportunity as the Commission's executive director to explore ways to reverse the odds for babies in the child welfare system. I am grateful for her trust as well as for the lessons she taught me about the necessity for leadership to create lasting reform.

Many people granted me interviews, shared materials, or reviewed all or parts of this book. I am extremely indebted to those generous individuals including Julia Alexander, Trista Borra, Jackie Bouissant, Wendy Breitner, Susan Chinitz, Terri Combs-Orne, Rob Conlon, Joan Cooney, Carole Cornelius, Don Crary, Azra Farrell, Heather Forkey, Selina Higgins, Beverly Jones, Joseph Kuna, Alexandra Lowe, Denise Patterson, Lourdes Rosado, Amy Rossi, Susan Scott,

Eldon Schulz, Judith Silver, Sheila Smith, Nancy Travers, and Margaret Zukowski.

Finally, I am indebted to my husband, Norman H. Stein, for his unwavering support for this project. Norman read every word of this book and used his skilled editing pen on many of its pages. I am grateful for his faith in this book and his faith in me.

To my children, Max and Becky

Introduction

JENNY'S STORY

In the winter of 1992, Jenny was born 1 month early to a 39-year-old mother who abused substances. At birth, Jenny weighed just a little over 4 pounds and was found to be prenatally exposed to crack cocaine. She had trouble both breathing and feeding and cried with a high-pitched screech for weeks after birth. Her mother's fourth child, Jenny had one brother who was almost 20 and two other siblings who were school-age. All her siblings had spent time in the foster care system. Her oldest brother was in prison at the time of her birth and her two other siblings were living with her grandmother, a woman in her 50s.

Jenny's mother never asked to see her after birth and left the hospital a day after delivery. Jenny remained in the hospital for several weeks so that she could gain sufficient weight and have her breathing stabilized. She was discharged to New York City's Special Services for Children (SSC), the city child welfare agency. The caseworker immediately contacted her grandmother—who never visited Jenny in the hospital—and requested that she care for Jenny as another kinship foster child along with the other two grandchildren. The grandmother agreed and Jenny was brought to her grandmother's house in the Bronx.

For the next few months, Jenny remained at her grandmother's house. Her grandmother received a kinship foster care stipend, the standard payment for any foster child, and a Medicaid card. She struggled with Jenny's incessant crying, feeding, and sleeping problems. Almost every week, she took Jenny to the emergency room because of the infant's breathing difficulties. Jenny spent several days in the hospital during those first few months of life in order to stabilize her breathing. Her grandmother and the hospital staff noticed that Jenny's growth rate was slow, as well. The SSC caseworker visited once over the first few months, but offered no tangible assistance except a promise to try to secure a higher foster care stipend rate due to Jenny's health problems.

The burden on the grandmother was great. Finally, overwhelmed and never receiving the higher stipend or any other assistance, she called the caseworker to say she could no longer care for Jenny. The caseworker came to the grandmother's home and, after some discussion, placed Jenny in the children's shelter and then in another foster home—this one run by strangers. The second placement did not last long—Jenny became sick within days and had to be rushed to the hospital to address her breathing difficulties. When she returned to the foster home, the problems of crying, feeding, sleeping, and breathing persisted, and the foster parent requested Jenny's removal. At 9 months old, Jenny was sent to her third home. This time the caseworker secured the higher stipend and placed Jenny in a home with a very experienced foster mother, a woman in her 50s.

Jenny's new home had five other children of varying ages. Several had special needs for which higher stipends were provided. The foster mother ran a tight ship with a very structured environment; sleeping and eating times were strictly enforced. Jenny's sleeping and eating improved with this structure but her breathing problems persisted. The foster mother, Mrs. M., was undeterred by the breathing problems and regularly brought Jenny to the hospital clinic or, if needed, to the hospital emergency room. So Jenny remained at Mrs. M.'s home. She reached every developmental milestone late—she did not walk until age 2, did not begin to talk until she was almost 3, continued to have speech difficulties, and remained very small for her age. Jenny never attended an early childhood education program.

After Jenny left the hospital, the Family Court had entered an order at SSC's request to place her in foster care. Jenny's mother was not present at that hearing or any subsequent hearings. The judge entered the standard order in New York in 1992 for a finding of infant exposure to drugs, requiring drug treatment for the mother and granting her visitation with the child every other week in the SSC office. Almost a year later, the court held its next hearing, a fact-finding hearing to determine if Jenny had been abused or neglected. Without opposition, the judge entered an order finding Jenny neglected because she was both drug-exposed at birth and abandoned at the hospital. A few months later, a dispositional order formally placing Jenny in foster care was entered, and it was extended five times over the next 9 years.

While Jenny was living with her grandmother, her mother visited her once. It was a short visit. She did not visit her daughter at the SSC office until Jenny was 1 year old and living with Mrs. M. Her mother brought candy and toys to the visit but it was a short outing. This pattern continued for the next several years—the mother would come to visit a few times a year with toys and gifts. On Jenny's birthday, her grandmother and siblings would also ask for a visit and bring her gifts. She had few other contacts with her family.

The spring after Jenny turned 5, Mrs. M. brought her to the local elementary school for kindergarten registration. She knew the routine from her older foster children and was given an appointment for the kindergarten screening. At the screening, the school staff immediately noticed Jenny's small size and her extreme shyness—she did not speak at all during the interview. The school staff suggested that Jenny was not ready for kindergarten and should return the following year. No recommendation about early childhood education, preschool special education, or any other service was made. Mrs. M. took Jenny home and she remained out of school for another year. The following year, Mrs. M. brought her in again for the kindergarten screening, and she was advised that Jenny was very behind but would be put in an appropriate kindergarten class. Kindergarten and first grade were lost years for Jenny. She sat quietly in her seat, never making contact with the teacher or other students. She did enjoy coloring and drawing, however.

At the beginning of second grade, the teacher noticed that Jenny could not read or write and knew little math—not even how to count. The teacher placed her in the "slow" reading group but not much more attention to her educational delays took place that year. At the beginning of third grade, the teacher became alarmed at how far behind Jenny was compared with the other children and requested an evaluation. This evaluation, performed in the middle of the school year, found Jenny to be functioning cognitively in the mild mental retardation range. At the end of that school year, Jenny was classified as a "handicapped child" and placed in a special education self-contained class. In fourth and fifth grades in the special education class, Jenny slowly began to learn letters and numbers. When challenged, she would sometimes develop breathing problems—now diagnosed as uncontrolled asthma—and exhibited some new behavioral problems such as refusing to do challenging work or having temper tantrums. Counseling was added as a service to her individualized education program (IEP), along with continued special education self-contained classes and speech therapy.

At Mrs. M.'s home, the routine continued. Jenny tried to call her "Mommy," but Mrs. M. was adamant that all the children should call her Mrs. M. Jenny now became upset on the occasions that she saw her mother, her grandmother, or her siblings. She did not understand her situation at all.

When Jenny was 10 years old, a new boy moved into Mrs. M.'s home. He was 12 years old and seemed to befriend Jenny. Jenny enjoyed the attention, but she became confused when he started coming into her bed at night and touching her. When she told Mrs. M., she was silenced and told not to make up stories. The boy's advances persisted until they started upsetting Jenny more and more. She finally became so frightened by his actions that one night she took a knife with her to bed. When he tried to touch her, Jenny stabbed him. They both screamed and Mrs. M. promptly called the police. The police arrested the boy and took the now hysterical Jenny to the hospital. She was placed in are the largest group of children to be reported to our child welfare system and to enter its out-of-home care arm known as foster care. Not only are they the largest group to enter care but also they remain in care and re-enter care at higher rates than older children. An alarming number of these children are prenatally exposed to drugs and alcohol and often are born prematurely or suffer the effects of low birth weight. Given this poor start in life, it is not surprising that they are far more likely than other young children to have serious medical conditions and developmental delays and disabilities. These data are followed by a chapter detailing the history behind the new face of child welfare. It describes the pendulum shifts in child welfare practice over the past 300 years. That history also discusses the birth and development of our nations' juvenile and family courts. This section ends by tracing a child's typical journey through the child welfare and juvenile court systems to give the reader grounding for the next parts of the book.

Section II of the book presents the promise of new research and laws that can reverse the negative odds for children like Jenny. Topics include the new scientific research of early childhood and brain growth that demonstrates the importance of the early months and years of life, the effectiveness of early intervention to prevent or ameliorate developmental delays, and the critical impact of nurturing, consistent caregiving on healthy child development. It details the new child welfare laws that place an emphasis on children's well-being and permanency. To realize the hope of these laws, the research requires a new collaboration among the child welfare system, the courts, and the child development fields.

Section III profiles collaborations that have built on the foundation of the research and the new laws. These partnerships forged with the child welfare system are beginning to change the forecast for young children in the child welfare system and promote their healthy development. In this book, *healthy development* is synonymous with *well-being,* an often misunderstood term. Healthy development means addressing young children's physical, developmental, and emotional needs and securing a permanent, caring, nurturing family. These components are intertwined. Children need parents with the capacity to observe their needs over time, to address those needs, and to advocate for and consent to services. This section contains four chapters, each highlighting professionals—judges and lawyers, pediatricians and other health care providers, and early interventionists—who have created links with the child welfare system to institutionalize multidisciplinary collaborations that promote the healthy development of very young children. Each chapter in this section begins with a study of an individual case in which a child's healthy development was augmented as well as a detailed examination of the process of creating portals for change.

Section IV also devotes a chapter calling for the creation of a new portal for healthy development—the early childhood education system. That system, particularly Early Head Start and Head Start—provides enormous promise for young children in the child welfare system. It is a comprehensive program that can address all aspects of children's healthy development including ensuring school readiness, supporting and modeling strong relationships, and serving as an ideal site for visitation.

The book concludes with a story of three siblings who entered the child welfare system in 2004. These children live in a county with strong collaborations among the child welfare, court, health care, early intervention, and early childhood education systems. The children's journey through the child welfare system resulted in their healthy development and family permanency. Their example illustrates the lessons of this book and what is truly possible.

At its heart, this is a book about the contours of change. It builds on my work of trying to improve the lives of children struggling with poverty and disability. My first book, *Stepping Stones: Successful Advocacy for Children* (Foundation for Child Development, 1990), contains five case studies of effective child advocacy. In each study, advocates not only highlighted major policy problems but also developed actual solutions to those problems. They used a multistrategic approach to place the given issue on the radar, but their solutions only became reality when they forged successful, long-term partnerships with officials working inside government. To be truly effective, these advocacy efforts had to be long lasting and self-effectuating, either by parents able to gain access to the reform or for the reform itself to have built-in perpetuating mechanisms.

One of the heartbreaks of that book was my inability to find any successful advocacy efforts involving the child welfare system. This deficiency underscores the greatest problem in the child welfare system—the lack of an adult who focuses on a given child throughout childhood while observing the child's development over time, identifying problems, seeking effective intervention, and advocating on the child's behalf. In short, this individual would maintain what all Americans assume are the qualifications of an *adequate* (not *excellent* and not *best*) parent.

The discovery that—unlike children with even the most severe disabilities—children in the child welfare system were the most likely to be forgotten and to have their healthy development ignored shaped much of my work for the last 16 years. In 1991, I became the executive director of a new national entity, a children's commission based in the judiciary and founded and chaired by New York's Chief Judge. The commission, recognizing the growing numbers of very young children involved in our court system—not just in child welfare cases but in custody, support, and visitation, too—chose to focus its energies on the youngest children whose lives and life chances are affected by the court system. Through this work, I discovered the demographic and early childhood research and the reality of life for young children in the child welfare system. I also was able to perform court-based experiments, as discussed in Chapter 6, to learn more about efforts to promote the physical, developmental, and emotional well-being of these children and their prospects for growing up in a caring, nurturing family—a "forever family."

This book is the outgrowth of that many-year journey. It is written to inspire and galvanize professionals—judges, lawyers, child welfare professionals, pediatricians and other health care workers, early interventionists, early childhood mental health specialists, and early childhood educators—to focus their practice on improving the lives of young children in the child welfare system. But, the book aims for more: to put young children in the child welfare system on the public radar screen and to support the public recognition that almost every time a child dies in foster care, that child is very young and often has serious medical problems or disabilities. This often-preventable pattern requires attention from the highest public officials and communities. It requires public policy and practice changes as well as redeployment of resources. But, perhaps most of all, it requires a change in public perception. My aim is to help the public recognize that because many children in our nation's child welfare system are very young and have disabilities, they cannot advocate for themselves and need the help of caring and committed adults. Many are adoptable, with a profile that is not much different from the children Americans cross oceans to adopt. If both our government and the public put these children on the radar screen, we can promote the healthy development of all young children in our nation's child welfare system. This is our imperative: We must reverse the odds and improve outcomes for babies in the child welfare system.

I

Sounding the Alarm

Background and Overview

1

Why the Odds Must Be Reversed for Young Children in the Child Welfare System

---

DEANA'S STORY

Deana was born 3 weeks early, and she weighed less than 4 pounds. She tested positive for cocaine. Her mother admitted to using both crack and alcohol during her pregnancy. Following policy, the hospital reported Deana's case to the child abuse hotline. The case was screened, but no further investigation occurred. After gaining sufficient weight, Deana was discharged from the hospital with her mother. The hospital staff scheduled several well-child visits in their clinic for Deana.

Deana missed the first and second-month visit, but she was brought to the clinic when she was 4 months old. The clinic staff noticed Deana's mother's intoxication as well as Deana's slow growth. The clinic called the hotline, and a child protective investigation substantiated the report. Child protective services (CPS) offered the mother in-home preventive services composed of a monthly caseworker visit. Deana was 7 months old at the first visit. Alarmed by the mother's drug and alcohol abuse, the caseworker decided that the infant was at imminent risk of harm and removed her from the home and placed her in foster care. A petition was filed with the court, and the mother appeared in court the next day. She begged for Deana's return and promised to attend drug treatment. She agreed to participate in the drug treatment court, which is a specialized court that monitors adherence to treatment for people who abuse substances.

During the next 8 months, Deana's mother participated in drug treatment and the drug treatment court. She left Deana with her mother or sister during the day. At times, she did not attend treatment or failed urine tests, but the judge did not order Deana to be removed from the home and continued to focus on the mother's ability to maintain sobriety. Neither the judge nor anyone at court or the substance abuse program saw Deana during these months.

One morning, when Deana was 18 months old, her mother noticed she was not breathing. Her mother's screams alerted neighbors, who called the police. Deana was brought to the hospital and was declared dead. A fatality review found that Deana had not seen a physician for more than a year. She was blind in one eye, had very poor muscle tone, and was not able to sit or move on her own. The cause of death was respiratory distress.

MALTREATMENT AND VERY YOUNG CHILDREN

Deana's case is not unique. More than 75% of child fatalities in the United States in 2006 happened to children under the age of 3 years (U.S. Department of Health and Human Services [DHHS], 2008). A special report written in 2006 underscores these numbers, finding that 45% of child fatalities occurred with children even younger—under the age of 1 year. The report finds that very young children are particularly vulnerable because of their "dependency, small size and inability to defend themselves" (Child Welfare Information Gateway, 2006, p. 2). These numbers are almost identical to those of previous years.

Although the fatalities of young children grab the media's attention and shape public policy, they do not tell the full story. Often ignored are the large numbers of infants and toddlers who are maltreated. In 2006, more than a quarter of a million children from birth to 3 years experienced substantiated cases of abuse or neglect and thereby entered the child welfare system (DHHS, 2008). A large percentage of those children were infants (i.e., under the age of 1 year). Indeed, in 2006, more than 100,000 of these children—11.4% of all victims that year—were infants who had been maltreated. Also troubling is that the rate for substantiated maltreatment is highest among these very young children—more than 16% experienced physical or sexual abuse and more than 70% were victims of neglect. More than a quarter of the neglect cases involved failure to provide the basic necessities of life—food, shelter, and medical care—and slightly more than 35% of those victims were infants who were being left alone without adult supervision. These very young children constitute the majority of all medical neglect cases and more than one third of all substantiated neglect cases. These children are most often placed in foster care.

PLACEMENT IN THE FOSTER CARE SYSTEM

The vulnerability of infants makes their experience in the child welfare system quite different from that of older children. They are far more likely to be removed from their homes and placed in the foster care system, which is the out-of-home placement arm of the child welfare system. Almost half of the infants who entered the child welfare system were removed from their homes and placed in foster care after their cases were deemed substantiated abuse and neglect. This is compared with slightly more than 20% of all older children. This reality skews the foster care system and defines the child welfare system in ways rarely noted (Wulczyn & Hislop, 2002). In 2006, infants under the age of 1 year constituted 16%—more than one of every six children—of those admitted to care. The majority of those infants entered in the first 3 months of life never having spent much, if any, time with their biological parents.

More than one third of all children entering foster care in 2006 fell between the ages of birth to 3 years. That same year, 47,536 (DHHS, 2008) children under the age of 1 year (more than half of all substantiated cases of abuse and neglect) entered foster care, the single largest age group. In addition, that same year, another 56,136 children from 1 to 3 years old entered foster care. Thus, in a single year, more than 100,000 very young children were placed into the foster care system away from their biological families.

Not only do infants and toddlers enter foster care at an alarming rate compared with other children but also their experience is quite different. Only 14,081 of the infants who entered foster care in 2005 exited, which left more than 32,000 still in foster care. Research tells us that these children will remain in care almost twice as long as other children. Half of the infants who enter foster care before they are 3 months old will spend at least 31 months in care (Wulczyn & Hislop, 2002), which is longer than the average length of stay of 28.3 months (DHHS, 2008). Indeed, the length of stay is greater than the age of most very young children.

Adoption data, however, tell another piece of the story. Of the children waiting for adoption, one quarter entered foster care in their first year of life, and more than half of all children waiting for adoption entered care before age 5 (DHHS, 2008).

A PROFILE OF VERY YOUNG CHILDREN IN THE CHILD WELFARE SYSTEM

For too long, research on all of the children involved with the child welfare system was nonexistent. The National Survey on Child and Adolescent Well-Being (NSCAW, 1997–2010), funded by the DHHS, is the first national longitudinal study to examine development and behavior patterns of all children under the age of 15 in the child welfare system and their corresponding service use. The study included children in foster care, children at home (children living with biological parents) with an open case receiving services, and children at home with a closed but substantiated case not receiving services. This study provides the first big picture of children involved with the child welfare system.

NSCAW findings indicate that children involved in child welfare services frequently have both mental and physical developmental delays. They tend to have smaller head circumference and decreased height and weight development. Other developmental statistics are also of concern—30% of children younger than the age of 3 in child welfare services were found to be falling significantly behind their peers in cognitive development (Stahmer et al., 2005). Furthermore, 53% of children age 3–24 months were found to be at high risk for developmental delay or neurological disability. The risk of behavioral delay is also high —27% of children 2–3 years of age in the child welfare system, whether in foster care or at home, have been reported by their caregivers as having behavior problems (DHHS, 2008).

Most alarming is the lack of services received by these children to address their developmental or behavioral delays. The study finds that children living with biological parents were the least likely to receive early intervention services, although those services were underused by all groups. The most serious results were found with the youngest children—only 20% of children under the age of 2 years with developmental delays received early intervention services. Children slightly older, 3–5 years, were 2.4 times more likely to use developmental services than the younger group (Zimmer & Panko, 2006).

A PROFILE OF CHILDREN IN FOSTER CARE

Far more long-term research exists for very young children who have been placed in foster care than for children in the child welfare system in general. Not surprisingly, their health, development, and behavior profiles are even more bleak than those children who remained at home within the child welfare system. The research finds that these children are our nation's most vulnerable children (Blatt et al., 1997; Harden, 2007; Silver, DiLorenzo, et al., 1999). Nearly 40% of children in foster care are born premature or low birth weight, which are factors that increase the likelihood of medical problems and developmental delays. The majority of these children were exposed prenatally to substance abuse, including crack cocaine, alcohol, and heroin. A child in foster care moves to different homes an average of three times during placement, further exacerbating risks to his or her healthy development (Pew Commission Report, 2004). Extensive data on the health, educational performance, and caregiving environments of children in foster care can be found in research conducted by academics, policy analysts, and service providers. Several studies confirm that compared with other children living in poverty, children involved with the foster care system are far more likely to have fragile health and disabilities and are far less likely to receive services to address their needs (Harden, 2007; Wulczyn, Barth, Yuan, Harden, & Landsverk, 2005).

In the NSCAW study, children in the child welfare system, whether placed in foster care or the care of relatives, when compared with all other children (including those living in high-risk parent care), are more likely to have physical, learning, and mental health disabilities that limit their daily activities (Kortenkamp & Macomber, 2002). A 2005 study using the same data set, but focusing only on children under age 6, found toddlers and preschoolers to have significant developmental and behavioral needs; however, less than one quarter of those children were receiving services to address those needs (Stahmer et al., 2005).

It is important to note that the data document that children enter the child welfare system already exposed to poverty, substance abuse, and parental neglect and abuse, which can undermine their healthy development (Goerge & Wulczyn, 1998). For many of these children, this exposure starts at birth. Similar to Deana, who was described at the beginning of this chapter, nearly 80% of these children were exposed prenatally to maternal substance use. As many as 40% of these infants are born either prematurely or with a low birth weight (Halfon, Mendonca, & Berkowitz, 1995; Silver, Amster & Haecker, 1999). Deana, for example, was born 3 weeks early and weighed less than 4 pounds.

The risks do not stop there. The data on the well-being of children in the foster care system confirm the disproportionate risks to their healthy development. Of these foster children, one third to one half are reported to have dental decay (Chernoff, Combs-Orme, Risley-Curtiss, & Heisler, 1994; Swire & Kavaler, 1977), and more than half have chronic health problems (Halfon et al., 1995; Silver, DiLorenzo, et al., 1999). These health problems can include serious conditions, such as asthma and elevated blood lead levels (Jaudes & Shapiro, 1999). Furthermore, these children exhibit twice the growth problems found in the general population (Blatt & Simms, 1997; Halfon et al., 1995). In addition, at least half of all young children in foster care placement exhibit developmental delays, which is approximately four to five times the rate found among children in the general population (Blatt, et al., 1997; Chernoff et al., 1994; Hochstadt, Jaudes, Zimo, & Schachter, 1987; Jaudes & Shapiro, 1999; Spiker & Silver, 1999; Takayama, Wolfe, & Coulter, 1998; U.S. General Accounting Office [GAO], 1995).

These delays have been identified more specifically through several programs that evaluate young children in foster care. They note especially elevated rates of motor development delays in 30% of foster care children, as well as language disabilities and delays in as many as 50% of them (Halfon et al., 1995; Hochstadt et al., 1987; Silver, DiLorenzo, et al., 1999). At the same time, studies on the mental health needs of children in foster care suggest that more than half have sufficient risks to warrant referral for psychiatric assessment or therapy (Blatt et al., 1997; Schneiderman, Connors, Fribourg, Gries, & Gonzales, 1998).

These studies reveal that the risks to well-being or healthy development are especially pronounced for infants and toddlers. Children ages birth–3 years had the highest rates of maltreatment (DHHS, 2008). Meanwhile, one third of all infants discharged from foster care reenter the child welfare system (Wulczyn & Hislop, 2002).

In addition, every event in the foster care experience—removal, visitation, placement and placement change, and reunification or adoption—has implications for emotional development and well-being (Rosenfeld et al., 1997). Research has found that a child's earliest experiences can have biochemical consequences in his or her developing brain (Shonkoff & Phillips, 2000). Maltreatment during infancy or early childhood can cause improper brain development that leads to physical, mental, and emotional problems (Jaudes & Shapiro, 1999).

Research also confirms that children who experience maltreatment are at an increased risk of behaviors that have an adverse impact on adult well-being, including smoking, alcoholism, drug abuse, eating disorders, severe obesity, depression, suicide, sexual promiscuity, and certain chronic diseases (Felitti et al., 1998; Runyan, Wattam, Ikeda, Hassan, & Ramiro, 2002).

Well-being indicators, such as school involvement and caregiver well-being and interactions, paint an equally grim picture for children in foster care. Research has shown that not only do children in foster care not perform as well as other children in school (e.g., lagging in achievement, repeating grades, failing classes) but also they are twice as likely to drop out of high school (Burley & Halpern, 2001). The special education services received by children in foster care are three to five times the national rate for all children (Goerge, Van Voorhis, Grant, Casey, & Robinson, 1992). Most disturbing of all, their life chances are bleak, resulting in high prevalence for dropping out of school, teen pregnancy, homelessness, and involvement with the criminal justice system (Courtney, Piliavin, Grogan-Kaylor, & Nesmith, 1998).

Despite their vulnerability, too many children in foster care do not receive services that can address or ameliorate their risks. Many children are placed with foster parents and relatives who report symptoms of poor physical and mental health. These foster families may provide little stimulation for young children (Kortenkamp & Macomber, 2002).

A significant number of these children do not receive even basic health care, and specialized needs are even less likely to be addressed. For example, findings from a U.S. General Accounting Office (GAO, 1995) report found that 12% of children in foster care had received no routine health care; 34% had received no immunizations; and, although 78% were at high risk for exposure to HIV, fewer than 10% had been tested. In another national sample, nearly one third of children with high degrees of behavior and emotional problems had not received mental health services, and 20%–40% had not received any preventive health or dental care (Kortenkamp & Macomber, 2002).

CONCLUSION

More than 250,000 infants and toddlers are touched by the child welfare system each year, and they are all particularly vulnerable to challenges to their healthy development. These children have far more health and developmental problems than other American children. No cohort of this endangered group is more vulnerable than the more than 100,000 who are removed from their homes and placed in the out-of-home placement system known as foster care. As was noted previously in this chapter, more than half of these children will experience serious medical conditions and significant developmental delays. They will remain in foster care for long periods of time, and they are more likely to be returned to care than older children. They often lack a consistent adult caregiver in their lives. The challenges to the healthy development of these hundreds of thousands of children remain off the radar screen of most Americans, public officials, and even the child welfare system. These numbers should serve as a wake-up call.

2

The History of Young Children in the Child Welfare System

OLIVER'S STORY

Oliver Twist was born in a workhouse to a dying young woman with "no wedding-ring." Indeed, no one knew her as "she was found lying in the street...but where she came from, or where she is going to nobody knows.... Wrapped in the blanket which had hitherto formed his only covering, he might have been the child of a nobleman or a beggar." But, his robes were yellow and "he was badged and ticketed, and fell into his place at once—a parish child— the orphan of a workhouse—the humble, half-starved drudge—to be cuffed and buffeted through the world—despised by all, and pitied by none....Oliver cried lustily."

He remained at the workhouse and was cared for by "hand" for the first months of life. He was then "farmed... to a branch-workhouse" with 20 or 30 other juveniles under the care of a female warden where he spent most of the day on the floor. He remained there until the age of 9. (Dickens, 1970, p. 1)

Oliver Twist may be the most famous young orphan in the history of the English-speaking world. Despite not being real, his story, like that of so many other young children portrayed in the popular culture of their day, such as David Copperfield, Jane Eyre, Jo Marsh's boys in 1870s America, Little Orphan Annie, or even the youth of Antwone Fisher (the author and screenwriter who wrote the true story of his life in the foster care system), reflects and shapes society's view of the child welfare system or the out-of-home placement system (Alcott, 1942; Black & Washington, 2002; Bronte, 2003; Dickens, 1970; Gray, 2008). Throughout history, the prevailing view has encompassed a pendulum swing from portraying harsh, bleak institutional life to benign schools to children being rescued by wealthy patrons to the limbo of modern foster care. These changes in beliefs by the popular culture were fueled by common perceptions of the era in which they lived, but each *change* maintains a consistent theme of unhappy children lost in a sea of indifference. Furthermore, each demonstrates that very young children were, in some ways, treated differently than older children since the 1800s. Only in recent decades has there been a melding of approaches to one single direction for children of all ages.

This chapter traces the history of child welfare efforts for young children in America. At this writing, there is no comprehensive written history focusing on young children in the child welfare system; rather, there are only more general histories that mention the youngest children in passing. In America, this system that attempts to deal with abandoned, orphaned, or troubled children has often been operated by sectarian methods, but even from earliest times it has encompassed some public funding. The child welfare system of reality, like that of popular culture, was guided by the common beliefs of the period. All too often, these children remained off the public radar screen, only to be spotlighted in times of scandal. Continuing until the 21st century, the short-sighted trend became characterized by scandals reaping system reforms and public attention waning over time.

This chapter is critical to understanding the present dilemma of young children in the child welfare system. Its intention is to explain how the system reached the point it is at today, with more than one third of all children admitted to care under the age of 3, and the majority of these children having serious medical conditions and developmental delays and disabilities.

THE COLONIAL PERIOD

During the colonial period, the death rate for young children was high—three fourths of all children died before they reached the age of 4 (Folks, 1978). Thus, parental investment in early childhood was quite conditional. Once a child reached the age of 4 or 5, he or she was viewed as a small adult ready for labor. As Hillary Rodham said in her famous *Harvard Educational Review* article, "Children were regarded as chattels of the family and wards of the state, with no recognized political character or power and few legal rights" (1973, p. 489).

Yet, even in this earliest period, orphans and children of "paupers" did receive public assistance with the English Poor Law governing the American response to these children. The youngest children were placed in almshouses or poor houses for the destitute, while older children, often as young as 5, but generally like Oliver Twist at the age of 8 or 9, were placed in indentured servitude. The practice of *binding out* was derived from English attitude and law, dating back to Henry VIII, under whom *statutes at large* read, "Children under fourteen years of age, and above five, that live in idelness *(sic)*, and be taken begging, may be put to service by the governors of cities, towns, etc." (Bremner, 1970, p. 64).

American colonial laws were mirroring those early statutes as early as 1646. It was written in the *Virginia statutes at large*, "…the justices of the peace should, at their discretion, bind out children to tradesmen or husbandmen" (Bremner, 1970, p. 65). Soon there were similar laws throughout New England.

Indenture reflected society's belief in the value of hard work and strict religious upbringing. The growth of slavery in the United States, however, reduced the need for indentured servitude, and its utility disappeared by the end of the colonial period. Institutions for orphans began to be founded during this period; although there were private orphan houses as early as 1729 (Bremner, 1970). The first public orphanage was founded in Charleston, South Carolina, in 1790 (Bremner, 1970, p. 275). Other publicly funded orphan houses, including those specifically for women, followed.

THE 19TH CENTURY

The 19th century dawned with young children still being placed in poor houses and older children still in some form of indenture; however, they were more likely to stay in poor houses until ready to leave for work. Studies of the poor laws in New York and other states during this period found serious problems (Bremner, 1970, p. 647). Children placed in those institutions were subjected to poor conditions, filth, illness, and minimal nutrition. The placement in institutions of young children with adults included not only exposure to debtors and destitute people but also "derelicts, criminals and the insane," as well (Bremner, 1970, p. 647). These findings constituted the first in a long series of scandals concerning children in out-of-home placement. As those reports stated, these conditions "disgraced the state and shocked humanity" (Bremner, 1970, p. 647).

A major response to these reports was the call for separate institutions for children. The early years of the century had seen the beginning of orphanages generally founded by sectarian groups in large east coast cities. These orphanages began to flourish as the reform response to the scandals. In 1811, a grant of state subsidy proved to be groundbreaking. In the *Laws of the State of New York,* it was proclaimed that "the Treasurer shall pay...to the trustees of the orphan asylum society in the city of New York, the annual sum of five hundred dollars...to the support of foreign poor" (Bremner, 1970, p. 281). This act set the precedent for public financing of orphanages in New York and nationwide.

Most orphanages were funded with some public dollars, although the majority were administered by religious organizations and segregated the children by race and, often, religion. Indeed, one of the first American orphanages was the Philadelphia Association for the Care of Colored Children founded by the Society of Friends in 1822; however, this shelter was burned by a white mob in 1838. The famous draft riots in New York City in 1863 caused the burning of the Colored Orphan Asylum (Mallon & Hess, 2005). There were also houses specifically for Jewish children, such as the Jewish Foster Home in Philadelphia (Bremner, 1970). As well, there were homes that were endowed specifically for "poor male white orphans" (Bremner, 1970, p. 657), and those that specifically administered to the sick, such as the New Orleans Howards Association, which provided for children with Yellow Fever during the epidemic (Bremner, 1970).

Orphanages as reformed poorhouses for young children were just one response to the growing presence of orphaned, abandoned, and destitute children. At the same time as state reports exposed dreadful conditions in poorhouses and Dickens was highlighting these issues in his popular writing and lectures in the United States, new services were being developed. Reformers such as Theodore Roosevelt, Sr., father of President Roosevelt, became involved in efforts to aid newsboys who hawked newspapers for pennies, for example. Newsboys often lived alone in squalor or on the streets. Programs were developed that helped these children by founding homes such as the Newsboys' Lodging Home, which provided shelter and meals (Morris, 1979; O'Connor, 2001).

During this period, a system of *placing out* children was developed that would later become the modern foster care system. Similar to orphanages, this forerunner of the foster care system was based on sectarian beliefs. In founding the Children's Aid Society (CAS) in 1853, Charles Brace Loring posited that the best way to save children was by placing them in Christian (i.e., Protestant) homes in rural areas to learn habits of work and morality (O'Connor, 2001). The timing for the founding of CAS mirrored an emerging pattern in child welfare—scandal followed by reform. A report in the early 1850s focusing on the youngest children found infant mortality to be more than 70% at Infants' Hospital on Randall's Island (off Manhattan Island) compared with the citywide percentage of 20% (O'Connor, 2001). The report further found that this high infant mortality rate was caused in part by unsanitary and overcrowded conditions (O'Connor, 2001). Thus, babies abandoned at the Infants' Hospital were dying at more than three times the rate of others in a city with many poor and immigrant children.

Loring's concern about these abandoned or destitute children and his devoted religious beliefs merged, and he created the famous Orphan Trains, which brought children, all poor and mostly immigrants of all ages to include largely Catholic and later Jewish children, to rural areas in the Midwest and West for new homes and new lives. By 1879, more than 40,000 children had been moved out west from New York City alone, and by 1930, roughly 250,000 had been placed nationwide (O'Connor, 2001).

Initially, CAS screened families and provided follow-up monitoring after placement. Families that would take children agreed to clothe, educate, and treat them as their own (O'Connor, 2001). Children, in turn, agreed to live with and provide labor to the new family. Most of the children involved were orphans, but many were not, and so these destitute street children often were ripped from their old lives to reside in distant places with new Protestant families. As the numbers of children participating grew, the screening and monitoring diminished, and local groups and families were given the task of matching children.

Although the Orphan Trains were applauded in the public domain and even produced some very successful people, including Governor John Green Brady of

Alaska and Governor Andrew Burke of North Dakota, there were critics of this system (O'Connor, 2001). Beginning after the Civil War, most of the criticism was from Catholics who saw the effort as proselytizing children, that is, converting Catholic children to Protestants (Hacsi, 1995). One response was to develop their own (i.e., Catholic) placing-out system, which in 1869 resulted in the New York Foundling Hospital that was developed by the Sisters of Charity of St. Vincent de Paul (Hasci, 1995).

Although the Foundling Hospital did establish an Orphan Train system that placed Catholic children in Catholic homes, it was far more than a Catholic response to CAS. It also instituted programs to assist abandoned and destitute infants. It placed a white curtained bassinet in its vestibule so that mothers could anonymously drop off unwanted babies. They also tried to engage mothers for the first few months of their child's life by encouraging breast feeding. Furthermore, they recruited wet nurses (i.e., women who were nursing their own infants who agreed to also nurse another baby) for infants without mothers, and even had the babies live with the wet nurses. These efforts lowered the infant mortality rate of Foundling Hospital babies to 26% comparable to the citywide level at that time (O'Connor, 2001).

The Foundling Hospital merely touched the surface of the huge citywide and growing national problem of abandoned babies. A harbinger for things to come, the Foundling Hospital received 45 abandoned infants in the very first month of its "white-bassinet-in-the-vestibule" program. In New York City, Bellevue Hospital received four abandoned babies each day in the 1880s. Ultimately, in the last years of the century, the total number of abandoned babies in New York City reached 4,000 annually (O'Connor, 2001).

The large numbers of infants and toddlers in the child welfare system at that time also began to change the shape of the CAS Orphan Trains. During its early years, the system was largely made up of children over the age of 5, with a predominance of even older children. The typical participant was an older child who was able to provide work for the new family, which was essentially a kind of informal indenture (Hasci, 1995). Although infants and toddlers were always part of the mix, they were the minority until the turn of the century. The emerging popular belief about the malleability of early childhood and a growing sense of the true vulnerability of babies during this period of development, however, made taking in young children more desirable. Reflecting the influence of the infant-focused Foundling approach, this trend also mirrored the popular view that adoption could work in early childhood, but that after infancy it would be problematic.

By the last years of the Orphan Trains in the post–World War I period, the vast majority of the children were infants and toddlers (O'Connor, 2001). This new view of early childhood reflecting the centrality and vulnerability of the early years became more widespread in the last part of the 19th century. This view was fueled not only by intellectual thought but also by the reality being bred of scandal. Beginning in the 1880s, *The New York Times* covered a story every week about an infant that was abandoned in a park, police station, church, or hospital. For example, newborn twins were left in a package at Grand Central Station in 1877 ("An Abandoned Pair of Twins," 1877), and in 1884, a bundle found lying on a Jersey City pier contained a 1-month-old baby ("Who Could Have Put It There?" 1884).

The sense that parents have an obligation to provide for their children's basic needs, and that, if denied, the state can intervene on a child's behalf flows from a belief that children are entitled to adequate care and treatment. This view that childhood, particularly in the early years, is precious underlies the *child saving* movement of the late 19th century. This movement traces its origins to the story of little Mary Ellen, a child found to be seriously abused who could only receive help legally by analogy to laws preventing cruelty to animals. Her ordeal led to the founding of the Society for the Prevention of Cruelty to Children (SPCC) in 1874 (Bremner, 1971).

SPCCs grew throughout the country in response to scandals about abandoned, abused, and neglected children, many of whom were very young. The SPCC lobbied for and secured state legislation to grant them police power to pick up and save children from the street, hospital, or other places where they could be subjected to harm. The SPCC ran shelters for emergency placements for children who were later placed in orphanages, often matched by race and religion. The exercise of the police power was potent. One can review the thousands of SPCC cases in the late 19th and early 20th centuries that underscore how truly powerful the organization was at that time. One of its most famous cases involved an investigation of Eleanor Roosevelt, who placed her babies in a bassinet outside as a way to provide them with fresh air, even in the winter. Even a wealthy and well-connected family such as the Roosevelts could find themselves the subject of an SPCC investigation (Cook, 1993).

The police power to investigate and remove children from environments that were deemed potentially unsafe was only a short-term solution at best for children who needed care. SPCC provided only emergency shelters. Continuous care was relegated to the existing child welfare agencies, such as orphanages, hospitals, or the Orphan Train programs. Orphanages proliferated during the 19th century with a 300% increase during the last half of the century (Katz, 1986). In fact, 247 orphanages or other institutions for children opened in the 1890s alone. By the 1910 census, more than 110,000 dependent, neglected or delinquent children lived in 1,151 institutions (Katz, 1986, p. 123).

Scandals in the treatment of children at those facilities and reports detailing serious problems multiplied throughout the country from the 1870s through the turn of the century. As a result, reforms enacted by state legislatures included the development of licensing and monitoring mechanisms for child-serving institutions. Some states, such as Pennsylvania and New York, prohibited children from placement in almshouses and later set state standards and required licenses for orphanages and other child-serving agencies. Other states, particularly in the Midwest, developed state-run services, such as the Michigan State School for Dependent Children, which was founded in 1871. Indeed, by the end of the century, two trends emerged. States in the East developed standards and licensing laws but provided government funding for services to abandoned, orphaned, and destitute children chiefly through licensed sectarian organizations. In contrast, in the Midwest and West, the government developed, operated, and funded the services either at the state or county level. State boards of charities supervised these public and private institutions, but the nature of supervision varied from state to state (Bremner, 1971).

The Role of the Juvenile Court

The Progressive Era of the late 19th and early 20th centuries advocated for a sea change in attitudes toward the poor. Societal problems were deemed not as a result of genetics, but as products of the environment. Problems such as poverty, child abandonment, juvenile delinquency, and crime were caused by the environment and social conditions and were the main determinants of human behavior—not heredity. Lincoln Steffens, a major leader of the Progressive Movement said that the aim was to provide "opportunities to do good" (McDonald, 1997, p. 6). Thus, progressives sponsored remedies such as the regulation of child labor, provisions for mothers' pensions, development of settlement houses, child care centers, playgrounds, and friendly visitors to help poor families.

Perhaps most emblematic of the Progressive Era reforms was the birth of the juvenile court. Founded in 1899 by a committee of the Chicago Bar Association, the children's court was an institution whose objective was to treat children not as criminals, but as neglected children whose behavior was a direct repercussion of identifiable, negative factors (Kahn, 1953; McDonald, 1997).

The early history of the children's court clearly indicated that it was to be different from traditional courts of law. At its heart was the belief that children should be treated differently than adults. This court was to provide individualized justice by tailoring rehabilitative rather than punitive remedies that recognized the individual needs of each child. It was to be a judicial "tribunal where law and science, especially the science of medicine and those sciences which deal with human behavior, such as biology, sociology, and psychology, work side by side" (Lou, as cited in McDonald, 1997, p. 2) and that its purpose was "remedial and...preventive" (McDonald, 1997, p. 2). This court was set up as a court of equity to determine the extent and nature of state intervention in changing the environment of a child and his or her family (McDonald, 1997).

Many of the juvenile court judges insisted on an intimate, informal, nonintimidating atmosphere within the courthouse. Judge Harvey Baker, for example, describes his 1910 Boston courtroom as "occupying a quiet corner of the main courthouse in the city, with a large and pleasant waiting room" (McDonald, 1997,

p. 5). He heard his cases in his chambers, rather than in the courtroom, while sitting on a platform about 6 inches high, typically with only a probation officer attendant. The child in question would stand at the end of the platform where Baker could see him "from top to toe" (Baker, 1910, p. 319). The judge sat near the end so that he would be close to the child and "could reassure him, if necessary, by a friendly hand on the shoulder" (Baker, 1910, p. 319).

In Buffalo, New York, in the early 1900s, the judge would visit children in hospitals, orphanages, or at home to understand the child's circumstances and fashion "individualized justice" (McDonald 1997, p. 6). This "new model for individualized justice" was "an oasis in the legal landscape" (Kahn, 1953, p. 93).

By 1919, 45 of the 48 states had juvenile courts (McDonald, 1997). As is evident from the CAS caseload of the Orphan Train, younger and younger children began arriving at the juvenile court doorstep. By the 1930s, the court was seeing many more cases of neglect and an increased number of very young children.

To further the court's rehabilitative promise, court administered services, such as probation and mental health evaluations, were established to provide judges with information with which to make judgments, as well as to oversee implementation of orders (McDonald, 1997). Initially, probation officers were merely "disinterested men and women of character" who could help set the "moral tone of the court" (McDonald, 1997, p. 10). Often SPCC volunteers played this additional role in conjunction with their existing task of investigation and supervision. Trained professionals, however, began staffing courts before World War I, even though the volunteers remained (Fox, 1996).

In addition to providing the court with information, many of these men and women saw their role as serving to provide human relationships to the children. Only later, as the field became more professional, did probation provide the court with administrative tasks, such as filling out petitions, daily oversight of cases, developing plans, and postdisposition supervision. The professionalization of probation—the unique service of the juvenile court—has seldom met its initial promise (McDonald, 1997). By the 1960s, the staff had become distant, overworked bureaucrats, which was a far cry from the volunteers who offered "direct services and hands-on good works, and provided human relationships" (Polier, 1987, p. 82) to the children that they served.

By the 1930s, many family courts had paid probation staff and court-annexed mental health evaluation services. Some courts actually provided direct, ongoing services, such as mental health intervention provided by the mental health clinic in Chicago founded in 1909 and the child guidance clinic in Boston known as the Judge Baker Clinic. However, in many cities, the development of such services was limited due to the power of voluntary sectarian child care agencies. In this period, a new service, was developed to divert cases from the court and direct children to services that met their needs. Expansion of various court-annexed services further fueled the debate about the court's role, with reformers at different periods calling for location of these services in the public schools or other agencies outside of the court.

The continuing debate over the role of the court reached a crescendo in the 1950s when many, such as Alfred Kahn, questioned whether the judges' role should be limited to adjudication rather than disposition. During this period, a number of proposals in New York City were developed to delegate dispositional responsibility to other entities. For instance, there was the Family Court Social Adjustment Agency, which administered investigative services (as the supervisory role of probation), including rehabilitative services, such as counseling and drug treatment. Another agency that was created during this time was the Foster Care Commission, which was founded to review cases. This kind of administrative delegation in which agencies outside the juvenile court were utilized to administer rehabilitative functions paralleled advancements happening in other countries, such as Great Britain and Norway (McDonald, 1997).

By the early 1960s, concern about due process reframed the debate. The New York State Family Court Act of 1962 (Laws of New York, 1962) for example, embraced the view of the court as a court of law. The Act insisted that the court should be governed by due process and tacitly implied the limitations of its original rehabilitative orientation. Over time, the court's role became purely judicial, more passive, and less able to fashion individual remedies. Ironically, during the next 20 years, this narrowing of the scope and nature of the court's review occurred at a time when state and federal law increased the jurisdiction of the court by requiring it to review virtually all cases of children in foster care. This gradual reduction of the court's role into a largely passive, supervisory body came at a time of rising general disregard of court-connected services. The availability of services, such as probation and mental health evaluation, diminished as many began to agree that it was not the court's place to administer such help; in fact, many believed that court-connected mental health services would be an obstacle to intervention because patients would not feel as free to express themselves as in treatments not connected with the court.

With the increased requirements of multiple reviews, even courts that sought to retain the original rehabilitative mission found it harder and harder to achieve that goal (McDonald, 1997). As former Judge Justine Wise Polier noted, the judges and the court had lost direct contact with the children, had diminished their responsibility for each case, and were, therefore, less able to shape and ensure the provision of dispositional remedies (Polier, 1987).

The Federal Role

While states and children's courts were struggling mightily to protect young children and develop individualized justice to enhance child development, the Progressive Era advocates also were looking for national solutions to the problems of child poverty and child neglect. Progressive Era lobbyists, such as Lillian Wald, met with President Theodore Roosevelt to seek redress for these problems. Their work led to the proposal of child labor legislation that was eventually rebuffed by Congress. However, at the end of Roosevelt's term, he was able to convene the 1909 White House Conference on the Care of Dependent Children. Attendees included an array of members of state boards of charities, settlement house staff, juvenile court judges, and others imbued with progressive beliefs.

The White House Conference on the Care of Dependent Children was a seminal event that lay the groundwork for the federal role concerning child welfare for the 20th century. The conference produced a consensus questioning the utility of institutions and positing the belief that children were best raised in families. The mantra of family preservation was central to its recommendations, which called for establishing a Federal Children's Bureau; the adoption of measures, such as mothers' pensions, to address poverty and prevent out-of-home placement; and the development of foster homes, rather than institutions, for children (Bremner, 1971; Folks, 1940).

The conference led directly to the enactment of a law in 1912 that appropriated $25,640 for a Children's Bureau—the first federal agency devoted exclusively to children (Bradbury & Eliot, 1956). Its charge was to "investigate and report…upon all matters pertaining to the welfare of childhood and child life" (Work of Children's Bureau, 1912, p. X9), including infant mortality, orphanages, and juvenile courts. Julia C. Lathrop was appointed the first chief of the Children's Bureau. As the first federal recognition of responsibility for the welfare of children, the program fostered greater development of licensing and regulation of child care facilities.

The first project of the Children's Bureau was to study infant mortality rates to determine ways to better the circumstances of very young children. In its early years, the Children's Bureau was responsible for the first legislation aimed at protecting children—the Sheppard-Towner Act of 1921 (PL 67-97)—its program provided grants to states "for the purpose of…promoting the welfare and hygiene of maternity and infancy" (Bremner, 1971, p. 1003). The act was a harbinger of future federal involvement to enhance maternal and child health. Although requiring states to adhere to standards, the act gave states autonomy in designing their own plans to aid mothers and children and adapting those plans to suit local needs.

The ramifications of the Sheppard-Towner Act were encouraging. From July 1924 to the end of June 1929, 1,594 permanent local child health centers, prenatal centers, or a combination of both had been established throughout the country. The Act also led directly to the establishment of many state child hygiene bureaus or divisions, an expanded birth registration area, and a huge increase in state appropriations specifically intended for "maternal and infancy work after the expiration" of the act (Bremner, 1971, p. 1009).

It should be noted that for all the good that the Sheppard-Towner Act accomplished, it was, in fact, opposed in 1922 in the *Journal of the American Medical Association* (JAMA) as a law that was "not in the interest of public welfare…an imported socialistic scheme unsuited to our form of government...[and that] unjustly and inequitably taxes the people of some of the states for the benefit of the people of other states" (Bremner, 1971, pp. 1020–1021). Ultimately, the JAMA saw the Act as "a type of undesirable legislation which should be discouraged" (Bremner, 1971, p. 1020–1021). However, this resistance was squashed in 1923 by the U.S. Supreme Court, which upheld the constitutionality of the Act (Bremner, 1971).

Encouraging the development of standards for child welfare services, the Children's Bureau also sponsored studies of health, nutrition, orphanages, and adoption, as well as publishing child-rearing pamphlets. Its objective became finding ways to allow all healthy children (even those born out of wedlock) to remain at home or be adopted. Indeed, adoption was supported by Children's Bureau funded research, and states were encouraged to pass laws to regulate the widely supported practice. Built on laws enacted in the post–Civil War period allowing for the transfer of parental rights, states such as Minnesota passed laws by 1917 requiring investigation of potential adoptive families and the filing of adoption petitions with the court.

The Children's Bureau encouraged experts to develop standards for adoption and out-of-home placement, and the founding of the Child Welfare League of America (CWLA) in the 1920s accelerated this effort. The formalization of practice brought about the reshaping of child welfare services so that agencies such as CAS would make every effort to fix families as well as to help build homes (O'Connor, 2001). However, reforming the services and their oversight by the court could not stem the flow of children into the child-serving systems. Placement in orphanages reached its height in the 1920s, when 142,000 children resided in more than 1,550 orphanages (Smith, 1995).

The issue of child health was once again thrust into the limelight at the very beginning of the 1930s with the White House Conference on Child Health and Protection of 1930. Ray Lyman Wilbur, appointed dean of the Stanford University Medical School in 1911, as well as chairman of the Conference, stated in an address that

> We must assist children in their own development...children should not be used as test-tubes for opinionated programs, with no worked out basis of science of fact, and that those who have developed methods without scientific preparation are often of the greatest harm in the handling of our childhood. (Cited in Bremner, 1971, p. 1079)

He called for a melding of science and experience in order to create programs and action that could work for the "good of children" (as cited in Bremner, 1971, p. 1080).

The conference included a survey on health protection for very young children that found that barely half of preschool-age children in urban areas had been taken to the doctor for any sort of preventive care or advice, and the percentage was even less in rural areas. Dental health examinations were found to be even rarer, with only one of every eight (13%) preschool-age children having received dental care. In the poorest economic group, only 4% of all preschool-age children had been to the dentist. Polls on vaccinations were also disheartening. On average, only 21% of city preschool-age children and 7% of rural preschool-age children had been given the then century-old immunization against smallpox. The newer diphtheria vaccination touted similar statistics, with 21% (city) and 18% (rural) preschool-age children having received the immunization.

However, for all of the rhetoric of the 1930 White House Conference, an article in *The Nation* at that time pointed out that despite the "blare of publicity that always attends these gatherings summoned by the President," the result was a string of 19 conclusions and an uninspiring "string of platitudes" (as cited in Bremner, 1971, p. 1083). These resolutions included abstract statements, such as, "Every child is entitled to be understood," and "Every child waif and orphan in need must be supported" (as cited in Bremner, 1971, p. 1083). Thus, the 1930 White House conference failed to fulfill the legacy of the earlier effort and had little impact on child welfare.

In contrast, the newspapers of the 1920s, just like every year since the 1880s, contained stories about abandoned babies and young children among immigrant and destitute families. In 1936, it was estimated that 4,000 babies were entering the New York City child welfare system (The City's Way with Its Waifs, 1936). At this same time, nationwide, more than a quarter of a million children lived in institutions or in some form of foster care (as cited in Bremner, 1971).

This trend did not abate until the fundamental views of society's obligations to those children changed with the passage of the Social Security Act of 1935 (PL 74-271). The passage of the Social Security provision known as Aid to Dependent Children (ADC), later known as Aid to Familes with Dependent Children (AFDC), created an income-based entitlement for destitute children for the first time. By the end of the 1930s, the number of children in the child-serving agencies plummeted. This decrease was most obvious in the extreme decline of babies abandoned in New York City. The number of abandoned babies in 1942 was half of the number in 1935 (Abandoned Babies Increasing in City, 1943). Thus, the provision of basic sustenance greatly reduced the number of infants abandoned by parents who were unable to care for them due to poverty. This decline reverberated for all young children. Parents, even those who were destitute, could raise their own children.

Although there was an increase in the number of abandoned babies during World War II due to war orphans and fears of illegitimacy, the number of children in the child welfare system remained low into the 1950s. This trend, however, did not eliminate media reports of abandoned babies, which continue to this day. Yet, by the late 1930s, fewer Caucasian children were placed in orphanages or other institutions, and adoption, particularly after the development of CWLA standards in 1938, became the norm for Caucasian children whose parents could not care for them for a host of reasons (e.g., birth out of wedlock, too many other children). Orphanages and other institutions, therefore, increasingly shifted their focus to minority children and children with disabilities.

After World War II, the concept of foster care limbo for many children, especially concerning children with disabilities and minority children, began to be recognized. Indeed, the segregation of the child welfare system during this period was quite notorious. After World War II, a public scandal ensued when hundreds of healthy *boarder babies* were left in hospitals for months and even years in New York City (Well Babies' Care Burdens Hospital, 1946). It was estimated by the Citizens' Committee for Children, a child advocacy organization founded after the war by Eleanor Roosevelt and a group of both professional and lay citizens, that more than 1,000 children, mostly young and minority, needed adequate placement. In New York City, the sectarian organizations of the time, which were predominately Catholic and Jewish, were unable to accept the largely Protestant African American children due to laws mandating religious matching (Bernstein, 2001). Those children, as a result, languished in foster care limbo. Indeed, much fanfare was produced by a New York City study that found adoptive homes for more than 500 African American infants, which proved that young African American children were adoptable and should not be forgotten in the foster care system (Jaffe, 1965).

Believing that funding restrictions were underlying some of these problems, amendments to the Social Security Act were enacted in 1962 that expanded the already established AFDC to include foster care funding for eligible children (PL 87-543). Probably even more significant was legislation passed in this period that established Section IVA of the Social Security Act that provided federal funds to match state dollars for foster care (PL 90-248). This provision required the placement of children in foster care by court order, thus expanding the role of the juvenile court in many jurisdictions and ensuring the court's gatekeeper role in foster care placement. These federal laws, later echoed in state laws, also required the court to place children in foster care while providing an oversight mechanism to prevent unnecessary placements (McDonald, 1997).

Thus, an emerging system of services—out-of-home care in foster homes—became the purview of the federal government. This new funding coincided with resurgence in concern about child safety and, specifically, child abuse and neglect. Echoing the child-saving cries of the late 1800s, child abuse became a national concern, but this time it was buttressed by support from the medical community, starting with a 1962 article entitled "The Battered Child Syndrome" (Kempe, Silverman, Steelle, Droegemueller, & Silver, 1962). This new funding source and the spotlight on child abuse spurred the growth of the foster care system, and, by the late 1970s, almost 500,000 children nationwide resided in foster care (Dicker & Gordon, 2000; Hacsi, 1995). Ironically, without this federal funding, the number of children in orphanages and in state and locally funded foster care had remained stable in the 1940s and 1950s, while the funding of the 1960s was a precipitating factor in the increase in out-of-home care.

The growing concern about child abuse in the 1960s resulted in the passage in 1974 of the Child Abuse Prevention and Treatment Act (CAPTA) (PL 93-247), which provided funds to states to develop systems of child protection, including requiring states to pass child abuse and neglect laws as well as to establish mechanisms for reporting child abuse and neglect. In addition, various states developed other mechanisms that included citizen review boards to monitor cases of child abuse and neglect. One year later, the Social Security Act was amended again and provided a funding mechanism for services to abused and neglected children known as Title XX (PL 93-647). This money was to go to only the most vulnerable children, which increasingly were children with special needs. Thus, by the late 1970s, a complex child welfare system had emerged that encompassed more children, included a host of funding streams, and created several more layers of oversight, including requirement of court-ordered placement.

The first comprehensive child welfare law passed by Congress was the Adoption Assistance and Child Welfare Act of 1980 (PL 96-272). The underlying premise of PL 96-272 was that many foster care placements had been unnecessary and that it was possible for most children to avoid placement and return home safely with appropriate family support and services. Designed to preserve families and promote permanency planning, the Act called for states to develop prevention and reunification programs and case plans of services for children and parents. It also required child welfare agencies to exercise reasonable efforts to try to keep families together. These efforts took the form of both services designed to prevent placement and services to reunify families after placement. The law defined the role of the court as a decision maker and monitor by requiring courts to approve all foster care placements, find reasonable efforts at every court proceeding, and review cases within 18 months of placement (Dicker & Gordon, 2000).

Although the foster care caseload declined by half in the early 1980s following the passage of the Adoption Assistance and Child Welfare Act of 1980 (PL 96-272), the foster care population more than doubled from the mid-1980s to the 1990s due to the epidemic of AIDS, increased use of crack cocaine, and escalated rates of poverty. Very young children comprised a large share of new admissions to foster care. The sheer volume of cases coupled with the complex needs of these children and their families resulted in children spending the majority of childhood in foster care (Wulczyn & Hislop, 2002). This new reality made the task of ensuring reasonable efforts toward reunification far more challenging.

In 1997, Congress passed the Adoption and Safe Families Act (ASFA) (PL 105-89), which signaled a pendulum swing away from the emphasis on family preservation toward permanency and adoption. ASFA strengthened the court's role as the central and ultimate decision maker in child welfare proceedings. ASFA also makes clear that a child's health and safety is a paramount consideration in every child protective proceeding and that courts have broad authority to address these issues. ASFA allows the court to find that reasonable efforts toward reunification with parents are not necessary in specific situations, such as abandonment; torture; and chronic physical, emotional, and sexual abuse. In addition, reasonable efforts toward reunification are not required if the parent has committed murder, voluntary manslaughter, felony assault that resulted in serious injury to the child, or if the parental rights to a sibling have been terminated voluntarily.

ASFA also tightened the time frames for decision making by requiring permanency hearings 12 months after placement and within 30 days of placement if the court determines that reasonable efforts to reunify are not required. ASFA also required that Termination of Parental Rights (TPR) petitions be filed when a child is in care for 15 out of the last 22 months unless compelling reasons exist, such as placement with a relative, the child being an adolescent who objects to adoption, or a failure to provide timely services to parents as enumerated in the case plan. As a result, courts must keep a tighter rein on cases and have access to information that can identify a child's and family's needs and barriers to permanency more quickly. Finally, ASFA provides fiscal incentives to states to increase adoptions (Dicker, Gordon, & Knitzer, 2001).

Of note, prior to the passage of ASFA, Congress developed the state Court Improvement Project (CIP), which provided federal funds for the first time to aid the nation's juvenile and family courts involved in these proceedings. After ASFA, CIP further reinforced the central decision maker role of the courts, and CIP funds became a major tool for ensuring the safety, permanency, and well-being of children in foster care (see Chapter 6).

BABIES IN OUT-OF-HOME CARE BEFORE THE 1980s

The history of child welfare in America is replete with a high concentration of babies—children birth–3 years—being abandoned, neglected, or otherwise deprived and placed in out-of-home care. The high numbers in orphanages in the 19th century underscores the reality that thousands, perhaps millions, of babies grew up in institutions during that time period. Only late Victorian thinking about the preciousness of early childhood began to change this pattern, which led to adoption and foster care efforts emerging for the youngest children.

As this chapter describes, by the early 20th century, the Orphan Trains and Foundling Hospital placement efforts included thousands of infants who were eventually adopted. These efforts remained segregated by race and religion, with healthy Caucasian newborns having the greatest likelihood for a family based childhood. Indeed, the emergence in the 1920s of regulated adoption practices either by law or by professional standards, both of which were aided by the Children's Bureau, created a separate system of out-of-home care for healthy Caucasian infants. Although adoption was cultivated for that group of children, institutional care for long periods of childhood remained the life experiences of minority children and children with disabilities.

The enormous decline in placement of babies by their mothers after the onset of ADC underscores the central role that poverty played in the child welfare system. Simply put, provision of an entitlement for funding for poor mothers resulted in fewer and fewer babies being placed in out-of-home care. Although a small rise in placements occurred during and right after World War II due to dislocation from the war and a rise in illegitimate births, the numbers remained far lower than before the Depression.

An increase was seen, however, in two specific groups—minority babies and babies with disabilities (Kramer, 1965). Often intertwined, these two categories of babies constituted much of the child welfare system and these children all too often spent their childhood in institutional settings through the early 1960s. However, even in these two groups, the presence of babies was declining by the early 1980s. Federal expansion of the Social Security Act and direct funding of foster care programs led to an increased placement of these children in foster homes and a decline in institutional placement. There were major changes in the delivery of services to children with disabilities in the 1970s, and from 1977 to 2003 the percentage of residents under 21 at state institutions dropped from 36% to only 5% (Rothman & Rothman, 2005).

BABIES IN OUT-OF-HOME CARE AFTER THE 1980s

The placement of babies in out-of-home care began to change slowly in the early 1980s. In 1984, *The New York Times* printed the first article detailing the trend of more infants entering the child welfare system and revealing that seven babies with AIDS were abandoned in New York City hospitals that year (Young Victims of AIDS Suffer Its Harsh Stigma, 1984).

One year later, far more coverage of this issue appeared. By July 1985, it was reported that 600 children nationwide were suffering either from AIDS or preliminary symptoms of the syndrome, and many were in hospitals because their parents were

> Too incompetent or too sick to raise them, and they [we]re placed in foster care before their illness [was] diagnosed. Other times they [were] abandoned in the hospital by mothers or foster families unwilling or unable to nurse them. (Young Victims of AIDS Suffer Its Harsh Stigma, 1984, p. A22)

"Sometimes," Dr. Arye Rubinstein of Albert Einstein Medical College in New York City was reported as saying, "the whole family is dying" (Gross, 1985, p. B10). Reports proliferated about infants left in hospitals for months and sometimes years. Initially diagnosed as demonstrating a *failure to thrive* (a term still used today with the acronym FTT), these infants begin to develop signs of AIDS and remain in the hospitals.

The stories increased in number until a *New York Times* article in August 1986 warned of the growing crisis (Kerr, 1986). New York City hospitals were

Overwhelmed by growing numbers of babies born to users of the drug crack...and infants remaining in their care for weeks or months after delivery, instead of days, because their parents [were] unable to care for them" and because foster families fearing AIDS were reluctant to take in children of drug abusers. (Kerr, 1986, p. B1)

By mid-1986, the number of reports of child abuse and neglect had gone up 30% (Kerr, 1986). In June 1986, 2,044 reports were filed in New York City with a rising proportion of the children under age 2 (Kerr, 1986). Indeed, the week before the *New York Times* article was published, 100 children were waiting in hospitals for placement; more than half of these babies were the children of drug addicts (Kerr, 1986). In Harlem Hospital, for example, there were 25 babies, 5 of whom had been in the hospital for more than 2 months (Kerr, 1986). Nearly 30 babies at Kings County Hospital Center in Brooklyn were reported in recent weeks to have waited between 1 week and 1 month to leave the hospital.

A Kings County professor of pediatrics, Dr. Leonard Glass, went on record stating that more than one third of the infants born to crack users suffer from neurological disorders, such as tremors, muscle rigidity, and stiffness. These are examples of common symptoms of toxic exposure from cocaine and are milder than heroin exposure because they dissipate in a few days.

By the end of 1986, Mayor Koch of New York City castigated Special Services for Children (the New York City child welfare agency at the time) for not acting fast enough to place infants in foster homes and urged that some system of conditional approval should be established for foster homes (Faster Track for the Boarder Babies, 1986). During the next months, calls continued for foster homes for the hundreds of babies abandoned in hospitals. Makeshift solutions were proposed from recruiting "foster grandparents" (Evans, 1987) to having friendly visitors in hospitals to spend time with the boarder babies to calling for group homes for infants throughout the nation (Daley, 1987). Meanwhile, the growing size of the problem coupled with the hysteria about AIDS led to dire consequences—a proposed group foster home for babies was burned by an arsonist (Purnick, 1987). The arson seemed to frighten the public and caused the child welfare world to find more viable solutions. By late May 1987, more foster homes were being found in recruitment drives; yet, reminiscent of early trends, babies in New York City were arriving in high numbers to both the Foundling Hospital and CAS. Pleas for foster families continued.

The hysteria continued around the country as calls for orphanages were revived and dire predictions about the future severity of disabilities of these children proliferated. Orphanages as well as special schools for children who had been exposed to drugs prenatally were proposed across the country (Smith, 1995). In response to the crisis, Congress passed the Abandoned Infants Assistance Act in 1988 (PL 100-505). This Act supports programs across the country as well as the National Abandoned Infants Assistance Resource Center. Even though the vast majority of the babies were from New York City, Chicago, and Los Angeles in the early 1990s, by 1998 those cities constituted only a little more than a quarter of all infants. In addition, the racial composition of these children also changed throughout the 1990s from 75% African American in 1991 to just over half in 1998 (National Abandoned Infants Assistance Resource Center, 2005).

Although the number of babies remained consistently high after the mid-1990s, there were different responses in different jurisdictions. Most noteworthy were places such as Atlanta, Phoenix, and Los Angeles that developed group residences or orphanage-like group living for babies. Often funded privately and staffed by volunteers, this response echoed an earlier time when babies were believed to be safe if in a secure setting. Once out of the hospitals and the glare of publicity, community attention faded. One such example is the Atlanta-based Project Prevent's *My House*. Although this project received donations and volunteers, it also received federal Abandoned Infant Act funds to help pregnant substance abusers receive prenatal care, drug treatment, and other services (Baker, 2000). Viewed as a haven for babies who have nowhere to go when it is time for them to leave the hospital, Project Prevent founded *My House* as a temporary emergency shelter for medically fragile infants. But, consistent with the history of this issue, these were not permanent solutions.

As in the past, as infants left the hospitals mostly because of reforms to foster care, including group or semi-orphanages as well as family preservation, the scandal ran its course and the issue of abandoned babies fell off the radar screen. It picked up every now and then when a baby was left in a park or a dumpster. Occasionally, the stories suggested the continuation of the trend of large numbers of infants simply abandoned (Collins, 2007). For example, in 1999, within a few days, 13 infants were left around Houston, Texas, 10 of whom were found alive (Yardley, 1999). The numbers from the mid-1980s to the late 2000s remain very high. In most years, one in six admissions to foster care was an infant under the age of 1, and the majority of these were under 3 months of age and came directly from hospitals (Wulczyn & Hislop, 2002).

Yet, it is not the trends but the individual harrowing stories that continue to grab public attention. The baby left in a trash bin behind a high school or on top of a park bench in the cold are the stories that galvanize public action and result in the passage of infant safe haven laws. These laws, also known as Baby Moses laws, were first passed in Texas in 1999. Ultimately, most states created their own versions of these statutes that permit placement of infants in hospitals, police stations, or other public facilities without criminal sanction (Child Welfare Information Gateway, 2007).

Yet, these laws have saved only 100 babies (National Abandoned Infants Resource Center, 2005) in contrast to the safe haven practices of 100 years ago. At that time, hundreds of babies were left at Foundling Hospital in the vestibule cradle or similar hospitals throughout the nation. The circumstances, however, lead one to surmise that we are dealing with a different situation. Yes, babies are being abandoned in large numbers, but the underlying reasons are different. As the letters left by mothers at the Foundling Hospital indicated, poverty and the stigma of out-of-wedlock births accounted for most of the placements (Collins, 2007).

Today's babies in the child welfare system face far more complexities and problems that cannot be solved as easily as providing an income support system. Although poverty is certainly a major factor in the plight of today's babies, it is only a part of a constellation of causes that range from parental drug and alcohol abuse to mental illness and cognitive limitations, as well as the challenges of the babies themselves who exhibit significant delays or have serious health problems or are hard to soothe. Yet, moving from scandal to reform is a historical cycle that must be broken (Bartholet, 1999). Indeed, without ensuring the healthy development of these babies by promoting their physical and mental health, development, and prospects for growing up in a loving, permanent family, that cycle will only continue.

3

A Child's Journey Through the Child Welfare System

JOEY'S STORY

Joey was born a few weeks early and weighed only 5 pounds. He was found to have a positive toxicology for crystal methamphetamine at birth. After a few extra days in the hospital, Joey and his mother went home. Joey did not receive any health care for the next 3 months, including immunizations.

One night, when Joey was 3 months old, his mother went out in search of drugs. She planned to be out for only a short time and left Joey asleep in his crib. She did not return, however, for hours. Joey awoke while she was away, and he began crying. He cried louder and louder. An exasperated neighbor called the police after banging on Joey's door and not getting a response. The police broke into the house to find a soiled, wailing Joey and called child protective services (CPS).

CPS saw Joey's state—dirty, whimpering, and very hungry—and took him into emergency protective custody. He was brought to the children's shelter in his rural county where he was examined by a physician and placed for the night. That evening, Joey's mother returned home to find Joey gone, but she found a notice advising her that he had been taken by CPS and that she needed to go to family court the next morning.

At the court hearing, the judge found Joey to be in imminent risk of harm and ordered him into foster care. His mother pleaded for his return. She was ordered into substance abuse treatment and given the right to visit him once every other week. At this point, Joey was placed in nonrelative foster care.

Three months later, an adjudicatory hearing was held to determine if Joey had been abused or neglected. Joey's mother did not appear at the hearing. The judge found that Joey had been neglected because his mother had left him alone, failing both to protect him and to provide the basic necessities of life during her absence.

These 3 months had been very difficult for Joey. He was moved from the children's shelter to an unfamiliar foster home. The foster parent was unable to soothe and comfort him, and Joey was moved again. At the time of the adjudicatory hearing, CPS was looking for yet another home for Joey because he was now having serious feeding problems and was still crying all the time.

Almost 6 months passed before the next court hearing, called a _dispositional hearing._ That hearing took only a few minutes because Joey's mother was once again not present. The court continued Joey's placement in foster care. No information was presented to the court about Joey's difficulties or his relocation to a number of different foster homes.

By this time, Joey was almost 1 year old, and he had lived in four different foster homes. Each had been unable to care for him. His child welfare caseworker determined that this had to stop, so she did two things. First, she referred Joey to the early intervention (EI) program in her county. Due to Joey's multiple problems (i.e., feeding disorders, growth difficulties, incessant crying), he was labeled "failure to thrive" and found eligible for EI services immediately. At the same time, the caseworker found a new foster family—a family that had fostered and adopted a child with disabilities. The family agreed to take Joey only if he received needed services. The child welfare caseworker, therefore, had an incentive to make sure the EI services, which included a nurse for the feeding and sleeping problems, began providing services for Joey in the home right away. It was imperative that the family received not only EI service coordination but also parent training and respite care so they could have some periodic time off from caring for Joey.

Joey began to gain weight almost immediately after his new placement and the start of EI services. Soon, he was sleeping and eating well and beginning to reach developmental milestones. By age 2, he was running and had begun to speak with some difficulty. He then received speech therapy as part of his EI services. At 3 years, he began a preschool special education program.

When Joey was 2 years old, his mother came to the extension of placement hearing in court and requested his return. She was still struggling with substance abuse, and the judge ordered her into treatment, but also gave her the right to visit Joey every other week in the social services office. She never entered substance abuse treatment, but every other week Joey would get bundled up—sometimes under protest—and brought to the visits.

His mother came once every 2 months. Whether or not she came, the period after the visit was difficult. Joey would cry and scream, and after a while, he began having temper tantrums. The foster family requested counseling services for Joey, and those services were provided by EI until Joey was 3 years old. Thereafter, he continued to receive counseling services under the preschool special education program.

This situation became intolerable for Joey and his foster family, and these often empty visits seemed harmful to him, so at the insistence of Joey's foster parents, his goal was changed to adoption when he was 3 years old. However, making this change on his child welfare case plan took months of advocacy by his foster parents. It took another year for the court to approve the change and months more for a Termination of Parental Rights (TPR) petition to be filed. Once the petition was filed, Joey's birth mother, who had been in and out of his life for so long, emerged to strenuously oppose the TPR. After losing the case at trial because of her failure to cooperate with her service plans, complete substance abuse treatment, visit Joey every other week, and evidence any ability to care for Joey, his mother appealed the court's decision, despite the fact that she had never had time alone with him during his 4 years in foster care.

The appeal process took almost 2 years and affirmed the lower court decision to terminate parental rights. At that time, Joey's foster parents had filed an adoption petition that took almost a year from filing to finalization.

CHILD PROTECTIVE SERVICES

Every child's journey through the child welfare system begins in the same way—with someone making a report to CPS. Every state has a CPS system that provides a mechanism for the reporting, assessment, and investigation of allegations of abuse or neglect (Dicker & Gordon, 2004a). In Joey's case, his neighbor called the police who then reported the case to CPS. The identity of the reporter will vary from those who are mandated or required by law to report possible abuse or neglect to neighbors and the general public. Nationwide, approximately half the reports are made by mandated reporters and half by other individuals, such as Joey's neighbor (DHHS, 2008).

In most states, specific categories of professionals are mandated reporters. These include professionals in the education, health care, child care, social services, mental health, and law enforcement professions. Since Joey had very little contact with the outside world as an infant, he was unlikely to be reported by one of these professionals. Indeed, the largest percentage of reports is from the education system, which can act as a second set of eyes for older children (DHHS, 2008). However, infants such as Joey have no contact with this system and must rely on surveillance during well-child visits with health professionals or by child care providers (Dicker & Gordon, 2000). Although reports from mandated reporters are twice as likely to be found valid because of their professional training, very young children are less likely to come into contact with mandated reporters (DHHS, 2008). Their invisibility to CPS due to lack of professional surveillance only compounds their inherent vulnerability.

When CPS receives a report alleging abuse or neglect, they will first screen the case to determine whether an investigation is warranted. Sometimes the case involves issues other than child protection, and sometimes there is insufficient information to proceed with an investigation. Approximately one third of all cases will be screened out at this point, and CPS will further investigate another two thirds of the cases reported. It is far more likely that mandated reports will be screened in than those from other persons (DHHS, 2008). In Joey's case, this screening process was done in the context of an emergency. The police contacted CPS and reported an infant left alone.

Once a case has been identified for investigation, CPS ordinarily will examine the case within 24–72 hours to determine whether the allegation is substantiated or unsubstantiated. In emergencies such as Joey's case, the investigation occurs much quicker. More than 60% of the cases will be found to be unsubstantiated, whereas nearly 30% will be found to be substantiated. A substantiated finding means that an investigation determined a likelihood that maltreatment occurred (DHHS, 2008). In Joey's case, an infant left alone, unsupervised, and without food is, on the surface, a substantiated case. Sadly, children with disabilities are far more likely to be maltreated than children without disabilities (DHHS, National Center for Child Abuse and Neglect, 1994).

Once CPS determines that a case is substantiated, it then must determine a course of action. Of greatest significance for very young children is whether a child such as Joey is at imminent risk of harm. If CPS determines that the child is at imminent risk, they can remove the child with emergency court approval or, in some circumstances, with court approval after the removal.

COURT PROCESS

In all instances, a court order must be obtained for a child to remain in out-of-home placement or foster care. (A small number of children may be voluntarily placed by parents, but courts also are required to review those placements.) This underscores the central decision-making role of our nation's juvenile and family courts in child protection cases (Dicker & Gordon, 2000). In a case such as Joey's, the court will hold a preliminary or intake hearing within a day of removal. According to the federal Adoption Assistance and Child Welfare Act of 1980 (PL 96-272), the court will initially consider whether the child can be returned home safely or is in imminent harm and whether it is in the child's best interest to be placed in foster care. The court will also consider the types of supports needed by the family.

In all hearings, the judge will also make a "reasonable efforts finding," that is, a determination that the child welfare agency provided services to prevent placement and, after placement, provided services to reunify the family. If the court determines that it is not in the best interest of the child to return home, it can choose to do one of several things. It can order foster care placement; order that the child be placed with an available relative; order visitation with the parents that may be supervised; or order assessments, evaluations, or reports of the child and family to be provided to the court by the next hearing date. The child could remain in foster care until this next court appearance, which often does not transpire for 30–60 days.

The next hearing is the adjudication, in which the court determines the merits of the abuse and neglect claims. In a case such as Joey's, adjudication is often delayed for a host of reasons, including lack of information about the child, parent, or the petition allegations. If the court finds that the allegations are true, or, as occurs in the majority of cases, the parent admits to the abuse or neglect, the court will hold a disposition hearing generally 30 days thereafter. As is evident from Joey's case, these time frames can take far longer, particularly when the parent does not appear in court.

At the critical disposition hearing, the court reviews mandated child welfare case plans for both the child and the parent, as well as visitation, other services, and orders. By this time, in Joey's case, he had been in foster care for 9 months. Unlike Joey's cursory hearing, the disposition hearing is a crucial point in which the court receives and considers the health and developmental needs of the specific child, while at the same time assesses the ability of the biological and foster parents to carry out those needs. In Joey's case, the hearing was very short, and the court did not receive any information about his health and developmental needs or his difficulties in placement. This is, perhaps, why it took Joey so long to settle into a more stable foster family.

After the disposition hearing, courts are required to conduct periodic reviews of the placement and compliance with court orders. At every hearing, the court must make a reasonable efforts finding, and every court review is an opportunity to bring vital information about the child's well-being to the attention of the court.

Under the federal Adoption and Safe Families Act of 1997 (ASFA) (PL 105-89), the permanency hearing was created to ensure that more expeditious decisions about children's lives are made by our nation's courts. At this critical hearing, the judge must determine the child's permanency plan, including return to parent, placement with a relative, adoption, legal guardianship, or other long-term placement.

Although ASFA requires a permanency hearing no later than a year after a child has been in foster care, in Joey's case no permanency hearing was ever held. The fact that Joey's case was not provided this critical hearing may be the result of his state's failure to implement ASFA in a timely fashion. Had the court held a permanency hearing for Joey, perhaps his stay in foster care would have been shortened. Indeed, under ASFA, if a child has been in foster care for 15 out of the most recent 22 months, state agencies must file petitions to terminate parental rights. The only exceptions to the 22-month rule would not apply in Joey's case because they include placement with a relative or failure to provide needed services to parents. TPR can only be obtained in the most serious cases, such as abandonment, parental mental incapacity, severe or repeated child abuse, or permanent neglect. The difficulty of achieving TPR is further underscored by the standard used to evaluate evidence by the court. The court must find by clear and convincing evidence that parental rights should be terminated. This is a very strict standard as it is only a notch below the criminal law standard of beyond a reasonable doubt.

Joey's mother's parental rights could have been terminated far earlier if ASFA requirements were followed because the facts of his case met the stringent standards of the law. Often, the petition, as in Joey's case, is contested and appealed, and the process can span years of a child's life. Once all appeals are exhausted and a court order is final for the TPR, a petition for adoption can be filed. All too often, the adoption hearing is delayed further, which keeps the child in the limbo of foster care. Again, it is essential that the court receive ongoing information about the child's needs throughout the child's time in foster care.

The persistence of Joey's foster parents, who are now his legal parents, is an important lesson in Joey's long journey in the child welfare system. Yet, for most of the hundreds of thousands of children, finding such ardent parent advocates is difficult. In the meantime, the wait has an impact on their childhood and imperils their long-term health and development.

II

The Promise of the Research and the Law

4

Promising New Research

DARREN'S STORY

Darren entered foster care at birth with a toxicology screen that was positive for cocaine. His birth mother abandoned him at the hospital, and his father's whereabouts were unknown. In his first 8 months of life, he was hospitalized several times for respiratory infections and other medical problems. He was described by nurses as withdrawn and unable to tolerate any changes in his environment. He was placed with a foster family who was also open to adoption. They were willing and able to meet his extraordinary medical and emotional needs, including constant nighttime monitoring for sleep apnea. The judge in this case was so concerned about the strain on the foster family that she ordered that an aide be provided to give the family respite.

When Darren reached 9 months of age, his biological mother reappeared and requested his return. The judge ordered substance abuse treatment and frequent visitation for the mother, who was compliant and became sober. Due to Darren's fragile condition, the judge ordered the visits in the home of the foster parents. Despite their collaboration and the biological mother's consistent efforts, Darren would not allow anyone other than the foster parents to hold him. At the next hearing, the biological mother told the judge that she understood the child's extraordinary needs and believed he was better off with the foster parents. Darren was adopted by his foster parents, but he has occasional contact with his biological mother according to an open adoption agreement.

Scientific research on the first months and years of life tells us that infancy presents an unparalleled window of opportunity to promote a child's healthy development and family stability. Yet, when the needs of the most vulnerable infants—those in the child welfare system—are undetected and unaddressed, their well-being and prospects for growing up in a permanent home can be jeopardized. Fortunately, abundant scientific knowledge about early child development is available to inform policy and practice. We now know that more brain growth and learning occur during infancy than during any other time of life, which builds a foundation essential to all future development. Yet, at the same time, in no other period do children rely so completely on the adults in their lives. The care received and attachments made during the first months of life for all children are critical building blocks for future development and adult well-being.

In 2000, the Board on Children, Youth and Families, the National Research Council, and the Institute of Medicine collaborated and published *From Neurons to Neighborhoods: The Science of Early Childhood Development* (Shonkoff & Phillips, 2000). This seminal work sought to evaluate and integrate all knowledge about the current science of early childhood development. It provides a consensus document that policy makers, academics, educators, professionals, and the public can use as a guide. Shonkoff and Phillips provide an analysis of the explosion of research in neurobiology, behavior, and social sciences concerning young children, and they underscore the following four core concepts:

- All children are born wired for feelings and ready to learn.

- Early environments matter and nurturing relationships are essential.

- Society is changing, and the needs of young children are not being addressed.

- Interactions among early childhood science, policy, and practice are problematic and demand dramatic rethinking.

This chapter focuses on those findings and related works concerning early brain development, the importance of early relationships, the applicability of the research to children who have been subject to abuse and neglect, and the possibilities for effective intervention for those children.

EARLY BRAIN DEVELOPMENT

The human brain develops most rapidly during the first years of life. By age 3, a baby's brain is 85% of its adult size (Hudson, Klain, Smariga, & Youcha, 2007). Between birth and age 3, the neural pathways that govern sight, hearing, and language are established. These pathways are extremely sensitive to external stimulation that influences brain development and affects memory, emotions, and learning. Indeed, babies have memories. From the first days of life, infants have what is called *perceptual memory* in which sights and sounds trigger both physical and emotional responses. From very early life, infants are trying to communicate their needs and feelings to adults (Youcha, 2005). Infants are very aware of the other humans with whom they interact. They are more likely to create expressions of joy, as well as positive vocalizations, when looking at their mother than at an object.

Babies, of course, have feelings. It is known that babies can communicate distress, but they also can make their feelings known through gazes, yawns, and cries. Infants as young as 3 months of age can show signs of depression and other psychological disorders. Babies even grieve when their caregivers disappear (Wingert & Brant, 2005).

The basic architecture of the brain is built over time, which is a process that continues into early adulthood. Its foundation involves the connections that form during early childhood, which will be highly influential in later years. Indeed, from birth to age 3, children rapidly develop foundational capabilities on which subsequent development builds. Children gain remarkable linguistic, cognitive, emotional, social regulatory, and moral progress, as well as cognitive and communication capacities during these 3 years. All of these critical dimensions of early development are intertwined, and each requires focused attention.

THE IMPORTANCE OF SELF-REGULATION, COMMUNICATION, AND LEARNING

From Neurons to Neighborhoods (Shonkoff & Phillips, 2000) highlights the importance of the development of self-regulation in young children—a key developmental task. Infants begin life totally dependent on adults for their very lives. They move from complete helplessness to eventually gaining control over their bodies and being able to communicate their needs. Scientists refer to this transition as gaining regulatory capacity. In early infancy, it means regulation of temperature, sleep patterns, and the ability to soothe oneself. Darren's case illustrates the critical nature of regulation and its impact on child well-being and family life. Over time, self-regulation involves the capacity to manage emotions and focus attention.

Learning ways to communicate effectively is another major developmental achievement. Self-regulation and communication skills support later critical developments essential for learning and school readiness (Shonkoff & Phillips, 2000). When young children are delayed in developing communication and cognitive skills, these difficulties will reverberate in other domains, particularly in the child's emotional and behavioral functioning. A strong body of research indicates that children's language and cognitive development are significantly influenced by variance in socioeconomic circumstances (Shonkoff & Phillips, 2000). This profound risk factor, in conjunction with the intersecting strands of development, underscores the importance of early identification and intervention for early communication and cognitive delays.

Learning language begins at birth and is a resilient process, with most children learning to speak without additional special help. Children across the world learn to speak in a similar pattern. Children between 10 and 15 months of age speak their first words in their own language. Most 18 month olds learn nine new words every day, and many can produce short phrases, sometimes even sentences. Interestingly, cross-culturally, the content of these short sentences is similar in content and in their adult mirroring structure. By the age of 3, most children speak in complete sentences.

Despite the universality of language learning, however, there can be hindrances that are either environmental or organic. Studies have established that babies who are spoken to have stronger vocabulary growth, emergent literacy skills, and written skills. The number and type of words heard has dramatic correlations to socioeconomic factors, maternal mental health, and parental education. Fortunately, deficits are amenable to early intervention. *From Neurons to Neighborhoods* (Shonkoff & Phillips, 2000) notes that children raised in orphanages are less likely to use language to express emotions and ideas or even ask for adult assistance; however, even children raised in low-stimulating orphanages who have noticeably delayed language abilities can rebound when placed in supportive, stimulating families.

THE IMPORTANCE OF EARLY RELATIONSHIPS

Although *From Neurons to Neighborhoods* underscores the importance of neuroscience research and its application to the early years of childhood, its most surprising findings concern the inherent significance of the earliest relationships in life. It finds that early relationships provide the foundation that determines whether a baby's brain is hard wired for social-emotional well-being or isolation and failure. The research tells us that babies require stability in their relationships and consistency in their daily routines. These requirements are illustrated by Darren's story at the beginning of this chapter.

Infant mental health principles are based on research and clinical experience that provide support that infants' emotional development occurs within the context of their caregiving relationships. Consistent early relationships and experiences are the foundation upon which all subsequent emotional development rests. The single most important predictor of a child's healthy development and growth is the emotional attachment he or she forms with a consistent, loving caregiver (noting, of course, that multiple attachments are possible and preferable), a person whom the infant may use not only as a source of comfort but also as a kind of base from which to explore (Appleyard & Berlin, 2007). A secure emotional bond with a loving caregiver helps infants feel secure and comfortable, able to seek help when necessary, but also capable of exploring on their own. Conversely, inconsistent, neglectful, or abusive parenting can result in one of several types of insecure or disorganized attachment styles, which results in a child who might be detached, overly dependent, or simply frightened (Appleyard & Berlin, 2007).

For infants, consistency in relationships is achieved through attachment; that is, the formation of an enduring emotional bond with a primary or small number of stable, responsive, and sensitive caregivers. There is a dance that caregivers and babies engage in repeatedly. All facets of an infant's daily life are involved in this dance—feeding, waking, sleeping, diapering—and they are all in concert with the particular mode of response by the baby's caregiver. Disrupted attachments not only contribute to social-emotional problems, but can have biochemical consequences in a developing brain.

Research indicates that from birth to 2 months of age, an infant's preferences are limited to familiar sights and sounds. Between 2 and 4 months of age, they begin to know differences among caregivers, but a preference is not strongly expressed. By 6 months, most infants show a preferred attachment and begin to develop anxiety when a stranger approaches or when separated from primary caregivers. Yet, after multiple disrupted attachments, it takes much longer for children to feel an accepted level of comfort with their caregivers (Dozier, Stovall, Albus, & Bates, 2001).

One can think of stress during early childhood as representing a continuum. Certain kinds of stress, such as waiting briefly to be fed, are a catalyst for positive development that build the ability to sit for reading activities in preschool. However, unremitting, uncontrollable experiences with intensely stressful conditions can overtax a baby's capacity to cope with and regulate the resulting anxiety. The impact of overtaxing a young child's capacity for stress or anxiety may be thought of as *toxic* stress, such as in situations that terrify a baby (e.g., exposure to violence) or result in chronic, enduring stressors (e.g., significant neglect of basic needs) (DC:0-3R). Toxic stress causes the body's stress response to go into lengthened activation; it raises an infant's heart rate and blood pressure and floods the body with stress hormones. It literally alters brain chemicals. When an infant experiences this mode for a prolonged period or too frequently, it can have an adverse impact on brain development and thus affect the baby both physically and mentally over time (Center on the Developing Child at Harvard University, 2007).

How the infant responds to such difficulties is moderated by the infant's relationship with his or her primary caregiver. When infants have secure attachment relationships with their caregivers, and those caregivers are available to soothe them and help them regain their equilibrium, they will be more resilient despite adversity. However, the absence of a caregiver whom an infant trusts exacerbates the infant's vulnerability.

Self-regulation, communication, learning, and early relationships are intertwined during early development. Self-regulation is achieved through consistency in caregiving and daily routines, such as sleeping and feeding. This consistency allows infants to gain a sense of security that reduces their stress when faced with new or challenging situations and helps them to self-regulate their emotions and behaviors. Babies born with low birth weight, who have mothers who abuse substances or have serious mental illness, who are exposed to violence, or whose stress has reached unmanageable levels are particularly vulnerable to problems with regulation. These infants often exhibit challenging behaviors, including excessive fussiness and sleep or feeding disturbances.

APPLYING THE SCIENCE OF EARLY CHILDHOOD TO BABIES IN CHILD WELFARE

From Neurons to Neighborhoods (Shonkoff & Phillips, 2000) sounds an alarm concerning young children exposed to abuse and neglect because research shows that environments characterized by these harmful behaviors impede development. Young children are especially vulnerable to the effects of maltreatment, and its impact on their physical as well as emotional development can have lifelong implications if not addressed. Children who are abused and neglected are more likely than other children to have mental health problems and other disadvantages in life, such as academic failure, involvement with the criminal justice system, substance abuse, and teen pregnancy (Widom & Maxfield, 2001). These effects can be observed in imaging data, which has shown that severely abused children actually have smaller brain volumes, with fewer connections between the right and left hemispheres, when compared with physically and mentally healthy children of the same age (Shonkoff & Phillips, 2000). Indeed, the longer the duration of the trauma, the greater the differences observed in terms of brain volume between children who have been abused and their peers.

Despite these grim findings, a number of studies have indicated that children who have been maltreated can flourish and progress when placed into caring homes with consistent caregivers. Although the impact of early maltreatment may persist in some regards, development can improve because it is a dynamic process involving interactions between the child and caregivers over time. The importance of providing training for caregivers in how to meet the needs of these children cannot be understated. Helping foster parents or kinship or relative providers learn how to understand and manage their infant's emotional and behavioral needs can assist them in responding more effectively to the infants. Substitute caregivers often tend to conduct themselves in ways that correspond to a baby's own actions. For example, if a baby who has low expectations of nurturing pushes his foster mother away, most likely she will perceive him as independent rather than insecurely attached. The baby, not expecting nurturance, is acting in a way that will not elicit the comfort or security he desperately needs to develop trusting relationships and, in turn, healthy emotional regulation (Dozier et al., 2001). Programs that teach foster parents to recognize the baby's need for nurturing and to respond to this need can enhance interactions between these infants and their caregivers and hopefully lead to a more secure bond. For infants in foster care, this guidance and support can mean the difference between a stable placement and placement disruption. It can also strengthen families for possible reunification or adoption.

Separation from parents, sometimes traumatic, coupled with the difficult experience of adjustment after placement, can render infants and toddlers "dramatically impaired in their emotional, social, physical and cognitive development" (Cohen & Youcha, 2004, p. 16). Changes in placement and visitation with their families are two key issues inherent in foster care that can compound infants' emotional difficulties. A 2003 study found that, for boys especially, placement itself did not increase the likeliness of delinquency in youths who have been maltreated. Rather, it was placement instability that predicted trouble with the law (Ryan & Testa, 2004). This discovery seems obvious: If attachment is one of the most critical developmental tasks of infancy, then multiple placements will undermine the centrality and consistency of crucial relationships. Placement disruptions break the bonds of children's relationships. As they are severed over and over again, children experience feelings of abandonment and distrust. Babies grieve when their relationships are breached. Children who have experienced abuse and neglect have an even greater need for sensitive, caring, and stable relationships; yet, many are unable to show that need. Their grief may manifest in heightened irritability and inconsolable crying, as well as in emotional withdrawal.

Guarding against placement disruption should begin as soon as possible with a prudent analysis of the birth parents' capacity to meet the child's needs. If out-of-home care is warranted, enhanced matching requirements must be in place to ensure that the foster parent has the capacity to care for this particular child. There also must be other policies that safeguard placements. In choosing a placement for an infant, agencies should explore challenges and be certain that at the bare minimum the caregiver is able to meet the infant's basic health and safety needs. In choosing a foster home for an infant, assessment should be made as to whether a foster parent has any physical, psychological, or cognitive limitations that could interfere with his or her ability to carry, lift, or feed the infant, as well as hear the infant cry or stay awake at night with the infant. The age of the caregiver or caregivers, as well as the number of other children in the home and their needs, can provide clues about a caregiver's capacity and resources. Finally, a foster parent's willingness to participate in a partnership with birth parents during reunification efforts (and to adopt the infant if reunification efforts fail) must be considered for the good of the child.

Making sure that foster parents have sufficient training in the requisites of attachment is critical. This education should include how to read an infant's or toddler's cues, how to establish an emotional bond with this child, and a general understanding of the importance of attachment in the child's life. Foster parents must adapt their own parenting style to facilitate attachment with each child. Parent education that is individually tailored and addresses the child's attachment needs should occur before reunification and during the adjustment period postreunification because this is a critical transition and there is a high risk of reentry into foster care for children under 3 years of age.

Research also underscores the importance of a foster parent's commitment to the child, which is paramount to the child's functioning. Developmental delays in cognition, learning, and social-emotional domains are common in children who experience multiple placements and fail to develop secure attachments to at least one caring adult (Shonkoff & Phillips, 2000).

Visits with parents are also strongly related to attachment. The regularity of visits is one of the best predictors of reunification for families. Yet, all too often, infants see their parents briefly, once a week or once a month. These brief court-ordered visits purport to be aimed at maintaining and building relationships between parent(s) and infant; however, they are actually tantamount to no visits at all. The youngest of children can barely keep an image of their mother in their minds for more than a day; therefore, a full month can feel like (or be) a lifetime. Parent visits are critical, and they need to begin soon after the child is placed into foster care (Wright, 2001). Frequent and extensive contact is needed to build and maintain relationships, and not just within an alienating or impersonal agency office (Beyer, 2008). These meetings should happen as often as possible and occur daily or every other day in a setting conducive to parent–child interaction (e.g., a cozy, private space rather than an agency office). The visits should last long enough to give the parent time to practice changing, feeding, holding, and comforting the baby. These visits are not merely a chance for the baby and the parent to establish or continue a relationship but also an opportunity for the parent to enhance his or her understanding of the particular challenges of being a parent and to work on his or her abilities to meet these challenges.

These interactions need to be supported to work. Parents, particularly those whose children are placed as infants, are likely to be challenged by substance abuse, mental illness, or cognitive limitations. They may need assistance to get to know their baby, to learn to read the baby's cues, to understand the importance of talking to their baby, and to have strategies to comfort their baby when distressed. They may need help on an even more basic level, such as learning to feed, hold, and change their child. Visits should be a learning opportunity as well as a relationship-building time (Beyer 2008). Visits also can be diagnostic because they can be used as a means to gauge the parents' capacity to care for their child. Visits provide valuable information not only to child welfare agencies and courts but also to the parents themselves. The visits can underscore the enormous difficulties posed by parenting each particular child and, therefore, render a parent better able to make decisions about the future. This is precisely what happened to Darren, described at the beginning of this chapter. His birth mother acknowledged her inability to care for a child with enormous needs; however, the option of an open adoption allowed her to continue to be present in his life.

RESEARCH-BASED INTERVENTIONS

Building Strong Parent–Child Relationships

The centrality of stable, consistent relationships to child well-being echoes throughout the research on early childhood development. Placing children in stable families allows them to catch up developmentally, particularly in the resilient language and cognitive domains. More persistent over time are the emotional delays that may be constrained by a caregiver's capacity to tailor his or her parenting style to suit the special needs of a specific child. Thus, at its core, healthy development requires the presence of a caring, capable, consistent caregiver, but that is only the starting point; other interventions may be needed.

The need for all children, especially young children, to have caring, consistent relationships, is at the heart of child welfare law and policy (see Chapter 5).

However, the current system is undermined by the use of career foster parents (e.g., Mrs. M. in the Introduction to this book) who have fostered many children and are less likely to make the necessary intense emotional commitment that babies need to promote a secure attachment (Dozier & Lindhiem, 2006). These *experienced* caregivers actually may be causing emotional harm to the babies by impeding the formation of a secure attachment. Research has shown that commitment is ultimately more important than experience, at least in terms of the youngest of foster children.

Ensuring permanency and commitment is an enormous challenge and the research has only begun to provide guidance on how it can be achieved. There is a wide body of research on the efficacy of adoption for abandoned, abused, or neglected children. In particular, there have been studies on children in orphanages in Romania and other eastern European countries that have found these children to exhibit considerable delays in cognitive and emotional development (Shonkoff & Phillips, 2000). Yet, when adopted early into loving, supportive families, these children often demonstrate significant recovery and make enormous developmental leaps, particularly in the cognitive and language domains (Shonkoff & Phillips). These positive responses are a direct result of having committed adults in their lives (Bartholet, 1999).

Even with these committed adoptive parents, however, emotional development is most likely to remain delayed, with approximately 15% retaining significant emotional disabilities (O'Connor et al., 2000; Shonkoff & Phillips, 2000). Yet, adequate stimulation coupled with stable relationships shows improvement in thinking, concentration, and inhibitory control. Provided that the new home is a stable and loving one, healing and improved skills are possible for most children who are adopted in their early years.

Although adoption is an important option for many young children who have been abused and neglected, many more will be reunited with their birth families. The challenge is to ensure that these children, too, have a family that can provide what children need most, which is a caregiver who is consistent, loving, stable, knows the child, and is mindful of the child's particular needs (Stone, 2007).

Research has only begun to document effective efforts to enhance the capacity of biological parents whose children have been maltreated. Most promising appear to be individualized clinical interventions that are consistent and regular to improve a caregiver's sensitivity. These sessions attempt to take into account the parents' own needs and unique life experiences, as well as the specific needs of the child, rather than being a cookie cutter training session (Shonkoff & Phillips, 2000). The Infant–Parent Program in San Francisco is one such program that targets young children involved with the child welfare system and provides intensive individualized therapy to mothers and children to build parental sensitivity (Lieberman, Silverman, & Pawl, 2005). The focus of the program is on the relationships between children and the parents, especially on how to create empathy and understanding toward the infant experience by using concrete assistance from therapists, as well as emotional support (Hinden, Biebel, Nicholson, Henry, & Stier, 2002).

Another promising effort has focused on improving foster parents' capacity to develop secure attachments for very young children in foster care. The Infant–Caregiver Project, based at the University of Delaware, runs the Attachment and Biobehavioral Catch-up (ABC) intervention program (http://icp.psych.udel.edu/parents/index.htm), which provides 10 intensive in-home sessions for parents, whether foster or biological, and their children with the goal of attaining a secure attachment. The intervention strives to help caregivers develop nurturing relationships, as well as to improve the child's psychological regulation. All sessions are videotaped and reviewed with parents. A parent trainer works with the family personally throughout all the sessions. Preliminary results indicate improved secure attachments for children and foster parents and promising prospects for birth parents involved in the program (Zero to Three, 2004).

Although the majority of parents of children who have been abused or neglected are required to attend parenting education programs, the research is scant in supporting the validity or efficacy of such programs (Barth et al., 2005). Typically, parents attend group sessions, often without regard to the age of the child or the presenting challenge of the parent, such as substance abuse or mental illness. These group classes rarely have standards for curriculum and accountability measures, and often the sole result is granting the parent a certificate of attendance. These programs are often one-size-fits-all and do not assess the child or the parent prior to beginning a parenting program to determine their needs. Furthermore, few programs have postsessions to measure changes in parental sensitivity or child interaction.

Importance of Basic Health Care

As emphatically stated in *From Neurons to Neighborhoods* (Shonkoff & Phillips, 2000), the single most important component of a child's healthy development is the presence of an enduring adult caregiving relationship. Yet, other services must also be in place to enhance the healthy development of the child. The most obvious is the provision of basic health care. Study after study reveals that children in the child welfare system, particularly those in foster care, have far more fragile health than other children and are far less likely to receive the health care that can improve their lives (Simms, Dubowitz, & Szilagi, 2000). As with all children, they require well-child health care, immunizations, and treatment of common childhood illnesses; however, many also have health concerns associated with poverty, such as low birth weight, increased risk of lead poisoning, and malnutrition.

Many foster children also face health risks specifically linked to parental neglect, including maternal substance abuse, physical or sexual abuse, and parental mental illness. Researchers have found that children with two or more identified risk factors are four times more likely than other children to develop social, educational, and health problems. On average, foster children at issue here have more than 14 risk factors including family factors such as poverty, social isolation, substance abuse, and mental illness as well as child factors such as disabilities and being under age 3 (Child Welfare Information Gateway, 2008; Dicker, Gordon, & Knitzer, 2001). Lack of attention to foster children's health needs compromises their healthy development and can also create additional stresses that may disrupt stable placements. Therefore, addressing those health care needs early has a number of benefits, and can reverse bleak prognoses, strengthen families, and enhance permanency (Dicker & Gordon, 2004c).

Because children enter the foster care system as a result of abuse, neglect, homelessness, poverty, and parental substance abuse and mental illness, all children should receive a comprehensive examination shortly after placement that addresses all aspects of child functioning. The Child Welfare League of America (CWLA) and the American Academy of Pediatrics (AAP) recommend that, beyond an initial health screening, there should be a comprehensive medical, developmental, and mental health assessment for each child within 30 days of placement in foster care (AAP, 2000a; CWLA, 1988, 2007; Evans, Scott, & Schultz, 2004).

The need for such a thorough examination is made clear by the fact that 60%–90% of all children entering foster care fail at least one of the areas of either the initial or the comprehensive exam. The AAP further recommends quality health care that includes comprehensive, continuous, and family supportive care that involves the biological parents when appropriate (AAP, 2000a). Family supportive care should consist of not only sharing the child's health information with the child's caregivers and providing education and training to support families in their ongoing care of the child, but also a *medical home* for the child in which health care is provided by a consistent practitioner who is familiar with the specific child and his or her circumstances. This kind of care should include all of the basics of Medicaid's early and periodic screening, diagnosis, and treatment (EPSDT) program, including complete and up-to-date immunizations; screening for vision, hearing, communicable diseases, lead exposure, development, mental health, and dental care; and treatment to address or ameliorate any diagnosed condition (Dicker & Gordon, 2004c).

Connections to Early Intervention

In addition to providing basic health care for maltreated children, there is consistent research that supports the effectiveness of early intervention (EI) programs for young children with developmental delays and disabilities (Shonkoff & Meisels, 2000). This body of literature holds that a set of interventions provided early in life can help resolve children's developmental delays. The research states that early intervention can mitigate, sometimes entirely, the risk factors that stem from a child's rocky beginning (Guralnick & Albertini, 2005).

Although much of the research has been on particular disabilities, such as Down syndrome, there have been enough studies that encompass all developmental delays that the results are clear: Intervening early with an array of programs can address or ameliorate developmental delays (Guralnick, 2006). The core principles of an effective program highlight inclusion, both within a family as well as within society, and, of course, the building of relationships. Furthermore, the program must synchronize and integrate support and services for the children and parents so that each family and child is getting exactly what is needed to promote healthy development. Effective EI programs have two components: 1) the provision of a range of therapeutic services based on need, such as occupational, speech, and physical therapies; and 2) the provision of those services within the context of a specific family (Shonkoff, J.P., & Meisels, S.J., 2000).

The EI programs for infants and toddlers with developmental disabilities, commonly known as Part C of the Individuals with Disabilities Education Act Amendments (IDEA) of 1997 (PL 105-17), embrace both needed components. Part C requires all states that choose to participate (currently all states and eligible territories) to use their funding to fully implement the requirements of the law. The requirements include an inclusive Child Find system set up by lead state agencies to find children in need quickly (2-day formal referrals to Part C) and ongoing, comprehensive evaluations to make sure that a child's needs are continually being met. Most importantly, an individualized family service plan (IFSP) must be drawn up within 45 days of referral for eligible children. The IFSP delineates all services (including frequency and duration) for both the child (e.g., physical, occupational, or speech therapies; special instruction) and the parents (e.g., parent training, counseling, support groups, home visits) as well as the critical service coordination.

Participation in Part C provides children and families with a wealth of opportunity, and child welfare caseworkers have an easier time ensuring that the needs of children with developmental disabilities are being addressed. Yet, despite its passage in 1986, states report the "underidentification and underenrollment" of eligible children who are a part of the child welfare system (Child Welfare Information Gateway, 2007). A major reason for this discrepancy is the frequent lack of consistent foster parents, medical care, and even child welfare caseworkers who are not always trained or well prepared to identify a special need or a developmental delay on the part of the child (Halfon, Mendonca, & Berkowitz, 1995).

Shonkoff and Phillips (2000) noted the high prevalence of developmental delays and disabilities among children involved with the child protective services system, and stated that it is imperative for these children to receive services under Part C. Indeed, they specifically recommended that all children who are referred to a protective services agency for evaluation of suspected abuse or neglect be automatically referred for a developmental behavioral screening under Part C. This is a broad assertion because it indicates that even a child for whom a report is unfounded or unsubstantiated is a member of a group at high risk for developmental delays. Yet, this recommendation is consistent with guidance from the AAP that recommends that developmental screens be performed on all children involved with the child welfare system, as well as referrals for those children to EI (AAP, 2000a). As will be discussed later in this book (see Chapter 5 on the law), this recommendation was modified to cover only those with substantiated cases, which involved hundreds of thousands of young children. However, it was added to the reauthorization of Part C of IDEA and to the reauthorization of the Child Abuse Prevention and Treatment Act (CAPTA) (PL 93-247). Both provisions require states to develop mechanisms for the referral of all children under age 3 involved in a substantiated case of abuse or neglect to Part C.

Early Childhood Education

The research has highlighted the importance of early childhood education for all young children, particularly those who are poor and vulnerable. Three major longitudinal studies have underscored how early childhood education programs can affect poor children in a positive way with long-term outcomes. These are the High/Scope Perry Preschool Study, the Abecedarian Study, and the Chicago Longitudinal Study, each of which is discussed here along with the programs or projects on which they are based. The research for these studies is also supported by cost–benefit analyses (Nores, Belfield, Barnett, & Schweinhart, 2005).

The High/Scope Perry Preschool Study followed its participating children, 123 African Americans who had been born into poverty, until they were 40 years of age (High/Scope, 2005). From 1962–1967, high-risk African American children were randomly divided into two groups (Parks, 2000). These children were chosen because of their low socioeconomic status and their high risk of failing out of school, despite a lack of biologically based disabilities. The first group was entered into the Perry Preschool, a high-quality preschool program whose curriculum relied heavily on participatory learning lesson plans. The second group, which was the control group, did not participate in any preschool program.

The program was a 2-year, half-day, Monday-through-Friday, preschool (Parks, 2000). There was one adult staff member for about every five or six children enrolled, which enabled the students to receive a lot of personal attention, including weekly home visits from the teachers that lasted an hour and a half. Parents were also incorporated in the program by participating in monthly group meetings with other parents, as well as with program staff.

The High/Scope Perry Preschool program was envisioned as an educational intervention, and early findings underscored its success in that area. Participants in the program had better academic performance than those in the control group. These results were categorized in a number of ways. Every year from ages 7 to 14, the children in the program group had test scores that were significantly higher, averaging a 16% difference (Parks, 2000). Furthermore, their mean grade point average (GPA) was significantly higher (a 2.09 versus a 1.68), and more of them graduated from high school (71% versus 54%).

However, program benefits extended beyond academic achievement. At age 27, individuals in the program group had greater monthly and household earnings and were almost three times more likely to own a house than the control group. Perry Preschool graduates were also far less likely to have been arrested for dealing drugs and had less contact with the police in general. These trends continued over time. At the age of 40, the Perry Preschool participants were more likely to earn more than $20,000 a year, to stay employed, and to have a savings account (High/Scope, 2005; University of North Carolina FPG Child Development Institute, 2007).

The cost–benefit analysis on this program is also impressive. Taking into account potential costs, such as the rates of the justice system, the higher amount of taxes paid, schooling, and the less frequent use of public welfare by the pre-school group, the return on public investment of the Perry Preschool program has been calculated to be 716%, with the costs topping out at $14,716, and benefits ballooning to $105,324 (Schweinhart, 2003). Clearly, investing in children early on pays off in the long run.

Another well-known longitudinal study showcasing how successful early childhood education can be is the Abecedarian Project (*abecedarian* means one who teaches or one who is just learning). This project was born out of the Frank Porter Graham Child Development Center (now the FPG Child Development Institute) at the University of North Carolina, which is a multidisciplinary center that was awarded a grant from the National Institute of Health to study the deterrence of mental retardation (Winton, Buysse, & Hamrick, 2006). The initial program, spearheaded by Dr. Craig T. Ramey, recruited 111 at-risk children throughout Chapel Hill and the greater Orange County area (University of North Carolina FPG Child Development Institute, 2007).

The Abecedarian Project was unique from the onset in that it started earlier and lasted longer than most other early childhood education programs of its time. Children were assigned to the control or experimental group between 6 and 12 weeks of age, and those that were enrolled in the program were intended to remain for 5 years. The program was also a year-long, full day program with free transportation and an extremely good teacher–student ratio (Winton, Buyssee, & Hamrick, 2006). The curriculum of the program revolved around play that involved lots of educational games that focused especially on language and cognition development while also trying to advance social-emotional and physical skills.

The Abecedarian students were shown to have improved cognitive test scores from their toddler years all the way into adulthood. All participants were assessed at the end of the program, as well as 8, 12, and 15 years later. At every point of assessment, the intervention group had higher IQ scores. As the children grew older, the experimental group proved more likely to attend a 4-year college, have a skilled job, and wait longer to have their first baby. They were also less likely to smoke or use marijuana (University of North Carolina, FPG Child Development Institute, 2007).

A third longitudinal study, the Chicago Longitudinal Study, followed more than 1,500 children who had participated in the Child–Parent Center (CPC) program in 25 different sites, as well as 550 children in a comparison group who participated in alternative full day kindergarten programs. This particular study followed these children until they were 20 years old.

The results of this 19-year study are impressive: the children who participated in CPC programs were significantly more likely to complete both high school and 4 years of college. Participating children were significantly less likely to be arrested for a felony and incarcerated as they grew into adulthood. These individuals were somewhat more likely to have stable employment as well as higher rates of health insurance coverage than were the comparison group. Finally, these participant were also found to be less likely to have one or more depressive symptoms (Reynolds et al., 2007).

The results of this study are all encompassing. Early childhood intervention and education has had an impact on the lives of participants far beyond what was once imagined. Not only did comprehensive services have an impact on the child's cognitive development, as is evidenced by the significantly higher number of program participants making their way through high school and 4-year colleges, but also the programs had an impact on adult well-being. Those who participated in the CPC programs were better educated, more likely to have stable jobs, and less likely to need public aid. Also, a key component for children in the child welfare system is the provision of comprehensive family services, which recognizes that positive learning experiences must continue at home with parents.

These early childhood programs have proven to have a positive impact on the lives of participating children. The problems of poverty, which often lead to poor academic achievement, an inability to attend college, early parenthood, and drug use, can be mitigated by an early focus on a child's educational development. Clearly, high-quality early education with programs that are comprehensive in scope and that also address children's health and emotional needs can change lives. Indeed, the two-generation aspect of these effective early childhood programs presents great promise for children involved in the child welfare system.

Finally, a growing body of research has demonstrated that effective early childhood education can support the development of social-emotional skills—the lack of which is a particular problem for children in the child welfare system. By designing a curriculum that identifies and addresses social skills, early childhood education programs can further support children's prospects for healthy development and permanency (Webster-Stratton, Reid, & Stoolmiller, 2008).

CONCLUSION

As indicated by the bounty of research discussed in this chapter, the first years of a child's life can determine the kind of life he or she will live. The research paves a path for policy makers, caregivers, or professionals to begin to ensure children's healthy development. This path makes clear that developing strong and stable relationships is key to healthy child development; however, other components are also vital for these most vulnerable children. These components include the provision of basic health care through a medical home, access to the two-generation entitlement of EI services to address or ameliorate developmental delays and disabilities, and enrollment in a comprehensive early childhood education program to promote school readiness, social-emotional development, and family support.

The research further provides guidance about evidence-based programs to address those goals. The central goal of creating strong and stable families for children in the child welfare system has only recently received research attention. In addition to a clear body of research supporting adoption, several other interventions show promise. For example, parents and caregivers can be taught to better care for their infants, to read their children's cues, and to be more attentive to their moods and needs. Other research clearly demonstrates the importance of addressing children's health needs, including complete immunizations, screens for vision and hearing and other potential health problems, and continuous care to treat diagnosed conditions in a medical home. It further supports the provision of an array of EI and family support services for children with developmental delays and disabilities and the families of these children. Finally, the wealth of studies has shown that it is not only advantageous for the children and their families to have access to quality early education programs but also for the rest of the community in which they live. The costs of these programs are high, but the benefits are far higher. These children can and will become well-functioning members of society, given the chance of a healthy, supportive childhood.

5

Powerful New Laws

NATHAN'S STORY

Nathan was born 1 month premature. He weighed 4 pounds and had a toxicology screen that was positive for cocaine. He was difficult to feed and console. Following established protocol, the hospital called the child abuse and neglect hotline about Nathan. Child protective services (CPS) determined that a petition needed to be filed in family court to protect him. At that preliminary hearing, his teenage mother, desperate to keep her baby, readily agreed to enter a residential substance abuse program. The judge ordered that Nathan receive a comprehensive health exam and follow-up health care, as well as a referral to the early intervention (EI) program. She also ordered a court-appointed special advocate (CASA) to ensure that Nathan's health and developmental needs were addressed. She further ordered substance abuse treatment for the mother and visitation that would increase with demonstrated sobriety. At the end of the hearing, the judge pointed to the clock at the back of the courtroom and said to the mother, "We are now at 1:00 p.m. At 12:00 midnight I must make a decision on permanency for Nathan. We will do everything possible to help you to learn to care for your son, but at 12:00 midnight I will make a final decision. Do you understand that you have 12 months to demonstrate that you can care for your child?" The young mother answered in the affirmative, stating that she was beginning her substance abuse program the next day.

Nathan received his comprehensive health exam and follow-up medical care. He was found eligible for EI services due to multiple medical (e.g., feeding and growth problems), cognitive, and communication delays uncovered during the multidisciplinary evaluation. He began to receive services at his foster home from a nurse who helped the family learn to feed and soothe him, and, over time, speech and occupational therapy services were initiated. The therapists taught the foster parent how to do exercises with Nathan. After participation in EI, Nathan's skills improved.

The young mother did well in the substance abuse treatment program and began to visit Nathan several times a week pursuant to the court order that allowed broad visitation commensurate with sobriety. Prior to the next court appearance, the CASA learned that the success of the EI services provided at the foster parent's home was cited by child welfare officials as a reason to delay reunification.

At the next hearing, the court ordered a change in Nathan's case plan to allow EI services to take place in his biological mother's home. During the next few months, EI services, including parent training and family support services to build a strong relationship with his biological mother, were initiated in the mother's home. Nathan continued to thrive and to receive EI services. At the next court hearing, the judge gave Nathan's mother permanent custody and care of her son. At the last report, Nathan, at 2 years old, continues to do well and has had no further contact with CPS.

CHILD WELFARE LAWS

Since 1980 Congress has passed a series of laws that can promote the healthy development of children, such as Nathan, who are involved in the child welfare system (CWS). The laws applied in Nathan's case promoted his prospects for healthy development and living in a permanent, loving, and capable family. These laws are powerful tools to ensure that children receive needed physical, developmental, and mental health care as well as EI, education, and family support services to address their needs and promote their prospects for growing up in a permanent, loving family. These promising laws can be placed into three broad categories: 1) child welfare, 2) health care, and 3) early intervention and early education. Each of these categories is summarized in this chapter.

Adoption Assistance and Child Welfare Act of 1980

All foster children in the United States have a court order approving placement in foster care. The court must review the child's needs and the parent's ability to meet those needs at every child protective hearing. This critical role was established by Congress in 1980 by the passage of the Adoption Assistance and Child Welfare Act (PL 96-272) and reinforced by the Adoption and Safe Families Act (ASFA) of 1997 (PL 105-89).

The foundation of PL 96-272 was the premise that many children were being placed in care unnecessarily. Designed to preserve families and promote permanency planning, the act concentrated on ways that children and families could receive appropriate support and services to avoid foster care placement. Requiring states to develop prevention and reunification programs, PL 96-272 necessitated the development of case plans for children and parents, as was illustrated in

Nathan's case at the beginning of this chapter. Tailored specifically for each child, the case plans were supposed to be consistent with the child's best interests and special needs and include a description of services offered. These services might include child care, counseling, or other necessary services, as well as services needed by the parents, such as substance abuse treatment or mental health counseling. Child welfare agencies are further mandated to exercise *reasonable efforts* to keep families together by providing services initially to prevent placement and, if placed, to reunify families.

Following the passage of the Adoption Assistance and Child Welfare Act, the foster care caseload plummeted by about 50% in the early 1980s, only to bounce up even farther during the mid-1980s to the 1990s because of the unprecedented epidemics of AIDS, crack/cocaine use, and poverty (Dicker & Gordon, 2000). As in recent years, very young children comprised a large share of the new admissions to foster care. The complicated and newly changing needs of these children, along with the suddenly huge volume of cases, meant that, despite the effects of PL 96-272, a large number of these young children spent much of their childhood in foster care placement (see Chapters 1 and 2).

The Adoption and Safe Families Act of 1997

In 1997, Congress passed the Adoption and Safe Families Act (ASFA) (PL 105-89), which signaled a shift in emphasis from biological family preservation to permanency for the child, including adoption. Coming after PL 96-272, ASFA further reinforced the central decision maker role of the court. Most significantly, ASFA makes clear that a child's health and safety is a paramount consideration in every child protective proceeding, and that the court has broad authority to address health needs.

While retaining the reasonable efforts requirement, ASFA allows the court to waive it in specific situations, such as when the parent has subjected the child to aggravated circumstances (e.g., abandonment; torture; chronic physical, emotional, and sexual abuse). In addition, reasonable efforts toward reunification are not required when the parent has committed murder, voluntary manslaughter or felony assault that resulted in serious injury to the child, or if the parental rights of the parent to a sibling have been terminated.

In addition, ASFA tightens the time frames for decision making to require permanency planning hearings 12 months after placement and within 30 days of placement where the court determines that reasonable efforts to reunify are not required. ASFA also requires that Termination of Parental Rights (TPR) petitions be filed when a child is in care for 15 out of 22 months unless compelling reasons exist such as the following: the child is placed with a relative, the child is an adolescent who objects to adoption, or there is a failure to provide timely services to parents as enumerated in the case plan. These new time frames require courts to keep a tighter rein on cases and have access to information that can identify a child's and family's needs and barriers to permanency more quickly. Finally, ASFA provides fiscal incentives for states to increase adoptions (Dicker, Gordon, & Knitzer, 2001).

The critical importance of children's healthy development is underscored by the federal ASFA regulations specifically holding states accountable for providing services to address the well-being of children and their families in concert with safety and permanency. These regulations are as follows:

- Families have enhanced capacity to provide for their children's needs.

- Children receive appropriate services to meet their educational needs.

- Children receive adequate services to meet their physical and mental health needs (Children's Bureau, Child and Family Services Review, 2007).

The regulations further demonstrate ASFA's recognition of the interconnection of children's healthy development, safety, and permanency. Indeed, all references to well-being in ASFA and its legislative history evidence the pairing of well-being with safety and permanency. The regulations begin to illuminate the term by referencing *well-being* as whether children are receiving needed health, mental health, and educational services and whether parents are receiving services to enhance parental capacity to meet those needs (Wulcyzn, Barth, Yuan, Harden, & Landsverk, 2005).

All 50 states have passed laws implementing ASFA. Most merely repeat its provisions; however, in response to the extensive body of research that links early childhood experiences to outcomes later in life, several states (e.g., Vermont, Minnesota, Oklahoma, New Mexico) have required that permanency hearings for young children (typically those under age 3, although potentially older) should occur within 6 months of placement rather than at the annual permanency hearing that is mandated by ASFA. These states undoubtedly are following California law first developed prior to ASFA that required hearings at 6-month intervals for children under age 3.

Perhaps the most sweeping post-ASFA legislation is New York's 2005 Governor's Permanency Act (Chapter 3 of the New York Laws of 2005, http:// www.ocfs.state.ny.us/main/legal/legislation/permanency). It requires permanency hearings after 8 months in care and 6 months thereafter, but, most important, it mandates provision of information on child well-being at permanency hearings. The New York permanency hearing report, which must be filed prior to the hearing, requires detailed information on children's physical, developmental, and mental health in addition to educational experiences, including EI (New York State Office of Children and Family Services, 2005).

The U.S. Department of Health and Human Services (DHHS) developed the Child and Family Services Review (CFSR) to ensure that states comply with ASFA. No state was found to comply with all the outcomes required to pass the CFSR review, and all of them had to implement Program Improvement Plans (PIP) (Children's Bureau, Child and Family Services Review, n.d.).

Child Abuse Prevention and Treatment Act (CAPTA)

In 1974, Congress passed the Child Abuse Prevention and Treatment Act (CAPTA; PL 93-247) to spotlight the problem of child abuse and neglect and to provide funds for states to develop child protection reporting systems. It is the key federal legislation to support states and communities in their efforts to prevent, identify, and address child abuse and neglect. In 2003, Congress amended and reauthorized CAPTA with the Keeping Children and Families Safe Act of 2003 (PL 108-36), extending its original goal of child safety to focus on child well-being and permanency.

Similar to ASFA, the new law does not offer a clear definition of well-being, but it does spotlight the importance of identifying and addressing a child's health and developmental needs. It also requires states to establish referral mechanisms to the EI program under Part C of the Individuals with Disabilities Act Amendments (IDEA) of 1997 (PL 105-17) for children under age 3 who are involved in substantiated abuse and neglect cases. (The 2004 IDEA reauthorization law [Individuals with Disabilities Education Improvement Act (IDEA) of 2004 (PL 108-446)] contains parallel provisions to CAPTA requiring policies and procedures for the referral of young children to Part C). CAPTA also awards grants to encourage linkages among state and local child protective agencies and public health, mental health, and developmental disabilities agencies to ensure that substantiated victims of child maltreatment have their physical health, mental health, and developmental needs appropriately diagnosed and addressed.

Court Improvement Project

In 1993, Congress developed the state Court Improvement Project (CIP) to address problems within the foster care system. Originally passed as part of the Omnibus Budget Reconciliation Act (OBRA) of 1993 (PL 103-66), Congress provided funds to the highest court of each state to assess and improve proceedings related to foster care, TPR, and adoption. This funding signaled congressional recognition of the central role of the court in improving the foster care system. The original allocation of $5 million nationally was doubled and then tripled during the interceding years.

As part of the Promoting Safe and Stable Families Act of 2001 (PL 107-113), the CIP program was reauthorized and funding increased. It further reinforced the courts' central role in ASFA implementation by obligating the state's highest court to promote the safety, permanency, and well-being of children in foster care. All 50 states participate in CIP, and those funds provide a vehicle for court reform activities, including training, passage of legislation, enactment of new court rules, development of collaborative mechanisms with child welfare and other agencies, mediation projects, and other innovative endeavors.

HEALTH CARE LAWS

Medicaid and Early and Periodic Screening, Diagnosis, and Treatment

The mandate to provide medical services to children in foster care has been clear under Title IV of the Social Security Act (PL 103-432), as well as the Adoption Assistance and Child Welfare Act of 1980 (PL 96-272) (Ruptier, 1997). ASFA further reinforces this mandate. All children under age 21 enrolled in Medicaid, including virtually all foster children and the vast majority of other children in the child welfare system, are entitled to receive the early and periodic screening, diagnosis, and treatment (EPSDT) program provisions of Medicaid. EPSDT is a comprehensive benefits package that requires medical, vision, hearing, and dental screenings to be performed at distinct intervals decided by the state that meet current standards of pediatric medical and dental care (U.S. General Accounting Office [GAO], 2001). The medical screen must include at least five components:

1.   A comprehensive health and developmental history assessing both physical and mental health

2.   A comprehensive, unclothed physical exam

3.   Immunizations

4.   Laboratory tests, including testing for high-risk exposure to lead

5.   Health education

In addition, EPSDT requires state Medicaid agencies to ensure the provision of necessary treatment for all physical and mental health conditions identified or diagnosed by the screenings and assessment as required by the needs of an individual child.

Building on EPSDT's requirement for a developmental assessment, many states use age-specific components, particularly for infants and toddlers (Johnson & Kaye, 2003). These are consistent with long-time federal guidance about the content of developmental assessments for young children that should include periodic screenings to assess developmental processes; gross and fine motor development; communication skills; self-help and reliance skills; social-emotional development, especially as it relates to the ability to interact with other children and parents; and cognitive skills (Rosenbaum, Proser, Schneider, & Sonosky, 2001). In addition, under EPSDT, states are charged with providing health education and anticipatory guidance to parents and even referral to related services, such as Head Start and the Special Supplemental Nutrition Program for Women, Infants, and Children (WIC).

In 1989, Congress amended the EPSDT statute in the Omnibus Budget Reconciliation Act of 1989 to include broad language enabling states to finance through Medicaid an array of services that might otherwise be ineligible for reimbursement, including EI and developmental screenings (PL 101-239). Thus, Medicaid and EPSDT provide an entitlement and reimbursement mechanism for physical, dental, developmental, and mental health screenings; assessments; and other services. Medicaid can also support administrative case management and the services of public health nurses for eligible children. These provisions bolster case plan requirements in child welfare law requiring the provision of services identified as "necessary and appropriate." Thus, fulfillment of the EPSDT provisions complements ASFA mandates and can provide measures to assess whether a child's physical, mental, and developmental health needs have been identified and addressed.

EARLY INTERVENTION AND EARLY CHILDHOOD EDUCATION LAWS

Early Intervention

Research shows that children who experience abuse or neglect are at high risk for a variety of physical, developmental, and emotional problems, including attachment disorders, social-emotional disturbances, cognitive delays, neurobiological changes in the brain, and failure to thrive (Jaudes & Shapiro, 1999). This risk is greatest for the very young. Therefore, many children in foster care are at grave risk of poor health and disability. Studies reveal one fourth of these children have significant delays in motor development, and almost one half have significant delays in communication and cognitive development (Halfon, Mendonca, & Berkowitz, 1995; Hochstadt, Jaudes, Zimo, & Schachter, 1987; Silver, Zukoski, et al., 1999).

In 1986, Congress passed the Early Intervention (EI) Program for Infants and Toddlers with Disabilities, also called Part H of the Education for All Handicapped Children Act of 1975 (PL 94-142; Horne, 1996). Now known as Part C of the IDEA, the new law provided financial assistance to states to maintain and implement a statewide, comprehensive, coordinated, multidisciplinary, and interagency system of EI for infants and toddlers with disabilities and their families.

The Education of the Handicapped Act Amendments of 1986 (PL 99-457), or Part C, provides an entitlement for children who are under age 3 and are experiencing developmental delays or who have a physical or mental condition that has a high probability of resulting in delay, which are eligibility requirements that almost half of all young children in the child welfare system can meet. The EI program is an entitlement that enables children to receive specialized assessments and services and allows their caregivers to receive services that can improve their ability to support healthy child development. The children's legal parents and relatives, as well as foster parents, may receive services under EI to enhance a child's development if the individualized family service plan (IFSP)—the blueprint for services—enumerates those services. In some jurisdictions, other caregivers, such as child care providers, also may receive support services (Dicker & Gordon, 2000).

The EI entitles eligible children to a rich array of services, including speech, occupational, and physical therapies; psychological services; special instruction; social work; assessment and counseling; assistive technology devices, such as hearing aids; nursing; nutrition; and transportation services. Service coordination or case management is a mandatory service under EI. Parents (including legal, foster and kinship parents) may receive a host of services to enhance their child's development, including parent training, counseling, support groups, home visits, and, in some states, respite care. The IFSP developed collaboratively by the evaluator, EI official, and the parent must enumerate these services, including their frequency and intensity.

Although the EI program is an amendment to IDEA, it is different in several ways from special education. First, it creates an entitlement to EI based on the research demonstrating the importance of providing services to two generations—both young children and their families. Thus, biological, adoptive, foster, kinship or relative caregivers and legal guardians can receive vital services under this law. Second, the EI program differs from special education in that its definition of *eligible child* is not limited to a child having a specific, diagnosed, categorical disability, but, instead, a developmental delay or a condition with a high probability of resulting in delay. The broad EI eligibility definitions reflect congressional findings that EI services can address or ameliorate delay and disability and reduce the need for special education. Indeed, the high probability category of eligibility includes not only accepted physical and mental conditions, such as Down syndrome and cerebral palsy, but also severe attachment disorders and fetal alcohol syndrome. Beyond children in high probability groups, states are also allowed to include infants and toddlers who—if not receiving EI services— are at risk for substantial developmental delays. States that choose to invoke the at-risk category use well-known biological and environmental factors, such as low birth weight or a history of abuse and neglect. Only six states (California, Hawaii, Massachusetts, New Mexico, New Hampshire, and West Virginia) are providing EI services to at-risk infants and toddlers. That number has actually fallen from nine in recent years as states such as Nevada and Indiana have revised their respective policies.

Finally, in contrast to special education, the EI program is not administered by local school districts, but by lead state agencies (Dicker, 1999). The lead agency is required to administer the program statewide and to implement a Child Find system to identify, locate, and refer eligible children. In many states, the lead agency is the education department, but states also have named their health, developmental disabilities, family, and social services departments as their lead agency (NECTAC, 2007).

Despite their documented need and eligibility for EI services, many children who have been maltreated do not receive them. Nationwide, states report underidentification and underenrollment of children involved with child welfare (Robinson & Rosenberg, 2004). There are several reasons that explain this lack of connection to vital EI services. First, children who have been maltreated often lack a lasting relationship with a caring adult who can observe their development over time and advocate on their behalf. Second, because a significant number of these children do not receive even basic health care, they lack access to pediatricians and primary care physicians who are often referral agents to EI (GAO, 1995). Third, child welfare professionals, foster parents, and court personnel who are responsible for the well-being of these children often are not trained to identify developmental needs and have limited knowledge about Part C services (Halfon et al., 1995). Fourth, confusion over who can grant consent to EI evaluation and services also can be a barrier for these children. Agencies providing child welfare services, for example, are prohibited from consenting to Part C (as well as special education) services (Dicker & Gordon, 2006).

In recognition of the risks faced by these children and their low enrollment in EI, the Keeping Children and Families Safe Act of 2003 (PL 108-36)—required states to develop

> Provisions and procedures for referral of a child under the age of 3 who is involved in a substantiated case of child abuse or neglect to early intervention services funded under Part C of the Individuals with Disabilities Education Act. [§ 106b(2)(A)(xxi)].

The 2004 IDEA reauthorization contains parallel language to CAPTA, detailing specific requirements for state EI programs. Underscoring the importance of enrolling children who have been abused and neglected, IDEA's Part C initial findings state that

> Congress finds that there is an urgent and substantial need to enhance the capacity of state and local agencies and service providers to identify, evaluate and meet the needs of all children, particularly ... *infants and toddlers in foster care* [italics added]. (§ 631[a] [5])

Also, EI must ensure "appropriate early intervention services...are available to all infants and toddlers and their families, including ... infants and toddlers with disabilities who are homeless children and their families" (§ 633) and meaningful involvement of underserved groups. The 2004 IDEA also requires the establishment of a state interagency coordinating council that includes at least one representative from the state child welfare agency responsible for foster care [§ 641(b) (1) (L)]. In addition, the CAPTA and IDEA amendments help to remove the consent barrier by allowing states to permit foster parents to consent to EI services and authorize courts to make orders for appointment of surrogate parents.

Congressional passage of the Part C referral provisions in CAPTA and IDEA opened the door to one of the richest entitlement services for children under age 3 involved in substantiated cases of abuse or neglect and their families. These provisions offer new tools to enhance policy and practice and ensure compliance with federal child welfare requirements that focus on child well-being. The provisions also connect child welfare staff to EI service providers who can assist in assessment, service delivery, and permanency planning to expand the array of supports and resources for children and their caregivers to promote safety, permanency, and well-being.

Head Start

Head Start (HS) and Early Head Start (EHS) are comprehensive early childhood and family support programs that serve children from birth to age 5, pregnant women, and their families. Unlike EI or Medicaid, they are not entitlement programs and, therefore, eligibility is limited by available funding. However, they are child-focused programs with a strong parental component and have the over-all goal of promoting healthy child development and school readiness for young children in low income families. HS is a federal program, operated locally under the aegis of the Office of Head Start (OHS), Administration for Children and Families (ACF), and U.S. Department of Health and Human Services (DHHS). HS comprehensive services include educational, medical, dental, mental health, nutrition, literacy, home visits, and parent support (DHHS, 2007).

The original HS program was founded as a centerpiece of President Johnson's War on Poverty in 1965. The EHS program, established in 1994, built upon that foundation (Condry & Lazar, 1982). The two programs share many requirements; however, EHS has additional requirements to facilitate its service to pregnant women and children from birth to age 3. In 2002, grants were awarded to fund 24 demonstration projects for 3 years to establish the Early Head Start/Child Welfare Services (EHS/CWS) Initiative (DHHS, n.d.). EHS/CWS provided a select group of already existing EHS grantees, in partnership with their local child welfare agencies, to demonstrate how to use the EHS model to serve children under the age of 3 in the child welfare system better. The initiative, established through a partnership between the HS bureau and the Children's Bureau, maintains the goal of expanding the service network in local communities to meet the needs of this unique population.

The Improving Head Start for School Readiness Act of 2007 (PL 110-134) reauthorized and renewed the HS and EHS programs in November 2007. It preserves the comprehensive nature of the program and identifies its purpose as "to promote the school readiness of low-income children by enhancing their cognitive, social and emotional development" through the provision of "health, educational, nutritional, social and other services" [§ 641(d) (2) (B)]. The act does not establish any new category of program, such as continuation or expansion of the EHS/CWS initiatives. It does, however, contain several references to children in the child welfare system that could be used to increase their participation in the programs. Specific language exists in the new law concerning the needs of "children in foster care" or "children referred by a child welfare agency" [§ 641(d)(2) (O), § 650(1)D)], including funds for training, inclusion in program strategic planning and needs assessments [§ 640(d)(2)(D)(i)], development of formal linkages with CAPTA agencies [§ 645(A)(ii)], promoting involvement of and providing family assessments to foster parents and kinship caregivers [§ 641(d)(2) (J)(i)], considering the needs of these children in modification of program standards as well as program monitoring efforts [§ 641(A)], and developing research and demonstration projects to test how best to serve these children [§ 649(a)(1)(B)].

These new provisions that reauthorize and renew HS and EHS raise awareness of programs to consider the needs of children in the child welfare system. Ideally, as programs develop their needs assessments, they will note the low participation of these children and include them in strategic planning. This effort will be augmented for EHS because of the specific requirement of linkage with CAPTA agencies. In turn, this information can lay the groundwork for increased outreach and enrollment of these children. In addition, the new funds targeted to training can enhance program capacity to address the unique needs of children in the child welfare system. Taken together, the 2007 Improving Head Start for School Readiness Act (PL 110-134) can stimulate greater enrollment of young children touched by the child welfare system in vital EHS and HS programs.

Preschool Special Education

Concurrently with HS, children between the ages of 3 and 5 who have one or more disabilities, including hearing and/or vision, physical development, language and speech, or learning, are eligible to receive special education and related services under the Federal Preschool Grants Program. This program is a downward extension of special education law for children age 3–5 and is administered by local education agencies (LEAs), which are similar to local school districts. After a multidisciplinary evaluation determines eligibility, the LEA, in concert with parents and the evaluator, develops a blueprint for the child's preschool special education known as an *individualized education program* (IEP) (Dicker & Gordon, 2000).

Early Childhood Programs

High-quality early care and education programs can enhance healthy development for children in the child welfare system, offer families information and direct services to assist with the problems of parenting, and create an additional opportunity for children to establish stable relationships with adult caregivers. HS and EHS, as previously discussed, are federal programs that provide comprehensive and developmentally appropriate preschool services for children from low-income families. Similar to EI, HS is child focused and family supportive, making the program a rich resource for foster children and their caregivers. Quality early childhood programs also have a two generation approach—providing early childhood education for the child and support for the parents. Other federal programs provide funding streams for child care to low-income children, including the Child Care Development Block Grant, Temporary Assistance for Needy Families (TANF), and the Social Services Block Grant (Title XX). In addition, under Title IV of the Social Security Act (PL 107-133), child welfare funds are available for child care programs.

USING THE LAW TO UNDERSTAND THE ROLES OF THE COURT AND CHILD WELFARE AND THE IMPORTANCE OF COLLABORATION

At its heart, the law identifies two pillars of decision making concerning children involved in abuse and neglect cases—the child welfare system and the courts. The child welfare system makes the daily decisions about children's lives, while the court renders the overarching determinations. The child welfare system investigates allegations of abuse and neglect and makes a determination about those allegations. It decides if services should be provided at home or if a child requires removal because of an imminent risk of harm. Once there is a decision to remove a child or to seek court supervision of an in-home placement, the court becomes the central decision maker concerning placement in foster care, approval of plans, delineation of visitation and services, determination of a permanency goal, and authority to terminate parental rights and grant adoption. Within those confines of court authority, child welfare renders daily important decisions about the child's life. It is child welfare that determines where a child lives and with whom; whether, where, and by whom a child receives services, including medical care; if they will grant consent to ordinary and customary medical care (nonroutine and/or invasive care may require court order or in some instances parental consent); and where a child attends school (Dicker & Gordon, 2000).

Thus, the court decides the overarching issues of placement, services, and visitation, but the critical daily decisions are made by child welfare professionals. Understanding this dynamic helps to underscore the importance of collaboration. Recognizing the scope of each decision maker's role and responsibilities is imperative in designing any effort to improve children's well-being. All professionals and agencies, such as health care, EI, early childhood education, and mental health, that touch the lives of children in the child welfare system must interact effectively with both pillars for decision making.

Putting together the pieces—applying the research and the law—to promote the healthy development of young children in the child welfare system cannot be achieved by any player alone. Effective collaboration that actually reforms policy and practice long term is difficult to achieve.

To be successful, any effort to advance a child's healthy development must contain extensive interagency and multidisciplinary collaboration, including court and child welfare links, development of a common base of knowledge through ongoing training and technical assistance, and creative use of existing programs and funding resources. Partnerships must be forged between child welfare and the courts, and among all relevant agencies and stakeholders. Every collaboration will be enhanced by involving court-linked strategies to maximize the authority and power of the courts as the central decision maker in every child protection proceeding. Judges are uniquely positioned to convene collaborations among child-serving agencies. The power of a judicial request is seldom ignored and judicial leadership can jump start and sustain community partnerships (Townsend & Carroll, 2002). Judges also can fashion court orders to address the specific well-being needs of children by tying the provision of services to meet those needs to promote safety and permanency (Dicker & Gordon, 2004b).

In addition, collaboration is necessary to ensure that child welfare and court personnel have information essential to a child's well-being or healthy development. For child welfare and court personnel, it is important that the connections between services that address health, education, and caregiving challenges and the achievement of safety and permanency are clear. This requires building the knowledge base about healthy development through training and technical assistance efforts and ensuring that all stakeholders share the same knowledge and understand each system's language while creating ongoing opportunities for discourse and relationship building among professionals (Townsend & Carroll, 2002). Collaborative partnerships can produce formal tools and strategies, including written protocols, checklists, and memoranda of understanding, as well as the colocation of professionals serving children.

Stakeholder collaboration also can develop formal mechanisms to track and monitor the delivery of well-being services and identify and creatively harness multiple funding streams on behalf of children involved in the child welfare system. Existing federal programs and dollars, such as EPSDT, IDEA, HS, and CAPTA, can fund collaborative partnerships, training, technical assistance, and services that promote the healthy development, safety, and permanency for these children. CIP, developed to assess and improve foster care proceedings, can be tapped to grow and sustain these efforts (Dicker & Gordon, 2004b). All of these federal building blocks also can support a research agenda to develop better knowledge about the most effective intervention strategies, their costs, and their benefits.

III

Portals for Healthy Development

The Case Studies

The centerpiece of this book are case studies—stories about real professionals often working in concert with parents who were able to put the pieces together to change policy and practice to ensure the healthy development of young children in the child welfare system. The research and the law frame the substance of that work—ensuring that children receive needed health care, early intervention (EI), and quality early childhood education; and that they have a permanent, caring relationship with an adult. The portal or gateway to receiving those research-based components for healthy development may vary from state to state. Juvenile and family courts charged with overseeing children's well-being and permanency are a clear portal to healthy development. But, so are the health, early intervention, and early childhood systems. Each can provide the entry point for needed services to augment healthy growth and development and reinforce the development of permanent relationships as stipulated by the research and the law. Professionals from around the United States are working in each of these systems—the courts, health care, early intervention and early childhood education—who have forged collaborations with child welfare to improve the lives of young children at issue here.

Three case studies of efforts of those diverse professionals are contained in the next chapters. Each chapter, like every chapter in this book, begins with a story of a real child (all names and some details are changed to protect confidentiality) whose life was improved by the profiled effort. Each chapter follows a long and circuitous path to show how professionals secure changes in policy and practice that have actually improved the lives of young children in the child welfare system. Each, too, is an ongoing story as these often decade-long efforts have just begun to bear fruit. Although the stories of the children who are the focus of these advocacy efforts are remarkably consistent regardless of location, the background, skills, and working environments presented are quite distinct. The profiled professionals found diverse ways to analyze and suggest solutions to the presenting problems and used multiple strategies from litigating, training, writing books and articles, advocating with the media, and lobbying to change policy. But, all needed to find a partner inside the child welfare system to not only create policy changes but also to transform those paper victories into actual practices that could improve the lives and life chances of these children. And all of these professionals or advocates have struggled to find ways to institutionalize the reforms amidst ever-changing environments with new priorities, new players, and fluctuating resources.

A fourth study calls for unlocking a new portal or gateway for healthy development—early childhood education. The research strongly underscores the potential of this gateway for improving the lives of children in the child welfare system. Through the portal of early childhood education, many of the services addressed in the earlier chapters can be brought together—health care, EI, and programs to enhance parenting skills—to advance the well-being and family stability of these most vulnerable children.

Finally, these case studies demonstrate that creating and securing the full potential of these four portals for healthy development can reverse the odds for young children in the child welfare system. As the details of the cases illustrate, these are doable tasks that require leadership, partnerships with child welfare services, persistence, flexibility, and support for families.

6

Using the Courts as a Portal for Healthy Development

The New York Case Study

JASON'S STORY

Jason was born in the spring of 2005 in Brooklyn, New York. He was born premature at 27 weeks and weighed 1 pound, 12 ounces. He had a positive toxicology screen for cocaine. Jason remained in the hospital for 3 months during which time he was treated for a heart defect and retinopathy. He was discharged at 3 months when he gained sufficient weight and was well enough to go home; however, his mother had abandoned him at the hospital and no one had visited him during his 3-month stay. Jason, therefore, was taken directly from the hospital into foster care.

Jason's case was assigned to the Babies Can't Wait (BCW) program in Brooklyn Family Court. At the time of the initial hearing, the BCW early childhood specialist (ECS) had reviewed the case and identified potential questions and issues for the judge. As a result, the judge ordered an investigation into why the child had not been taken into care during his 3-month hospital stay when he had no family or visitors. She further ordered that a court appointed special advocate (CASA) be assigned to the case to provide information to the court, which is in response to the Permanent Judicial Commission on Justice for Children's infant checklist questions (see Figure 6.3 later in this chapter), as well as to ensure that the child was referred to early intervention (EI) services.

At the time of his hospital discharge, Jason was placed with a foster care agency that specialized in children who were medically fragile. The agency provided a foster mother who had experience with children with similar issues. As Jason's mother's whereabouts remained unknown, the judge also ordered a diligent search for the mother, father, and other relatives. Several weeks later, however, this search was called off when it was discovered that the mother had been raped and murdered.

Following the court's directive, CASA learned about Jason's many complex health issues and the three separate medications he was being given at the hospital clinic for his retina and heart problems. As arranged upon hospital discharge, he was receiving regular and intensive specialized medical care. CASA also urged the child welfare caseworker to make the EI referral, but it was not until CASA walked Jason's caseworker through the referral process that it was finally made. Delays ensued, and when CASA followed up, they learned that Jason had been found ineligible because he was not significantly delayed for a 1-month-old child, which would be his age if he had been born full term. However, at this time, a psychologist working for the private child welfare agency overseeing Jason's care found that he was significantly delayed in all domains and, therefore, needed services.

Thirty days after the initial hearing, the ECS met with CASA to review the case and discovered that his birth father had never been found and no family existed to care for Jason. In addition, Jason was in need of laser eye surgery and the ECS and CASA made sure that consent for the surgery was secured from Administration for Children's Services (ACS). Despite these adversities, Jason was doing well in his foster home, and the ECS and CASA agreed to work again on the EI referral.

Until the first 6-month permanency hearing, CASA and ECS met monthly to review his case. The eye surgery went well, and after persistence by CASA, including submission of the private agency psychologist assessment, Jason was finally found eligible for EI. At the permanency hearing, the judge reviewed CASA's report that included the completed infant checklist acknowledging that Jason visited the pediatrician once a month and received EI services that included speech, physical, and occupational therapies; special instruction; and parent training in his foster home. The judge inquired about changing the child's goal to adoption and learned that the foster mother was interested in adopting Jason. The judge ordered continuing services, including CASA monitoring, in addition to beginning the adoption process.

When Jason turned 1 year old, he weighed only 12 lbs, but he was gaining weight. Jason's heart and eye problems were monitored monthly, and he continued to receive an array of EI services and do well in his foster home. In addition, all paperwork for the adoption process had been filed. Several months later, the judge presided over a pleasant hearing that was held on one of New York City's adoption days (festive Saturdays when dozens of adoption cases are heard by judges and court staff volunteering their time). Jason's adoption was granted, and his foster mother became his mother.

As Jason's case illustrates, our nation's courts are at the front line for addressing the well-being of the more than 100,000 children under age 3 who spend days, weeks, or, more likely, years in foster care (Dicker, Gordon, & Knitzer, 2001). All of these children are placed in foster care by court order due to allegations of abuse, neglect, or abandonment. Although the research reveals that the vast majority of young children in the child welfare system have serious health conditions and disabilities, courts rarely receive this information and are seldom understood as having the power and potential for enhancing children's health and development.

As the central decision maker in every child protective case, the court—as in Jason's case—requires information about the child's physical, developmental, and emotional needs as well as the parent's capacity to meet those needs. The court requires this information for all children in order to make meaningful decisions. Ensuring the well-being of children involved in the child welfare system requires harnessing the power of the courts, pioneering judicial leadership, and creating court-linked mechanisms that promote a steady focus on the well-being of children.

In most states, courts have broad powers to review individual case plans and order services to ensure a child's well-being (Publication Development Committee, Victims of Child Abuse Project, 1995). Judicial leadership can shape the courtroom climate and community expectations about the centrality of child health and development in case review and permanency planning. Judges can order information about a child's health needs and order services to ensure that these needs are addressed. They can inquire about how a child's health needs have an impact on safety and permanency by asking about the capacity and learning requirements of a caregiver—whether biological, foster, or adoptive parent—to meet that child's needs. Judges can reach beyond the courtroom to develop relationships and collaborations with experts and resources in the fields of pediatric health, child development, and education. These well-being partners can assist the court in obtaining and translating information about the needs of children and how that information will have an impact on caregiving. They also can help link children and their families to services and provide caregivers with opportunities for supervised involvement in their child's routines.

This chapter spotlights the influence of our nation's courts in the lives of children in the child welfare system. It further describes strategies developed by the New York Permanent Judicial Commission on Justice for Children to harness the power of the court by focusing attention on the healthy development of young children.

THE PERMANENT JUDICIAL COMMISSION ON JUSTICE FOR CHILDREN

From 1991 until 2007, I had the privilege of serving as Executive Director of the Permanent Judicial Commission on Justice for Children (referred to as Commission in this chapter), the nation's first multidisciplinary children's commission based in the judiciary. Chaired by New York's Chief Judge Judith Kaye, and cochaired during its first 8 years by New York University's Wagner School Dean Ellen Schall, its mission remained constant—to improve the life and life chances of children affected by New York's courts.

The Commission was originally established 3 years earlier in 1988 by Chief Judge Sol Wachtler in the aftermath of a notorious case of child abuse resulting in murder (Lyall, 1988). In appointing the Commission, Judge Wachtler recognized that the courts too frequently were an emergency room on the front lines of our nation's troubles. In order to solve the problems brought to the court's doorstep, the Commission needed to be permanent and composed of a multidisciplinary membership, including physicians, psychologists, officials from other branches of government, and children's policy experts, as well as judges and lawyers. Yet, for 3 years, the Commission remained a debating society, unable even to agree on the definition of a *child*. At that point, Judge Wachtler asked his colleague on New York's highest court, Judge Judith Kaye, to chair a reconstituted Commission. Dean Schall and I were asked to join her for this endeavor. It then became a viable entity.

Since justice for children is a limitless, lofty goal, we knew we needed to target our efforts, and we resolved early to produce reforms, not reports. At the outset, we agreed to focus our attention on the needs of young children who were increasingly involved in court proceedings. In order to identify specific, doable tasks to address the problems of young children who pass through the courts, the Commission embarked on a series of key interviews of experts around New York and the nation who were knowledgeable about young children living in poverty and their relationship with the courts. Those interviewed bemoaned the lack of services for young children displaying developmental delays, particularly those in foster care, and voiced dismay at New York's failure to implement the federal EI program now known as Part C (Individuals with Disabilities Education Act Amendments [IDEA] of 1997 [PL 105-17]). They also identified the problem of children spending idle time waiting in our state's courthouses, precluding parents from participating in court proceedings, impeding efficient administration of justice, and jeopardizing the well-being of the children. Thus, the Commission's agenda was set for the next decade—to address the needs of young children by implementing Part C in New York, to make the environment of the courthouse more hospitable to children, and to develop mechanisms to address the needs of young children in the child welfare system.

Early Intervention

The Commission's first project was one that I had hoped would be suggested by the key informants—to implement the 1986 federal law, the Early Intervention Program for Infants and Toddlers with Disabilities, now referred to as Part C of IDEA. Unlike any other state, New York used the family courts to enter orders for preschool special education services, with the state and counties splitting the costs and receiving no federal reimbursement.

Based on the opportunity presented by the federal law and the pivotal role of the court in the existing system, the Commission began its first project. The methodology established for this effort echoed through the next 15 years of Commission activities. First, an Early Care Working Group was established that was composed of Commission members and outside experts. The group studied the existing system and found it to be seriously flawed and riveted with geographic and economic disparities regarding access to services. It then studied the federal law and research around the nation on the effectiveness of EI programs for infants and toddlers with developmental delays. In an unprecedented move, two Commission members who were state legislators suggested that the Commission cosponsor legislative hearings on proposed bills. So, in our first year, Judge Kaye as well as Schall and I presided along with members of the New York State Senate Committee on Children and Families, the New York State Assembly Committee on Health, and their staffs at two legislative hearings that verified the inequities of the existing court-based system and the promise of implementation of the federal law.

After a protracted legislative battle, New York implemented the federal law with the passage of Chapter 428 of the Laws of 1992 and Chapter 231 of the Laws of 1993, including most of the Commission's proposals. These laws created an entitlement program for children with developmental delays or disabilities to ensure that they had access to a comprehensive system of educational, therapeutic, and family support services (Dicker & Schall, 1996). I represented the Commission on two vital implementation bodies. First, a task force appointed by Governor Cuomo to establish a rate reimbursement mechanism, and second, the regulatory drafting task force. As a result, New York's EI system is a national model serving more than 30,000 young children like Jason, and funding an array of services including family support services, such as respite care and parent support groups specifically advocated by the Commission.

The Children's Centers Program

The success of the EI effort galvanized the Commission to take on the daunting task of solving a problem within the courts of the presence of hundreds of children in the hallways, waiting rooms, and even courtrooms of New York. Using the method established by the EI work, a Commission working group was appointed that was composed of both Commission members and outside experts. The group conducted a study to verify the problem and engaged in a unique process known as an *idealized design process* to construct a new service called Children's Centers in the Courts.

Under Commission co-chair Schall's leadership, the idealized design process proposed a Children's Centers program that provides a two-pronged service. The first part is the establishment in courthouses of a safe haven for children where they can constructively engage in a quality drop-in early childhood program while their caregivers attend to critical court business. The second prong of this service is to connect children and families to vital services, such as Head Start, Special Supplemental Nutrition Program for Women, Infants, and Children (WIC), and Child Health Plus.

Tapping the legislative staff contacts made during the EI effort, I was able to secure $300,000 of funding in the Child Care Block Grant allocation that could be used for Children's Centers in the courts. Once those funds were placed in the Department of Social Services's (DSS) budget, I began a series of meetings with DSS staff to develop minimum requirements for the program and to draft a Request for Proposals (RFP). In an unusually quick turnaround, we were able to issue the RFP in the fall of 1993. Six Centers opened in the spring of 1994. That same year, we began to build a statewide system using child care funds for start-up and enhancements, such as training, equipment, and court funds for operations. By 1995, we had more than a dozen Centers operating throughout New York (Kaye, Schall, Dicker, Nadel, & Kennedy, 1996).

After the program was fully established, the Centers took on the task of providing a literacy-enriched environment (New York State Unified Court System, 2000). We became the first court system to participate in President Clinton's America Reads Challenge and the first court to be selected for the national Reading Is Fundamental (RIF) program, which gives an age-appropriate book to each child who visits the Centers. By 2006, 32 Centers were operating in New York's courts and were visited by more than 54,000 children.

The Court Improvement Project

In 1993, the Commission was given the opportunity to tackle the challenging problem of addressing the needs of foster children. This was an issue touched on by the EI work, but one that was not chosen as the focus until the Commission was well established. The Commission was designated by New York's Court of Appeals (New York's highest state court) to spearhead the federal Court Improvement Project (CIP). CIP's mandate was to assess and improve proceedings related to foster care, termination of parental rights, and adoption. During the first phase of this project, the Commission once again convened a multidisciplinary working group and conducted a series of research endeavors. First, all available social sciences and court data were reviewed to construct a profile of New York State's foster care population. The research found that the foster care population was disproportionately young—almost 40% of the admissions were children under age 5 and 25% were under age 2. These young children were more likely to enter foster care and remain in care longer than older children (Heidt, 1995).

The identification of the disproportionate number of very young children entering foster care shaped the next research effort—a project that both conducted court observations and reviewed case files for more than 400 foster children in five counties in New York State, 300 of whom entered foster care in the first year of life. This research found that the court received little information about the children and families involved in cases; they received only ordered services in a minority of cases, and those services were generally for parents, not children. Even in instances in which services were ordered, compliance was very poor by both social services and parents. In addition, ample evidence was found that scant attention was paid to the health and developmental needs of children, particularly young children, in court proceedings, and that court orders seldom contained specifications for services to young children. All of this inactivity happened against a backdrop of endemic delay with cases often taking more than 6 months just to get to disposition (Permanent Judicial Commission on Justice for Children, 1998). Most troubling of all, those involved in the court process that is focused on children's safety overlooked the critical link among safety, healthy development, and permanency.

The Commission responded to these grim findings by developing two broad categories of initiatives. First, two pilot projects (one in Erie County, Buffalo, and the other in New York City) to reform court proceedings were developed. Second, statewide initiatives to improve the health and development of children in foster care as an integral component of court improvement strategies were created.

The Healthy Development for Children in Foster Care Initiative

To develop a strategy that addresses the needs of children in foster care and improves the delivery of health services for these children, the Commission convened a Health Care Working Group. Following the successful EI and Children's Centers efforts, this broad-based group was convened with Commission members, as well as pediatricians and health policy experts. The initial Working Group meetings explored existing standards of health care and health care delivery models to children in foster care throughout New York State and the country.

Judge Kaye urged the Working Group to develop a strategy in which the court could exercise leadership to ensure the healthy development of children in foster care. Her guidance focused the Working Group's efforts on developing court-based innovations, the unique characteristic of the Commission's prior successes. In response to Judge Kaye's charge, the Working Group explored how to use the authority of the courts to enhance the healthy development of these children. It also used its knowledge of the overburdened court and child welfare systems to develop a simple tool that would spotlight the most basic health needs of children involved in child protection cases.

The research revealed that no guide on the basic health needs for children in foster care aimed at court and child welfare professionals existed. A pediatrician on the Working Group, Steven Blatt, and later a Commission member, suggested a checklist of basic questions that parents might ask for their own children. A strategy that would require at least one person in every child's case—attorneys, caseworkers, CASA volunteers, or even judges—to ask questions that parents would ask about their own children's health was the next step. Out of that discussion, the concept of a checklist was born, and Judge Kaye endorsed this concept.

Elysa Gordon, the Commission's Senior Policy Analyst, and I worked closely with the New York State chapter of the American Academy of Pediatrics (AAP) to choose the checklist questions and write a companion booklet, *Ensuring the Healthy Development of Infants in Foster Care: A Guide for Judges, Advocates, and Child Welfare Professionals* (Dicker & Gordon, 2004c). We wrote several drafts for the working group's review because we wanted to tap the expertise of pediatricians and child development specialists to identify the most critical guideposts for children's health.

The checklist questions reflect the Commission's core mission to assist the court in improving outcomes for children. To ensure the legitimacy of the checklist and encourage its use by judges and attorneys, the questions were made consistent with the Child Welfare League of America (CWLA)/AAP standards, the legal standards for health care as outlined in the federal Medicaid law through the early and periodic screening, diagnosis, and treatment (EPSDT) provisions, as well as the requirements for health care for children in foster care under New York law (U.S. General Accounting Office [GAO], 2001).

The checklist was designed to contain primarily those screenings and services that children in foster care are entitled to receive under the law. In addition, the checklist was based on the court's authority under state and federal law— the Adoption Assistance and Child Welfare Act of 1980 (PL 96-272) and the Adoption and Safe Families Act (ASFA) of 1997 (PL 105-89)—to make inquiries about the health of children in foster care and write court orders for services to address their needs. The checklist was also based on the law to assure judges, attorneys, and child welfare workers of their authority and obligation to ask the questions. In essence, the checklist is to be viewed as an augmentation of existing responsibilities and not an additional burden.

Judge Kaye, while giving her keynote address at the November 1999 Millennium Conference, unveiled the booklet and checklist. (See Figure 6.1 for the complete checklist.) During the conference, which was sponsored by the U.S. Department of Health and Human Services (DHHS), Children's Bureau, the National Council of Juvenile and Family Court Judges, and the Department of Justice, Office of Juvenile Justice and Delinquency Prevention, she stated that the goal of the booklet was to expand awareness of the importance of health issues for children's life prospects. Addressing these needs would both enhance their physical health and decrease the probability of placement disruption. In essence, it would increase the likelihood that these children will grow up in stable, loving, permanent homes.

To facilitate full use of the checklist, a multidisciplinary training was developed and implemented for court and child welfare professionals on child development; available community resources; and the ability to use information about

1. Has the child received a comprehensive health assessment since entering foster care?
2. Are the child's immunizations up-to-date and complete for his or her age?
3. Has the child received hearing and vision screening?
4. Has the child received screening for lead exposure?
5. Has the child received regular dental services?
6. Has the child received screening for communicable diseases?
7. Has the child received a developmental screening by a provider with experience in child development?
8. Has the child received mental health screening?
9. Is the child enrolled in an early childhood program?
10. Has the adolescent child received information about healthy development?

Figure 6.1. Checklist for the Healthy Development of Children in Foster Care. (From Dicker, S., & Gordon, E. [2004b]. Building bridges for babies in foster care: The Babies Can't Wait Initiative. *Juvenile and Family Court Journal, 55*(2), 30. Retrieved March 31, 2008, from http://www.nationalcasa.org/download/Judges_Page/0510_building_bridges_for_babies_0036.pdf; reprinted by permission.)

a child's health needs in making decisions concerning placement, visitation, services, and permanency. In addition, there are several companion materials to the checklist, as well as presentations that were made at meetings sponsored by national organizations (Dicker & Gordon 2000; Dicker, Gordon & Knitzer 2001).

It also became clear that the court needed assistance in implementing the checklist by asking the questions, gathering information, and translating the results of screenings and evaluations relevant to permanency decision making. The Commission developed its Court Appointed Special Advocates (CASA) project to harness the resources and expertise of CASA volunteers to use the checklist (Dicker & Gordon, 2004b). CASAs are specially trained community volunteers appointed by a family court judge to assist in finding safe and permanent homes for children in the child welfare system. Once appointed, the CASA becomes an official part of the judicial proceedings, working alongside the judge, attorneys, and social workers as an appointed officer of the court for a particular case to help identify a child's best interests. We trained all the New York State CASA directors to use the checklist, and the directors have trained their local volunteers. As a direct result, CASAs throughout New York State are routinely using the checklist and making the child's health and developmental needs known within their court reports.

CASA involvement has inspired judges to write court orders that specifically request developmental and health screenings, as well as referrals to health and EI services for individual children as deemed appropriate. The CASA project has facilitated the use of the checklist, which has strengthened the CASA program by increasing its availability as a resource for judges. As a result of the Commission's outreach and training efforts, judges, attorneys for children, parents, CASAs, and child welfare agencies nationwide are using the checklist to identify the health needs of children in foster care.

BABIES CAN'T WAIT: CREATING THE INITIATIVE

Despite the progress made by the checklist, a surprising result emerged—the checklist was not being used as often for the youngest children in foster care. All too often the sole question asked in court was, "How is the baby doing?" and the child welfare caseworker would reply, "The baby is fine." It was clear that a new, targeted approach was needed for infants because the baby was *not* fine.

To garner Commission support for such a targeted approach, I invited researcher Fred Wulczyn to the October 2000 meeting of the Commission to present his key findings on infants in foster care. I also invited Professor Michael Wald, a visiting professor at New York University Law School that semester and a national expert on child welfare to respond to Wulczyn's presentation (Goerge & Wulczyn, 1998). Dr. Wulczyn reported to the Commission on his research studies that showed that infants, identified as children under age 1, were the largest group of children to enter, remain in, and re-enter foster care. They constituted one in five admissions to care. Most alarmingly, he reported that if these infants were discharged to their families, nearly one third would return to care. At the conclusion of the presentation, Professor Wald suggested the need for a specialized focus on infants in foster care. The Commission endorsed a new initiative to find ways to enhance the permanency and development of infants in foster care.

Phase I of Babies Can't Wait

Several months later, we were able to secure a grant from the prestigious Robert Wood Johnson (RWJ) Foundation to begin a project that I would name *Babies Can't Wait*. This very small grant—just $48,500—from such a prestigious foundation gave the project instant credibility. It was made possible through a series of serendipitous events. First, the Commission formed its own 501c(3) supporting organization to raise outside funds. Next, there was longtime involvement of the RWJ Foundation in the problems of young children from low-income families in the Bronx, which was the site of the planned project (Dicker & Gordon, 2004b).

The Bronx was chosen not only for its potential appeal to the RWJ Foundation but also because of the resources lodged in that very poor and diverse borough of New York City, including the presence of a network of early childhood and health care resources for infants anchored by the Albert Einstein College of Medicine and the leadership of the Bronx Family Court.

We embarked on a multipronged research initiative before even appointing an advisory group for the project. Commission Deputy Director Azra Farrell and Elysa Gordon scoured the Bronx to learn about the child welfare system, the court, and resources for infants. They developed and executed a case review project to profile infants in foster care in the Bronx. Through the contacts we made from our healthy development checklist work, they were able to gain access to the Administration for Children's Services (ACS) demographic research. We learned that in 2000, 491 babies out of the 1,300 citywide under age 1 who entered the foster care system were from the Bronx.

A review of the case files for 10% or 48 of these cases was initiated. During the summer of 2001, Commission staff reviewed in depth the case files for these 48 infants who entered foster care from April 2000 to March 2001. Findings mirrored the national trends and highlighted current practice and gaps in services. That is, the majority of these infants had been placed immediately in foster care after being released from the hospital after birth. They were taken from their birth mothers because of a positive toxicology for substance abuse. Most of the mothers averaged four children, and the average age of the mothers was 34 years. Most of the parents had already had parental rights for older children terminated. The majority of the infants were living in nonkinship foster care; and less than 20% of the files contained reports on the infants' development or medical issues or held court orders for services to the babies.

These findings shaped our view of the challenge and our approach to the future advisory group. That group would not only guide the work but also serve as a forum to share ideas and expertise. Judge Clarke Richardson, Supervising Judge of Bronx Family Court, would chair the advisory committee and soon become a member of the Commission. He would be joined by another Bronx judge; lawyers from legal aid who represent children; parents' attorneys; attorneys and other staff for ACS; CASA volunteers and Bronx-based experts in infant health, development, early intervention; and early childhood providers. One of those members would play a key role in shaping the project—Dr. Susan Chinitz, Director of the Early Childhood Center at Albert Einstein College of Medicine.

The first meetings of the advisory group involved learning about each other, sharing the Bronx case file research, and understanding the array of services in the Bronx. After several meetings, the advisory group identified three tasks for the project:

1. Arrange a series of multidisciplinary training classes for everyone in the court and child welfare systems that focus on infant well-being and development.

2. Compose a checklist and booklet for infants that is modeled on the previously developed Healthy Development checklist that concentrates on the babies involved in the court process and their specific needs.

3. Work in partnership with the child welfare system in attempts to change policy and practice regarding infants.

The *Babies Can't Wait* Training Series

The multidisciplinary training series became the first task of the advisory committee's first year. Dr. Chinitz and advisory committee colleagues drafted a proposed training series for the advisory group to review. Since nothing like that had been attempted nationwide, they had to invent the topics and syncopation for the training. Deputy Director Farrell and I then took this outline, turned it into the *Babies Can't Wait* curriculum to be held on-site at the courthouse, and limited it to a 1-hour format during the court's lunchtime to encourage attendance. The lunchtime series, titled *Infant Health and Development: What Courts and Child Welfare Personnel Need to Know* (as cited in Dicker & Gordon, 2004b), aimed to educate those involved in the court process about this issue. The concentration of the training underscored the medical, developmental, and emotional needs of infants, as well as offering information on services designed to deal with those requirements. The five-part series enlightened attendees—judges, lawyers, and child welfare caseworkers—about the possible risks of biological and environmental factors in the lives of developmentally vulnerable foster care toddlers and infants. The training sessions include the following five issues.

1. *Understanding the health care needs of infants:* This session, presented by a pediatrician, outlined the specific health risks and problems facing infants in foster care, components of the pediatric health visit, and strategies to enhance the health of infants in foster care. The instructor reviewed the environmental and biological risks faced by infants in foster care, identified common diagnoses found among infants in foster care, and suggested basic questions to determine an infant's health status. Particular attention was given to the complications of prematurity. The instructor also discussed issues related to consent and confidentiality. The session concluded with case studies to help participants gain skills in assessing health risks and developing a problem list and plan.

2. *Understanding infant development:* This session, presented by a developmental psychologist, provided a basic understanding of brain and child development in the first year of life and developmental disorders in infancy and early childhood. The instructor reviewed the developmental tasks and milestones of infancy and defined the distinction between a screening and an assessment. The session concluded with an introduction to the EI program and the scientific evidence of the effectiveness of well-designed EI.

3. *Understanding the emotional needs of infants:* This session, presented by a clinical psychologist and a social worker, underscored the emotional needs of infants and offered insight on how their needs have an impact on permanency decision making, including permanency goals, visitation, and services. The instructor highlighted the importance of early relationships for an infant's development and emotional well-being. Participants gained an in-depth understanding of attachment.

4. *Accessing the EI program and early childhood education programs for infants:* This session, presented by an EI official, reviewed the developmental disorders in infancy and early childhood and provided an overview of the EI program and early education programs for infants. Participants gained specific knowledge of the federal and New York State EI law; the design of the EI program; the program's eligibility requirements; and protocol for referral, evaluation, and service planning. The instructor outlined how the program can be used as part of permanency planning and decision making. Participants also received practical information on the Head Start program and other home visiting services.

5. *Case study:* This session brought back the expert instructors to sit on a panel chaired by Judge Richardson and the other committee judge, attorneys, a CASA, and myself. Using an infant case, we enabled participants to reinforce the learning of the four earlier sessions (Dicker & Gordon, 2004b).

More than 80 professionals comprising Bronx Family Court judges, court attorneys, CASAs, legal aid attorneys and social workers, parents' attorneys, ACS legal and program (including caseworkers) staff, and advocates attended the training. The excellent attendance, including all of the Bronx judges, was no doubt encouraged by Chief Judge Kaye's attendance at the first session. The evaluations of the training were uniformly excellent. Most interesting was the response to the question: "What one piece of information that was provided to you will you incorporate into your practice immediately?" Participant answers included asking whether an infant has received a medical evaluation by a pediatrician and other specialists at the earliest possible point in the court proceedings, whether the infant received developmental testing and a referral to the EI program, and the importance of minimizing removals and changes in placements.

After the initial training, it was clear that booster sessions were needed to reinforce and clarify the learning. Between May and December 2002, the Commission held six monthly consultation clinics that brought back the instructors to the Bronx Family Court to answer further questions about infant health and development. Not only were the booster clinics useful in reinforcing what had been taught during the training series but also they provided additional chances for building relationships between the court and local service providers. These new, expanding relationships were illustrated by one session at which a judge asked the instructor, a pediatrician, a key question: "What should I be asking to determine if it is safe for an infant with a positive toxicology to return home?" The response of the pediatrician included several realistic questions for the judge to ask that would help clarify the issues and shape court practice. They included the following: Does the mother have a substance abuse addiction, does she accept that diagnosis, and is she compliant with treatment? What supports does the mother have, particularly at 3 a.m., when the infant is awake and crying? What is the mother's track record with her other children regarding her ability to be

1. What are the medical needs of this infant?
2. What are the developmental needs of this infant?
3. What are the attachment and emotional health needs of this infant?
4. What challenges does this caregiver face that could impact his or her capacity to parent this infant?
5. What resources are available to enhance this infant's healthy development and prospects for permanency?

Figure 6.2.   Checklist for the Healthy Development of Infants in Foster Care. (From Dicker, S., & Gordon, E. [2004b]. Building bridges for babies in foster care: The Babies Can't Wait Initiative. *Juvenile and Family Court Journal, 55*(2), 35. Retrieved March 31, 2008, from http://www. nationalcasa.org/download/Judges_Page/0510_building_bridges_for_babies_0036.pdf; reprinted by permission.)

compliant with school attendance, medical appointments, and treatment regiments (Dicker & Gordon, 2004b)?

Infant Checklist

While we were developing and presenting the training series, its learnings were shaping the second project—creating an infant checklist. Using the wealth of research available about the needs of infants and the characteristics of infants in foster care, Gordon and I began to draft an infant checklist. We created a list with five key questions known as the Checklist for the Healthy Development of Infants in Foster Care. (See Figure 6.2.)

This updated infant checklist, similar to the original Healthy Development checklist, was based upon the recommendations of the AAP committee and the American Academy of Child and Adolescent Psychiatry. It is an instrument created to collect, record, and, importantly, monitor risk factors that have an impact on the permanency possibilities and the healthy development of infants in foster care. Starting in April 2002, the judge on the advisory committee tested the infant checklist on all new infant cases. A CASA volunteer was appointed to every one of the judge's infant cases to better assist the court in completing the checklist questions and keeping specific data. Using their feedback, we were able to expand the original five infant questions to a more detailed checklist. Figure 6.3 illustrates this revised checklist.

The more detailed questions on this checklist enabled CASA and, later, judges, lawyers, and child welfare caseworkers to learn more about the children and families and better target decision making. For example, asking more detailed questions enabled CASA to learn more about the cases in that particular judge's court. Most infants in these cases were born with positive toxicology; one third of the infants were born low birth weight; 10% of the infants had a biological mother who was identified as having a mental health diagnosis and had been hospitalized for that condition; and only 21% of the mothers indicated that they had

---

The Medical Checklist

- What health problems and risks are identified in the infant's birth and medical records (e.g., low birth weight, prematurity, prenatal exposure to toxic substances)?
- Does the infant have a medical home?
- Are the infant's immunizations complete and up to date?

The Developmental Checklist

- What are the infant's risks for developmental delay or disability?
- Has the infant had a developmental screening/assessment?
- Has the infant been referred to the EI program?

The Emotional Health Checklist

- Has the infant had a mental health assessment?
- Does the infant exhibit any red flags for emotional health problems?
- Has the infant demonstrated attachment to a caregiver?
- Has concurrent planning been initiated?

The Caregiver Capacity Checklist

- What are the specific challenges faced by the caregiver in caring for this infant (e.g., addiction to drugs and/or alcohol, mental illness, cognitive limitations)?
- What are the learning requirements for caregivers to meet this infant's needs?
- What are specific illustrations of this caregiver's ability to meet the infant's needs?

The Resource Checklist

- Does the infant have Medicaid or other health insurance?
- Is the infant receiving services under the EI program?
- Have the infant and caregiver been referred to Head Start or another early childhood program?

Figure 6.3. The Revised Infant Checklist for the Development of Infants in Foster Care (From Dicker, S., & Gordon, E. [2004b]. Building bridges for babies in foster care: The Babies Can't Wait Initiative. *Juvenile and Family Court Journal, 55*(2), 36. Retrieved March 31, 2008, from http://www.nationalcasa.org/download/Judges_Page/0510_building_bridges_for_babies_0036.pdf; reprinted by permission.)

received any prenatal care. Not only did CASA garner vital information about the infants through the process of asking these important questions and following up, but they also raised consciousness about valuable services for these children and their families. This repeated use of the checklist resulted in every infant involved having up-to-date immunizations and almost 80% having an assigned pediatrician, a visit to the pediatrician planned, and a referral to the EI program.

In 2004, Gordon and I wrote an infant booklet as a tool to underscore the unique needs of infants and the resources accessible to deal with those needs, as well as a means to help judges, attorneys, and child welfare professionals. Copublished by ZERO TO THREE: National Center for Infant, Toddlers, and Families, the booklet, *Ensuring the Healthy Development of Infants in Foster Care: A Guide for Judges, Advocates and Child Welfare Professionals* (Dicker & Gordon, 2004c), is an outcome of the partnership between the Commission and the Bronx Advisory Group, whose members extensively reviewed the booklet drafts.

BUILDING PARTNERSHIPS WITH CHILD WELFARE

At the outset of the Babies Can't Wait Initiative, Farrell and I notified our colleagues at ACS about the RWJ Foundation grant. Two Administration for Children's Services (ACS) officials would become critical—Alexandra Lowe, Special Counsel to the Deputy Commissioner for Foster Care, and Lisa Parrish, Deputy Commissioner for Foster Care. In the spring of 2001, they agreed to provide us with the most up-to-date ACS data about infants in foster care in the Bronx. That information helped to shape our first task, which was the file reviews, along with the development of the infant profile, as well as the membership of the advisory group. They also helped facilitate the first meeting of private not-for-profit providers—virtually all infants in the Bronx are cared for by these private agencies—at Bronx Family Court to inform them about the project.

In April 2002 at the suggestion of Parrish and Lowe, I was invited to meet with the new Commissioner, William Bell, who was a new member of the Commission, to brief him on the BCW project. The meeting included all ACS key leadership, and, in addition to Parrish and Lowe, all the other deputy and assistant commissioners attended. Bell quickly agreed to join us in this project, and he asked his staff to convene a parallel ACS working group. That working group would consist of ACS staff, Commission staff, and outside infant development specialists, including Chinitz from the Bronx advisory group. Their charge, according to Lowe, would be "to spread the word about infant's developmental and permanency needs beyond the Bronx" (A. Lowe, personal communication, October 3, 2007).

The ACS working group began to meet monthly in the late spring of 2002. Its first task was to adapt the original Bronx training for ACS staff and providers. In October and November 2002, two series of training sessions, attended by hundreds of child protective and private agency staff, were held. These trainings used the core Bronx sessions with the same expert instructors. At the start of each session, either Lowe or Parrish would welcome the trainees and reinforce the importance of the sessions for ACS's work. I would follow by summarizing the prior session and introducing the present session. At the end of each session, we left time for questions, and Lowe and I would provide backup, particularly about practice implications, to the day's speaker. These sessions have been repeated and revised since 2002 to ensure that ACS staff and staff from provider contract agencies have been exposed to knowledge about infant health and development.

Having successfully produced the training and inculcated it into the curriculum, the ACS working group was eager to take on the third task of the Bronx advisory committee—reshaping child welfare policy concerning infants. Lowe and Parrish suggested that ACS actually apply the learning to a subset of cases, that is, those cases that would eventually become the BCW placement unit. They determined that approximately half of the infants coming into care were not living with relatives or siblings and could be the perfect candidates for applying the basic concepts of ensuring the healthy development of infants. The BCW unit would be composed of infants under the age of 1 placed in foster care who did not have siblings in care and for whom no kinship placement was available. Abandoned babies would be included in this group. Indeed, this placement unit's main charge was to follow the Parrish mantra that "An infant's first placement should be his or her only placement," which echoes the research presented at the training that emphasized the importance of attachment for infants for their healthy development (Parrish, 2002).

Thus, making informed and wise initial placement decisions for the BCW infants was critical. At Lowe's suggestion, the working group would develop criteria for the selection of homes for the BCW infants. In the spring of 2003, Lowe drafted a document titled *Factors to Consider in Selecting a Recruited Pre-Adoptive Foster Home in Which to Place an Infant Coming into Care Alone with No Siblings Already in Care* (Lowe, 2003). The document lists six factors for consideration. Its first tenet is that infants should be placed with foster parents in their early 50s or younger who would have the physical and emotional capacity to care for the child long term, if necessary. Second, it emphasizes looking at the other children in the home, including the number of and ages of all the children and any special needs with respect to keeping the foster parent from becoming overwhelmed. Next, the infant's own special needs must be considered, including whether the baby has been assessed for potential developmental disabilities, whether the foster parent is able to accommodate the infant's special needs, and whether the foster parent has the capacity to participate in EI services. At the same time, information about the baby's prematurity, low birth weight, and parent's drug and alcohol use must be factored into the placement decision. In addition, the document asks whether the foster parent has a dependable support system, especially relatives or close friends, who are able to help the foster parent care for the infant as well as the other children in the home. The requests identify those who could provide that respite. Finally, foster parents have to pledge to a family-to-family collaboration with the birth parent while time-limited reunification efforts are ongoing (including visiting and communication with the birth parent). At the same time, these foster parents also have to be agreeable to adopting the infant if those reunification efforts are unsuccessful.

The document underwent considerable refinement during the next 3 years by the BCW working group and the ACS executive staff. The final version of the protocol was promulgated in November 2006 (Chahine, 2006). Most of the questions have remained. The 2006 document borrows more specifications from the infant checklist and booklet requiring availability of hospital records and specialized training for foster parents to meet an infant's needs. After all of this effort, however, the BCW placement unit is only a placement unit that determines where children go. Ironically, despite all the work to shape policy, the unit has not been tracked by ACS. There were serious shortcomings after changing leadership (Lowe and Parrish moved on to other efforts), and the high level of focus of BCW within ACS was eroded.

Close of Phase I of Babies Can't Wait

As the grant drew to a close, the Commission held its last advisory group meeting in December 2002 to reflect on the project and designate a leader in the Bronx to sustain its activities. Group members stated that the project provided tools to increase awareness of the needs of infants and resources for family support through the trainings, the checklist, and links to experts in the community. Bronx Family Court Supervising Judge Clark Richardson noted that the project had broken down the barriers among the court, child welfare, and services worlds. It also raised the level of knowledge of court players with judges, attorneys, and child welfare workers asking general questions of Chinitz and her colleagues to better understand specific issues (S. Chinitz, personal communication, June 25, 2007). Most significant of all, it forged a lasting relationship that resulted in ongoing court consultation with Chinitz. Through a grant made possible by the collaboration between Chinitz and court players, Chinitz is now available 2 days a month at Bronx Family Court and by e-mail to provide information on child health, development, and emotional issues to all involved in the court process. This has resulted in providing expedited expert information to everyone involved in cases, identifying issues for evaluation, and securing appropriate evaluations and services on cases.

PHASE II OF BABIES CAN'T WAIT

As the RWJ project drew to a close in December 2002, the Commission staff handed the reins to the Bronx advisory committee. In 2003, we continued its two central features with CIP funds—the training for the courts and ACS and our active participation in the ACS/BCW working group.

   In the spring of 2003, we were given an opportunity to build the BCW citywide expansion when Judge Joseph Lauria, Administrative Judge of the New York City Family Court, asked me to participate in a visit by the New York Community Trust (NYCT) to Manhattan Family Court. At that meeting, I had the opportunity to discuss the BCW project and express our hope for its expansion to all of New York City. The NYCT was particularly intrigued with our idea to place an ECS in the court to assist judges on individual infant cases, as well as organize the advisory committee, trainings, and clinics. They hoped that position could become institutionalized as a resource for the court on all cases. I shared their hope and also persuaded them to fund CASA as part of the BCW Phase II initiative with the stipulation that CASA would be involved in at least 50 infant cases a year in the boroughs (Permanent Judicial Commission on Justice for Children, 2003).

Phase II began in January 2004 virtually at the same time as the publication of the infant booklet. Trista Borra, a Commission staff member, spearheaded this second phase to begin in Queens. Queens is a unique place because it is the most diverse county in America, with people from almost 200 countries speaking as many languages; yet, it has a neosuburban quality at its fringes (Official Home Page of the Queens Borough President's Office, n.d). Borra hired an ECS to work with her in Queens. They followed the initial structure established in the Bronx, but with a crucial divergence—the supervising judge, in contrast to Judge Clark Richardson in the Bronx, showed little interest in the project, and other partners were harder to engage.

Due to the lukewarm reception of the project, Borra and I determined that we needed a formal project kickoff prior to the first training. On April 14, 2004, Judge Kaye welcomed the group, I explained the project's history, and Judge Clark Richardson spoke of the importance of the project to the Bronx Family Court. He emphasized the resources that the project brought to the Bronx, particularly the relationships developed with Chinitz and other experts that provided enormous assistance to the court. He also underscored the importance of the trainings and booster clinics by adding that the exposure of the court to the latest scientific knowledge about infants reverberated for all cases and made the judges more aware of all children's health and developmental needs.

Despite the quality of the trainings, the efforts of the ECS and CASA, and the recruitment of a diverse advisory committee, the Queens project made little headway in the court without judicial leadership. In fact, the most important work was done by Borra and Dr. Jean Clancy, Queens director of EI. Through their efforts, a practice for referring all infants to EI was established. A special telephone number at EI would be poised to accept foster care referrals, and Clancy would be available to troubleshoot any concerns. This would lay the groundwork for a citywide practice for referrals to EI. That has resulted in children in foster care securing EI services at a rate of nine times that of other New York City children (S. Chinitz, personal communication, June 25, 2007).

By the end of 2004, it was clear that the project needed to move on to another borough. Brooklyn, with its large number of infant cases—more than 200 infants entering foster care each year—needed the work of the ECS. At the beginning of 2005, Borra and I met with Supervising Judge Jane Pearl to plan the BCW project for Brooklyn. She enthusiastically welcomed the project to Brooklyn. Several judges there were interested in working with the project, but one, Judge Susan Danoff, was very enthusiastic about serving as lead judge for the initiative.

In contrast to Queens, the enthusiastic support of the supervising judge and other judges enabled the BCW project to thrive and even expand the initiative. Judge Danoff in concert with Borra developed a specialized court project for infant cases. She would assign CASA to all cases, but her project would do more. She would use the ECS extensively and devise model court practices and orders for infant cases. Prior to the first hearing, the ECS would review the case and suggest questions for the judge as was evident in Jason's case at the beginning of this chapter. At the first hearing on all infant cases, the judge appoints CASA to report on the health and development of the infant using the infant checklist on a special data gathering tool developed by Rob Conlon of the Commission and orders a referral to the EI program, a comprehensive medical examination, a due diligence search for both parents, and asks the questions suggested by the ECS. Thereafter, the ECS and the CASA meet monthly to review every infant case. At the initial hearing, the judge calendars the case for review every 30–60 days. The ECS continues to track the case as it proceeds, flagging issues for the judge, monitoring the work of CASA, and troubleshooting with EI, as in Jason's case, to resolve any problems and help to identify other resources for the case.

As a result of these initiatives, CASAs have provided the court with timely information on infants' needs. By asking the checklist questions, CASAs have ensured that the vast majority of infants have up-to-date, complete immunizations, a medical home, and referrals to EI. The frequent court reviews have resulted in fewer placement changes for the infants, allowing them the critical developmental opportunity to create attachments to their caregivers. The growth of the project's many initiatives in Brooklyn and its strong support from the court and the child welfare community made us extend its stay in the borough. Indeed, the role of the ECS was not only embraced by Judge Danoff but also favored by all the abuse and neglect judges.

Judge Danoff explained it well:

> The Babies Can't Wait initiative has been an example of excellent, outstanding court improvement. As [the Commission's] statistics have shown for the year 2005, as compared with 2003, the majority of babies (67%) evaluated for early intervention required services, usually in the form of physical therapy, occupational therapy, special services, and the like. What is most important, however, is that through Court Appointed Special Advocates (CASA), the Court has been given a vehicle to provide children coming under the Family Court's jurisdiction with services, and that but for the Babies Can't Wait project these children would never have been evaluated for delays and would never have received the chance of leading normal, productive, and enhanced lives....Another aspect of the Babies Can't Wait project was the invaluable assessments provided to me by the Early Childhood Specialist for each case. Each day I have many cases, and, although well-intentioned, we can occasionally forget to address each important issue. But, routinely, the Early Childhood Specialist gave me a memo which highlighted the issues and helped the attorneys, caseworkers, parents and me to

focus the discussions had in court. Frankly, without the Early Childhood Specialist's participation, I am sure I would have missed many points of discussion. (Permanent Judicial Commission on Justice for Children, 2006, pp. 3–4)

The results of the Brooklyn initiative are encouraging. At the outset of the project, Borra and her staff collected baseline data reviewing 53 (approximately 20%) of 2003 infants' cases. The profile found that although 13% of the cases had a referral for EI, none of those cases had any follow-up information on EI or other ordered services. A review of an equal number of 2005 cases found that 98% of the cases were referred to EI; 100% of those had received a developmental screening or evaluation, and 67% of those evaluated were found eligible for EI services (Permanent Judicial Commission on Justice for Children, 2006).

During 2004 and 2005, Borra met with Judge Pearl and the other judges to try to establish an ongoing ECS type of position in Brooklyn. It was agreed that a master of social work (M.S.W.) position should be established that would not only perform the ECS tasks but also supervise M.S.W. degree students, thereby growing the resource for more judges. I targeted CIP resources to fund the position, and Judge Lauria approved its presence in his court budget. Borra drafted a job description that was extensively vetted by the court community in 2005, and interviews began in 2006 for the new position. A full time M.S.W. now works in the Brooklyn Family Court on an established court staff line funded by CIP. She assists three abuse and neglect judges first on infant cases and then on other cases as needed, provides social work expertise, shapes questions for judges, and identifies resources. The project has been so successful that additional M.S.W.s were hired in 2008.

In 2004, Borra began representing the Commission on the ACS/BCW group. Although its leadership had changed, practice breakthroughs did occur, including enacting policy requiring all children age birth-to-3 who are the subject of an indicated child protective report to be automatically referred to EI, creating the protocol of factors for consideration for BCW placements and developing other tools to aid child protective workers, including a palm card and questions to ask in all baby cases (Permanent Judicial Commission on Justice for Children, 2006).

LESSONS LEARNED

The 6 years of BCW were years of strides for infants in child welfare in New York City. Babies are now on the radar screen of the courts, ACS, EI, and other providers. More work remains because infants are still entering care, albeit in smaller numbers, and they still remain in care for a long time (NYS Council on Children and Families and the Permanent Judicial Commission on Justice for Children, 2006). Understanding what succeeded and what failed during the BCW project will be instructive for future reform efforts.

First, judicial leadership was a key component in the BCW project. Judges play a crucial role not only as central decision makers but also as community leaders shaping the courtroom climate and community expectations. The pivotal judicial leader in this chapter was Chief Judge Judith Kaye. She focused the Commission's efforts on developing court-based initiatives, gave her approval of the project by attending early trainings, and championed the project by spotlighting it in her public pronouncements. Leadership by local judges was critical as well. Administrative Judge Joseph Lauria lent his support at every juncture to BCW. Supervising Judge Clarke Richardson's chairing of the Bronx advisory group, encouraging judges to attend trainings, and issuing directives to the court on the project all served to set the tone for leadership and collaboration. His efforts were echoed by his Brooklyn colleagues—Supervising Judge Pearl and Judge Danoff—in their strong endorsement and expansion of the project. The challenges of the Queens project only underscore the necessity for judicial leadership and support.

Second, building collaboration with child welfare and the early childhood community was vital for success. To shape the project and provide ongoing opportunities for discourse and relationship building, the Commission convened a highly inclusive advisory group comprising representatives from the court, child welfare, and local child development experts. The advisory group ensured that the project reflected the voice of all of those involved in serving infants in foster care and their families and fostered an unprecedented, ongoing relationship between the court and community resources. Recruiting local child development experts as instructors gave the court and child welfare professionals a better understanding of and access to community resources. It also provided an opportunity for the court to receive ongoing booster sessions, as well as consultation and support on specific problems beyond the trainings. The instructors reported that their knowledge of the local court process and culture and their access to community judges, advocates, and child welfare professionals improved their ability to shape clinical recommendations and resolve difficult cases. Indeed, this new relationship between the judges and experts, such as Chinitz, resulted in tangible benefits for children who were able to secure timely high-quality evaluations, services, reports, and testimony to the court.

Although the early childhood experts played an unprecedented role in the development of the BCW, its success would have been greatly limited without the support of ACS. At the outset of the project, we approached ACS not only to serve on the advisory group, but also to help shape the project by tapping their data and information about the community. Later, through partnerships with high-level ACS officials, we were able to collaborate on every facet of the project. Indeed, when the ACS commissioner determined to commence a parallel BCW working group, ACS took ownership for the issue of enhancing the development and permanency of infants. This partnership that continues through strong ACS ownership of the BCW brand has proven to be instrumental for any future success.

Flexibility in building and sustaining the project has been essential. At the outset, we could not have predicted the strength of our ACS partnership, but we seized the opportunity. Nor could we have predicted the direction that Chinitz's long-term collaboration with the courts would take. In addition, the Brooklyn effort was so successful that it created new M.S.W. positions within the entire court system.

Taking the project to scale was an important lesson. Since the Commission is a statewide body, many of its members brought word of the *Babies Can't Wait* Initiative back to their communities. In Westchester County, under the leadership of Supervising Judge Joan Cooney, CASAs began using the infant checklist on every infant case. The Commission launched the project in Erie County (Buffalo) in July 2003 when Commission member Administrative Judge Sharon Townsend brought its learning to Erie County. She initiated the development of a *Babies Can't Wait* project as part of Erie County's larger Model Court Stakeholders Group. Erie County has added members of local EI programs and child care resource and referral agencies to its planning group. It replicated the *Babies Can't Wait* training curriculum in May 2004, using local experts as instructors. A similar effort was replicated in Monroe County (Rochester). Word of the Commission's *Babies Can't Wait* Initiative also spread to the New York State Office of Children and Family Services (OCFS). Due to a finding of noncompliance by the federal Child and Family Services Review (CFSR), OCFS organized a committee to write the required Program Improvement Plan (PIP) that included Farrell from the Commission staff. The PIP refers to the Commission's work, and one provision specifically calls for an automatic referral system to the EI program for all young children in foster care. The Commission–OCFS collaboration has led to the convening of a statewide conference known as Sharing Success. This annual conference now in its sixth year is attended by judges, lawyers, and state and local department of social services staff to highlight successful court and child welfare reform initiatives. Presentations about the BCW project were made the first morning of the first conference by Parrish and myself to emphasize its statewide importance and ensure that all attendees were exposed to its learning. As a result, several additional counties will be initiating BCW projects. This collaboration has led to unexpected partnerships between OCFS and the courts, resulting in the passage of the 2005 Permanency Law (New York Laws of 2005). This law requires that permanency hearing reports contain information on children's health, development, and education needs and services, including referral and receipt of EI services.

The BCW Initiative also has influenced child welfare and court practice. More than the Healthy Development of Foster Children Initiative, BCW has strengthened the ability of courts and child welfare professionals to make the connection between healthy development and permanency. The connection was clear for babies because individuals could understand how an infant who cries constantly could have an impact on a caregiver's ability to parent that infant, creating stress on the family and undermining family stability.

Thus, the work has only begun. Promoting the healthy development and permanency of infants in the child welfare system requires judicial leadership, strong collaborations with child welfare, a broad array of community resources, flexibility in seizing opportunities to strengthen and grow the program, and, most importantly, prolonged and persistent efforts. Babies in the child welfare system deserve this enormous commitment.

7

Using Health Care as a Portal for Healthy Development

The Arkansas Case Study

JOHN'S STORY

When John was 2 years old, the police were summoned to his house. They found him being beaten by his mother's live-in boyfriend. The police arrested the boyfriend and brought John to the hospital. There, they found bruises on his face, shoulder, buttocks, and genitals. His skin was also checkered with eczema and bug bites. Child protective services (CPS) was called and sought a court order due to apparent physical and sexual abuse. The court, without John's parents present, found him to be in imminent harm and placed him in emergency foster care.

John's mother, grandmother, and aunt were notified of his condition, and they sought to visit him in the hospital. The judge granted visitation under supervision. When John left the hospital, he was placed in foster care. His mother, grandmother, and aunt, now living together, were granted weekly supervised visits. Since John's foster mother worked, he was placed in child care where he received no special services. His bruises were cared for by the foster mother and were healing.

After John had been in foster care for 30 days, he was brought by his child welfare caseworker to the Arkansas Project for Adolescent and Child Evaluation (PACE) site for the required comprehensive examination. The Division of Children and Family Services (DCFS) worker brought John's complete social services file and medical records that the DCFS medical unit had secured, including his birth records from Tennessee and a 6-month-old hospital record reporting blisters on his genitals. The DCFS worker arranged for John's birth mother to be available by telephone to consult with the PACE team. The team consisted of a physician's assistant, a psychologist, a speech-language pathologist, and a social worker.

The evaluation began with a social history that relied on the records and the interview with the social worker augmented by the phone call to the mother. That history indicated that this was John's first placement in foster care, that the alleged perpetrator was now in prison, and that his mother was living with her mother and sister. The mother was not in contact with John's biological father, but she said that the man was observed to exhibit failure to thrive (FTT) when he was young. She said she had always been concerned about John's small size. She reported that John did not have a regular physician, and she could not recall his last shots or his last physician visit, other than the hospital visits. The search of the state immunization database showed no listing at all for John.

After the social history, John was given a physical examination. He was very small for his size, measuring less than 3% for height, less than 5% for weight, and less than 1% for head circumference. His body still had scars and healing bruises from head to toe. His facial features were misshapen and malformed. The DCFS worker advised the team that his mother had similar malformed facial features. He appeared and acted far younger than his age. His fine and gross motor skills were observed to be seriously delayed, with tests placing him at a 6-month-old rate. His speech was unintelligible, and he failed an audiological screening.

Due to his age, the psychologist and speech-language pathologist worked together to perform the next steps of the evaluation. They found that he was significantly delayed in many domains with a cognitive developmental equivalence age of 7 months. In some of the testing, he was in the lowest range of intelligence, often at the 1% level. After the evaluations were completed, the team met to discuss their initial findings. They were concerned about John's size and FTT, the continuing healing of his bruises, his failure to pass the hearing test, his overall significant developmental delays, and the ramifications of the abuse.

After meeting as a team, they met with the DCFS worker and put the mother on the telephone to share their preliminary findings. They recommended an immediate visit to his primary health care provider, which needed to be established by the DCFS medical unit, to address the failure to thrive and physical and sexual abuse issues, including the bruises. They also recommended an immediate hearing test and a referral to the early intervention (EI) program. The mother did not ask any questions, but she was cooperative on the telephone. The team then wrote the evaluation report. A total of 4 hours was spent evaluating John. The written report was sent to his DCFS worker, the DCFS medical unit, and to the DCFS Office of Chief Counsel.

In the next few weeks, John's new primary care physician saw him concerning John's growth and bruises, and steps were taken to help his foster mother with his diet. John began to gain a little weight. He was also taken for an audiological exam that noted a significant hearing loss. He was then brought to an audiologist for hearing aids. Only days after his comprehensive exam, DCFS referred John to the EI program, and he was found eligible. He was placed in a center-based, full day EI program where he received intensive speech therapy, physical therapy, and occupational therapy, in addition to special instruction. His mother, grandmother, and aunt began visiting him at the EI program with the consent of DCFS. At the program, his grandmother was taught exercises to augment his therapy because his mother was unable to learn the required therapies.

After 6 months in care, the court held a hearing on John's case. The judge and the lawyers had all received copies of the PACE report, and progress on its recommendations were noted. John had been making strides in the EI program, and his hearing aids were of great benefit. John's mother, grandmother, and aunt were present at the hearing. They each spoke about how well John was doing, and how they felt ready to take him home. The judge ordered increased visitation without supervision and overnight stays with John's family with the clear proviso that the perpetrator never be allowed near John. All agreed.

At the permanency hearing a few months later, the court noted that John's health and development, particularly his speech and hearing, continued to progress. His family was receiving the support they needed to enhance John's development. The judge was concerned about the birth mother's abilities and her apparent slow intellect, and, therefore, determined that the grandmother should be given custody. The judge continued court supervision of the case for a year. After the hearing, John was reunified with his family and now lives with his grandmother, mother, and aunt. He still attends the EI day program and receives needed health and developmental services. His family receives EI services to enhance John's development and support the family's stability.

John's story is about the centrality of health care for a young child. John's health and development truly were intertwined with his permanency. Addressing his health care needs made it possible for him to be reunited with his extended family. Providing health care also had lifelong implications because without identifying his hearing loss and other developmental delays, his future prospects would have been far grimmer.

It is axiomatic that the healthy development of young children begins with the provision of adequate health care. Yet, children in the child welfare system are at grave risk for chronic and acute medical problems and all too often do not have access to health care that could advance their chances for healthy development and their prospects for a stable and permanent home (U.S. General Accounting Office [GAO], 1995; Halfon, Mendonca, & Berkowitz, 1995; Silver, Amster & Haecker, 1999). Indeed, until John's comprehensive examination by PACE, he was not fully immunized, his growth deficiencies were not identified, his hearing loss was not flagged, and his many developmental delays were not noted. Once these many health-related problems were identified, John's life was transformed.

The lack of health care services to children in foster care is particularly alarming because all children in foster care are eligible for early and periodic screening, diagnosis, and treatment (EPSDT) under Medicaid law (Medicaid Early and Periodic Screening, Diagnosis and Treatment Act Amendments of 1989, Omnibus Reconciliation Act of 1989, PL 101-239). EPSDT is a comprehensive benefits package that requires medical, vision, hearing, and dental screens to be performed at distinct intervals that meet current standards of pediatric practice. The American Academy of Pediatrics (AAP) and the Child Welfare League of America (CWLA) have partnered to create health care standards for children in out-of-home placement (CWLA, 1988, 2007). Indeed, in recognizing the extraordinary health needs of this population, AAP has developed specific practice parameters and guidelines for health care delivery to children in foster care, recommending more frequent pediatric visits and screenings than required for all children under EPSDT (AAP Committee on Early Childhood, Adoption and Dependent Care, 2002). This was vital for John because his many medical and developmental problems required immediate and frequent follow-up. Without stringent adherence to these standards for follow-up, John's health would not have improved.

At the heart of these requirements is an initial assessment to identify acute problems at placement and a critical comprehensive medical examination within 30 days of placement. That critical comprehensive examination provides the baseline for all future medical care for the child as it is composed of an assessment of the child's medical, developmental, mental health, and educational needs. These are key guideposts for follow-up services and identification of placements that can address children's needs.

While virtually all children in foster care have health insurance through Medicaid, the program offers little to no financing for the health care management functions, such as coordinating care or even scheduling required follow-up appointments for these children. Medicaid provides no financing for advocacy and interdisciplinary collaboration on their behalf. Also, despite Medicaid funding, securing needed medical records, sharing information with other providers and foster parents, and performing needed developmental and mental health screens pose enormous challenges to ensuring the provision of adequate health care to children in foster care (Risley-Curtiss & Stites, 2007).

Even though the law and standards are clear, neither the CWLA, the AAP, nor any national entity has been able to create health care services for children in foster care; instead, these efforts have happened on the ground. In reality, the health care system for children in the child welfare system is a national checkerboard—vastly different depending on the state and even the county.

Few exceptions exist to the lack of a statewide system of health care (e.g., Utah has a statewide program that uses public health nurses to coordinate health care for children in foster care) (Georgetown University Child Development Center, 2000). PACE, which provided services to John and is profiled in this chapter, was the ancillary result of a decade-long lawsuit to improve Arkansas's child welfare system. Indeed, only one provision of the class action case known as *Angela R. v. Clinton* (1991) flagged the lack of health care for Arkansas's children in foster care. The case found that only one fifth of the children in foster care had received the comprehensive assessment required by EPSDT. Not surprisingly, few received any follow-up health care. The litigation was a catalyst that created a national model for health care for children in foster care. In this case, the power of the litigation was harnessed by advocates, dedicated public servants, and creative health administrators to develop the program. This is the story of that remarkable, but almost unnoticed, effort to create a vital service to ensure the healthy development of children in foster care, such as John.

THE ANGELA R. LITIGATION

The Angela R. lawsuit was filed in federal court in July 1991, but its roots go back for more than a decade. The lawsuit followed years of effort by Arkansas Advocates for Children and Families (AACF), a state-based advocacy organization that was founded in 1977 by a group of concerned Arkansans and was modeled after the Children's Defense Fund (CDF). From its inception, AACF understood its unique role operating in one of the nation's poorest states (Arkansas was often the 48th or 49th state on every indicator of child well-being at that time) and saw its mission as spotlighting the many serious challenges to the well-being of Arkansas's children. At AACF's founding in 1977, and for most of the next decade, Hillary Rodham Clinton would serve as its president.

At its founding, AACF had only a part-time staff. Since funding was so precarious, Don Crary, a former minister and early childhood researcher, was hired as an acting director. Crary was able to garner a small grant from the Carnegie Foundation that gave credibility to the fledgling organization. His first project reflected recognition of AACF's unique role as the sole voice for children in the state. Crary initiated a broad, sweeping study on the status of children in Arkansas called *Arkansas Children Have Problems* (Arkansas Advocates for Children & Families, 1979). That study highlighted problems in health, education, safety, child welfare, and juvenile justice.

Through the efforts of Amy Rossi, M.S.W., working with Crary, AACF was able to write a federal grant proposal (D. Crary, personal communication, April 2, 2008). When secured, those federal funds enabled AACF to focus on an issue underscored in that first report—the lack of due process in the court system responsible for cases of child abuse and neglect and juvenile delinquency. This effort began in the legislative session of 1981 when AACF collaborated with the University of Arkansas at Little Rock Law School clinic to draft new provisions of the Arkansas Juvenile Code that deal with the most serious violations of due process with the juvenile court (Dicker & Crary, 1990).

Despite these reforms, the problem of a dysfunctional court system that operated differently throughout the state—often without judges trained in the law, any counsel for children, a record of the proceedings, or rules of evidence—was exacting a toll on both the child abuse and neglect and juvenile delinquency systems. AACF began to develop a multistrategic effort to reform the court, beginning with an unsuccessful campaign to amend the Arkansas constitution. That effort was followed by targeted studies and highlighted problems for the media. Yet, the issue appeared frozen. Only litigation promised any chance of defrosting this issue. In late 1985, Grif Stockley, an attorney with Central Arkansas Legal Services, began to work with Crary and Rossi to plan a class action lawsuit challenging the constitutionality of the court system. On January 20, 1987, this team secured a declaration from the Arkansas Supreme Court that the juvenile court was unconstitutional. Governor Clinton appointed a commission to draft a new system, and Hillary Rodham Clinton led a successful campaign to pass a constitutional amendment establishing a new court system (Dicker & Crary, 1990).

CHILD WELFARE IN ARKANSAS

Creating a new court—a success for AACF and its allies—did not change the failures of the Arkansas child welfare system. During the 1980s, AACF conducted a series of comprehensive studies detailing the problems in the foster care system and secured countless newspaper articles reporting on the studies and problems in the system. These efforts resulted in Governor Clinton's appointment of an expert panel that proposed 75 specific recommendations for child welfare system reform. Yet, despite years of advocacy, child welfare remained a low priority (Shores, 1998).

The Litigation

In the spring of 1991, a team of national and local legal service attorneys working with Grif Stockley came to Arkansas to contemplate litigation against the child welfare system. However, as was AACF's strategy, litigation was never used as a surprise tactic but as a step in a multistrategic process. Thus, harnessing their long-term relationship with Hillary Rodham Clinton and Governor Clinton, Rossi (now AACF executive director) and AACF requested a meeting with the governor.

At the meetings, the attorneys told the governor of their intention to file a lawsuit unless major changes were made in the child welfare system. The advocates brought a series of demands to the meeting with the governor. These included huge staff increases (Keesee, 1991) and allocating at least $12 million to the child welfare budget (DHS to Overhaul Child Welfare, 1991). Governor Clinton responded with skepticism about the ability of any state to effectively reform the child welfare system or the notion that hiring 100% more staff or adding more dollars would reduce the number of abused children or repair broken families

(Morris, 1991). However, troubled by the problems the advocates raised and the possible political ramifications, the governor appointed another expert panel.

Despite this open atmosphere and AACF's strategy of giving the governor time to try to resolve problems, the advocates did not wait for the panel's recommendations but chose to file a lawsuit in July 1991. The timing was precipitated by yet another death of a child in foster care. Rossi recalled,

> The critical event in my mind was that during the negotiations, there was still another child who died in a foster home. This child had asthma, and the foster mother wasn't fully informed about the risks involved, and the child didn't have his inhaler. The child had an asthmatic attack...got into dire shape and the foster mother called for an ambulance...he died after 24 hours in the hospital. It was absolutely a horrible but emphatic example of how the system failed children with their medical needs. Had anyone looked, they would have seen that he had been in the hospital on numerous occasions. (A. Rossi, personal communication, August 15, 2007)

The death underscored the centrality of children's health in these cases. Yet, the filing of the litigation, in retrospect, was also at an opportune time—a few months prior to Governor Bill Clinton's announcement for the presidency.

The complaint filed by Stockley and the local legal service attorneys, along with the San Francisco based National Youth Law Center, addressed nearly all aspects of Arkansas's child welfare services and foster care system (*Angela R. v. Clinton*, 1991; Matthews, 1992). While individual children's deaths and poor health conditions were highlighted at the beginning of the complaint and later were the bait for news coverage, improved health care was a low priority for the attorneys. Indeed, health care was near the bottom of the complaint's allegations (located on page 77 of a 93-page document). The health allegations were general, asserting that children are required under federal law to receive *proper care*. They did allege some specifics, including that almost half of the children did not receive the required comprehensive exam, including basic eye, hearing, or dental screens during the first 60 days of placement, and that one third received no physical exam at all during the first 10 days in care.

A few months later, the governor's panel concurred with the advocate's allegations and the state entered into 4 months of comprehensive biweekly settlement discussions that focused on the substantive areas of the complaint. Heavily relying on the governor's expert panel report, these discussions produced a detailed proposed settlement entitled the *Arkansas Child Welfare Reform Document* (Shores, 1998). It created a five-member Arkansas Child Welfare Compliance and Oversight Committee to ensure full compliance. The consent decree addressed every problem in the child welfare system, with health merely one item on the long list of 245 mandates in the agreement (Shores, 1998).

In February 1992, the governor called an unprecedented special session of the Arkansas Legislature to focus on child welfare, implementing what came to be known as the *reform document* and requesting additional legislative appropriations and approval of the oversight committee through 1994. With the appropriation of $15 million dollars for the child welfare system—more money than originally requested by AACF and the attorneys in 1991—the oversight committee approval was secured.

Compliance and Oversight Committee

During the last year of Governor Bill Clinton's administration, and during the next years of Governor Jim Guy Tucker's terms, the oversight committee was a consistent force pushing system reforms. The oversight committee established by the consent decree and approved by the legislature brought together a unique group of individuals for several years of intense work. It was chosen by the plaintiffs, the defendants, and the legislature and would include several familiar faces, including longtime advocates Crary and Rossi; Beverly Jones, a child welfare official from Anne Arundel County, Maryland, who had served on the governor's expert panel and would serve as chair; Terri Combs-Orne, a professor of social work at Johns Hopkins University; and Samuel Magdovitz, Assistant Director of Community Legal Services of Philadelphia. All involved identified Combs-Orne as the one person with expertise in health care (T. Combs-Orne, personal communication, October 2007).

During the first 6 months of the oversight committee's tenure, beginning in August 1992, it met every few weeks in Little Rock. Those were labor-intensive times, with the oversight committee surveying family service workers, issuing questionnaires about services, reviewing case records, and trying to understand existing data and data needs (Shores, 1998). While it saw its first task as augmenting in-service training for workers, it did learn of slow progress in securing health care for children because of difficulties in collaborations with health care providers and the lack of accurate information (Shores, 1998).

As envisioned, Combs-Orne became the key spokesperson, pushing the health care issue at oversight committee meetings. The oversight committee was united when she raised any health issues (T. Combs-Orne, personal communication, October 2007). By April 1993, it issued its first report specifically criticizing the Department of Human Services (DHS) for failing to develop a mechanism to guarantee the comprehensive exam within 30 days as required by the reform document (Shores, 1998). Something as small but as significant as the form DHS uses to document children's medical appointments by listing the dates of appointments, but not the diagnoses, treatment or intervention, or follow-up care, was scrutinized by the oversight committee (Shores, 1998). With this form, it was impossible to know about children's health care needs or whether they had been addressed. In addition, the panel flagged another problem—not providing foster parents with information about the child, including their health needs and special needs. This lack of information sharing would also be monitored because developing a medical passport was a key issue for the oversight committee (A. Rossi, personal communication, July 2008).

Soon after the first oversight committee report was issued, it became clear to DHS Director Tom Dalton that change was needed. He appointed Jones, the chairwoman of the oversight committee, to head the DCFS (Shores, 1998). Appointing Jones, who had served on both the governor's expert panel and chaired the oversight committee, was a bold move. Jones recalls consulting with fellow oversight committee members Crary and Magdovitz and touching base with other members (B. Jones, personal communication, November 1, 2007). Some of the oversight members balked at this appointment, fearing it was a conflict of interest or that it could water down their efforts. Crary, however, applauded the appointment, believing that finding someone with Jones's deep knowledge of child welfare as well as Arkansas's problems was essential for change (D. Crary, personal communication, October 2007). Jones worried about establishing a trusting relationship with the DCFS staff who, all too often, saw the monitors as interlopers (B. Jones, personal communication, November, 2007). She worried, too, about the changing nature of her relationship with members of the oversight committee. The relationship between Jones and the panel during the next years would be tense at times, and despite the once close relationship of the oversight committee members to their former chair, the panel's criticisms would continue.

The critical oversight comments brought a strong response from Jones, who stated, "It is always easier to identify the issue and suggest the changes. The more difficult task is implementing the changes. I think we have made significant progress, but we have a long way to go" (Shores, 1998, p. 30). These often heated exchanges underscore a central issue in making change. Recognizing the key role of the inside government implementer to move the agenda is often difficult for advocates and even for a judicial oversight committee to accept. Yet, without Jones's and Dalton's commitment, any change would have been impossible.

During the next 2 years, the oversight committee reviewed dozens of reforms. For fiscal years 1993–1995, more than $70 million was authorized for child welfare services. Despite these large expenditures, the oversight committee's reports still highlighted serious problems, noting "the current level of compliance is dangerous to the health of individual foster children" (Arkansas Child Welfare Compliance and Oversight Committee, 1994, p. 41). The 1994 annual report raised concerns about the nonexistent system for performing the required comprehensive exams and follow-up treatment and questioned the reliability of information contained in the medical passport given to foster parents. In addition, the report raised questions about two DHS/DCFS implementation proposals: 1) the capacity of the Arkansas Department of Health to collect medical information, and 2) the viability of a proposed contract with the Arkansas Children's Hospital to perform the comprehensive examinations. Jones and Dalton heeded those concerns and nixed both proposals; however, the problem of untangling the challenge of implementation remained.

Fortunately, at this juncture, Jones received a call from Dr. Eldon Schulz, Director of the Dennis Developmental Center at the University of Arkansas Medical School (UAMS) (E. Schulz, personal communication, March 31, 2008). Dr. Schulz had learned from a newspaper article about the problems and particularly the need for development of a medical passport. He called Jones and told her that he could help. Schulz had completed his fellowship at the University of Massachusetts at Worcester and had been involved in an effort to develop a medical passport for children in foster care. He had traveled throughout Massachusetts to train child welfare caseworkers on the use of the passport. Through this effort, he learned about foster care and become steeped in the CWLA and EPSDT requirements. He offered to share that learning and help craft a program in Arkansas (E. Schulz, personal communication, March 31, 2008).

This conversation led Jones to initiate formal and informal discussions with Schulz and his colleagues from UAMS, along with members of the oversight committee (B. Jones, personal communication, November 1, 2007). With the advice of Schulz and his colleagues, the implementation problems began to unravel when it was recognized that the UAMS satellite system could serve as the basis for a statewide system, and, furthermore, that the lynchpin of this system and the key to the CWLA requirements was the comprehensive examination.

Final Consent Decree

During 1994, a new consent decree was negotiated. As noted in the oversight committee's 1994 annual report, there was a bitter struggle to finalize it. However, the oversight committee's recommendations, augmented by the ideas from UAMS, were translated into new health provisions of the consent decree. The health care provisions in the final consent decree, which were later approved by federal Judge George Howard in 1994, appear at the end of the document. The final decree obligates DCFS to develop new health care policies and procedures and complete an initial health screening within 24 hours of placements for severe maltreatment cases and within 72 hours for all other cases. Within 60 days of placement (a more doable provision), a comprehensive examination is required that is consistent with CWLA standards. In addition, DCFS is required to collect records from hospitals, other health providers, and schools, as well as all assessments and the development of a health plan for every child. Periodic assessments of health and ongoing treatment are also required. Foster and biological parents are encouraged to attend these health visits so that information can be shared with them. The decree further requires the development of a medical passport to be filled out by professionals and given to the caregiver at every health visit. Copies of it must be kept for records.

In late 1994, pursuant to the 1992 Arkansas legislation, the oversight committee was disbanded. Counsel negotiated a modified order designating a new panel headed by Jones, the agency director, with an outside policy research organization to produce annual reports to the legislature and the governor. Governor Tucker was forced to resign in 1996, and the new Republican Governor Mike Huckabee was inaugurated. The panel Jones chaired under the new consent decree became effective on January 1, 1995. It was a weaker entity without the membership of active outside advocates.

The outside policy research organization continued to write critical reports for the next several years, and the media highlighted those reports, but little happened. Monitoring by the new panel became less potent by the next change of events. Congress passed the Legal Services Corporation Act Amendments (PL 95-222), which placed severe restrictions on the ability of programs funded by the Legal Services Corporation. Unable to participate in class action litigation, Stockley and his Arkansas lawyer colleagues could no longer participate in the Angela R. litigation. Their national partner, the National Center for Youth Law based in San Francisco, was also hampered by those restrictions because national back-up centers rely heavily on the enforcement efforts of local programs. In essence, the legal oversight vanished when the oversight committee disappeared. In many ways, without the teeth of long-term monitoring, the power of the court decree was seriously eroded.

Of note, although those often ignored reports from the outside monitoring firm contained minute details of the implementation hurdles, they reported advances in health care for children in foster care. For example, in 1997, the report found, "There is a greater emphasis on meeting the health care needs of children in foster care and almost all informants report that access to health care resources for assessments and basic needs has improved." The only explanation given for this "modest success" was "structured partnerships with other organizations and disciplines," citing "the relationship with the UAMS for conducting and following up on health assessments" (Center for the Study of Social Policy, 1998, pp. 16, 20). How did this happen?

BIRTH OF PACE

After the failure of every effort at implementation, it was clear to the oversight committee and Jones that DCFS alone was unable to ensure timely comprehensive examinations, follow-up care, medical passport development, or compliance with the health components of the consent decree (B. Jones, personal communication, November 1, 2007). The fateful telephone call from Schulz from UAMS led to the slow development of the framework for a statewide program anchored by the UAMS network of clinics and revolving around the comprehensive examination. This outline could be converted into a workable statewide system with children not traveling excessive distances. Jones and the oversight committee believed that exams requiring more than 50 miles of travel would not be accomplished, and the decree requirements would again remain unsatisfied (B. Jones, personal communication, November 1, 2007).

The central issue was two-fold: ensuring that all children 1) receive a comprehensive health care assessment first within 60 days of entering placement, and 2) receive the needed care required by the assessment within 90 days. Of course, individual children's information needed to be placed in the child's records and shared with DCFS workers, the court, foster parents, and others who needed the information. Yet, devising a system that ensured that children actually received a comprehensive exam that could screen for basic health needs and diagnose problems, as well as receive recommended follow-up care, was critical. This was particularly important because the litigation had uncovered a troubling reality that only 20% of the children—even less than the half initially alleged in the complaint filed in 1991—had received the required EPSDT comprehensive exam, and few of those had received the recommended follow-up evaluations or services.

Developing the PACE Program

During much of 1994 and 1995, DCFS and UAMS worked to set up the parameters for a program that could be implemented. Schulz invited Susan Scott, a speech pathologist, and other colleagues at the Dennis Developmental Center to help devise a workable health care system for children in foster care.

The group decided that their first step would be to understand all available research on children in foster care and identify any models for providing health care. The research confirmed what they suspected—the majority of children in the child welfare system had serious physical, developmental, and mental health problems. Yet, all the models they uncovered were based in a given county, city, or region. No statewide models for providing services existed. The team would have to take the lessons from this research but invent a new statewide model (S. Scott, personal communication, August, 14, 2007).

Since Arkansas is a rural state, children in foster care are spread out throughout the state and clustered in the few urban areas, particularly the one metropolitan area of Little Rock. The team realized that the permanent clinical sites already affiliated with the UAMS system could be tapped in those parts of the state, but that professionals would need to travel to other parts to provide statewide coverage. This model reinforced the vision of the consent decree and the oversight committee that the central mission of the health care system was to provide the comprehensive examination. From that comprehensive exam flowed an identification of the child's needs and follow-up care.

Further comprehension of the research on the needs of children in foster care convinced the UAMS collaborators that the exams not only needed to be performed in sites throughout this rural state, but by a multidisciplinary team that would be anchored in a permanent site but could travel around the state. These multidisciplinary teams would need a physician, nurses, psychologists, speech-language pathologists, psychological examiners, and, due to the large number of very young children in care, professionals with early childhood experience. They would need to perform not only a comprehensive examination with the EPSDT/CWLA components, but also a psychological examination to identify developmental delays and disabilities as well as mental health problems.

Schulz and his colleagues eventually wrote a proposal based on all this work and negotiated a contract with DCFS/DHS (UAMS Department of Pediatrics, 1995). Schulz agreed to become the medical director of this new program, and he appointed Susan Scott the program's executive director. In July 1995, with a contract in place, Scott opened the doors of PACE in 16 sites throughout Arkansas. That contract for almost 2 million dollars to be renewed annually had DHS covering all administrative costs—the costs of administrative staff, sites, travel, and the few non–Medicaid eligible children. UAMS would cover the salaries of its clinical traveling and fixed site teams, all UAMS pediatric employees (Arkansas Department of Human Services, 1995).

Early Operation of PACE

It quickly became apparent that using the required consent decree standards and proposal design only provided the foundation for a workable system. In discussions with DCFS, it became clear that the most practical issues, such as scheduling appointments, had to be solved for the program to function. Initially, DCFS workers were charged with setting appointments with the PACE team, but it quickly became obvious that the appointments were not being made, or, if they were made, they were not made within the 60-day required window. All agreed that DCFS needed additional staff in a new health care management unit to work with UAMS. This staff would schedule appointments as soon as children entered care; later their mission would be greatly expanded.

Scheduling appointments was merely step one. Ensuring that the children were brought to those appointments was much more difficult. Not only were children being denied their right to a timely 60-day comprehensive assessment but also precious medical resources were being wasted because clinical services had to be provided for reimbursement by Medicaid. Scott realized that she had to quickly remedy this no-show problem. Jones agreed to get DHS to pay for all no-shows so UAMS could get reimbursed for their time (S. Scott, personal communication, August 14, 2007). This mechanism also provided a fiscal incentive to DCFS to make sure that children actually attended scheduled exams, thereby ensuring compliance with the consent decree. Jones readily admits that the court consent decree gave her an enhanced ability to move ahead, solve problems, and get more money (B. Jones, personal communication, November 1, 2007).

The no-show problems were also an impetus to secure a strong DCFS medical unit that would not only schedule appointments, but also use its resources to push localities to get children to those examinations. It became logical for this unit to take on more ministerial responsibilities, including scheduling follow-up exams as recommended by the comprehensive evaluations.

Yet, the implementation problems mounted. Scott had to resolve additional Medicaid issues. Under Medicaid in Arkansas, a primary care physician (PCP) was required to make all referrals, including for the comprehensive examination and follow-up care. Given the dearth of pediatricians and medical homes serving the children in foster care, the requirements of the consent decree that the comprehensive exam occur within 60 days became impossible to achieve.

The power of the court consent decree and DCFS/DHS's commitment to its full implementation facilitated a waiver of the PCP requirement for the comprehensive examination. Although the PCP would be involved in follow-up care, he or she would not be needed to schedule, perform, or approve the 60-day exam. In addition, as it became clear that the children had extremely high medical needs, Scott negotiated an enhanced Medicaid rate for clinical services for these children. Again, Jones was very receptive to this idea, given her commitment to enforcement of the consent decree. Indeed, Jones, Scott, and others acknowledge the strong partnership forged among DCFS, DHS, and UAMS in the early days of PACE. The positive language in the compliance committee's reports reinforced the collaboration. Furthermore, Jones's quarterly reports to the Arkansas legislature on the consent decree always mentioned the success achieved by PACE as more and more children received timely, comprehensive examinations and necessary follow-up care (B. Jones, personal communication, November 1, 2007).

This smooth relationship between DCFS and UAMS continued even after Governor Huckabee was elected for a full term in 1996. Major changes were underfoot within DHS, however, when Jones resigned in 1998. The PACE program continued with Scott as its founding and sole director for more than 12 years.

Ongoing Operation of the PACE Program

Since the late 1990s, the PACE program has become an institutionalized part of the foster care system in Arkansas. An elaborate data system was created and overseen by Schulz to track and understand the needs of children in foster care (E. Schulz, personal communication, March 31, 2008; Schulz, Evans, & Russell, 1999). Once a child is placed in care, the DCFS medical management unit schedules the 60-day comprehensive exam (S. Scott, personal communication, July 9, 2007). Scott has computer access to admissions data and double checks to ensure timely scheduling. During the 60 days between placement and the exam, the DCFS medical unit, and often the UAMS staff, gathers all medical information, including hospital records, school records, prior assessments (children are reassessed if returned to care after 6 months or, if upon a quicker return to care, a new problem is identified), and other health records. The day of the assessment, the team is given a file containing all the medical information. The child is brought to the exam at one of 16 sites—3 fixed and 13 traveling that could be in a clinic, school, or hospital—by a DCFS worker. Many times, children are also accompanied by foster and birth parents, which is strongly encouraged by PACE to provide a more complete history of the child as well as to enable parents to learn about recommendations for follow-up care and to receive guidance about the child's needs. DCFS medical unit staff and PACE try to meet often with local and regional DCFS staff to underscore the importance of parents attending these comprehensive exams.

The first part of the exam involves the parent and the DCFS worker providing a history. After that, the child is given a complete physical examination that follows all CWLA requirements. This is followed by a full assessment given by a psychologist as well as a speech-language pathologist. The team generally performs about 4 or 5 comprehensive exams per day. Once the exam is finished, there is a meeting for the team to review their findings, after which they meet with the DCFS worker as well as the parent. At this meeting, they review the test results, and give the parent a summary sheet. At the end of the day, a longer 10- to 15-page report is written and immediately e-mailed to the DCFS medical unit. Within a 2-week span, it is also sent to the DCFS director, as well as the local DCFS administrator. Recently, a new agreement also allows the information to be sent to the juvenile court, so that it can be considered within the context of judicial decision making as well.

From July 2006 to June 2007, 2,281 comprehensive exams were performed, reaching the almost 1,000 new children entering foster care, as well as executing reassessments of more than 1,000 children returning to care (PACE Report, 2007). The recommendations are also entered into the DCFS database and the Child Health Reporting Information System (CHRIS).

The DCFS medical unit is charged with notifying the PCP of the recommendations and gaining his or her consent to the recommended follow-up care. The unit then schedules the follow-up appointments with a cardiologist, pediatrician, dentist, or other needed specialists. This follow-up system is critical and must be evaluated periodically to ensure that it is functioning well. When this system collapsed in urban Pulaski County in the late 1990s, a patient care coordinator was hired to improve the scheduling and ensure follow-up care.

Indeed, the issue of follow-up was one that even the weaker internal panel raised, as well as UAMS. UAMS agreed to keep cases for 90 days after the comprehensive exam and to develop its own mechanism to test adherence to recommendations. It randomly selects a sample of 10 cases per month in each of the 10 regional areas to follow. It then determines whether recommendations for follow-up appointments were made and completed and that actual care was provided. It also enters the outcomes in CHRIS. Since the late 1990s, an average of 90% of follow-up recommendations from the comprehensive examination was completed for children in foster care (PACE Report, 2007).

LESSONS LEARNED

A central lesson of the Arkansas story is that persistent advocacy by Crary, Rossi, and their AACF colleagues was vital to highlight the problems in the child welfare system. After all other efforts failed, litigation proved to be the only strategy available to resolve an intractable issue. Although litigation can be a catalyst for change, alone it cannot ensure change. The *Angela R. v Clinton* (1991) case was the spark that spotlighted the problems of children in foster care in Arkansas, including their poor health conditions. Yet, neither the litigation nor its monitoring mechanisms were able to build a new health care system for children in foster care.

Grim stories of children's health problems and even their deaths are used to attract attention to the problems of children in foster care. For years, stories focused on serious health problems of Arkansas's foster children. The lawsuit's complaint begins with stories of the terrible neglect and disregard for the health of these children to illustrate the grim reality of foster care. Yet, the complaint and its aftermath illustrate that all too often children's healthy development is seen as an ancillary issue rather than central to child welfare. This reflects the long history of child welfare in America. The use of scandals of children's deaths are lures to garner public attention and enactment of reforms, which are seldom achieved. Yet, providing children what they truly need for healthy development—adequate and timely health care and, most importantly, a permanent, loving family—is the real challenge. John's story at the beginning of this chapter illustrates this challenge.

The Arkansas story stands for the proposition that if only a few people keep going beyond the horror stories and pursue the health care needs of these children, these issues can find a place on the radar screen. Once these issues were raised at each oversight committee meeting, a unified front for change was created. Indeed, if flagged, these health care issues are so clear that they cannot be ignored. Yet, to really solve them requires not only raising the issues and pointing to tried and true solutions, such as existing standards, but also commitment of government officials and partners in the medical community. By 1994, DHS/DCFS had admitted time and time again that the health care system was broken, and they demonstrated that no matter how many times the oversight committee criticized their actions, they could not make the system work. Only when DHS/DCFS partnered with UAMS and accepted the help of Schulz and his colleagues did reform begin. Only after UAMS vested Susan Scott with the responsibility of implementing the proposed outline for a program did change begin to take shape. Only after DHS/DCFS worked closely with Scott to iron out all problems, including the sticky issues of funding, was an effective program born. Finally, only through a decade of hard work by professionals within UAMS and state government has the PACE program provided children step one in their healthy development—basic health assessment and follow-up care to address their health and developmental needs. As John's story illustrates, providing this comprehensive health assessment and follow-up care is critical to healthy development and permanency.

8

Using the Portal of Early Intervention for Healthy Development

The Philadelphia Case Study

RAYMOND'S STORY

Born nearly 2 months premature, Raymond weighed less than 3 pounds at birth. His mother's pregnancy had been complicated by her use of drugs, such as heroin, cocaine, and marijuana, as well as her ongoing methadone habit. Raymond remained in the neonatal intensive care unit (NICU) for more than a month as he went through withdrawal from opiates, received a transfusion for anemia of prematurity and phototherapy for jaundice, and experienced problems with feeding. Raymond also suffered from retinopathy of prematurity, which placed his vision at risk.

Raymond was discharged when he was a little more than 1 month old to his mother's care. The discharge plan included a referral to a pediatric ophthalmologist for eye surgery to correct the retinopathy and referral to the hospital's NICU follow-up program in 2 weeks to monitor his growth and the other distinctive health and developmental needs confronting this medically complex infant. When Raymond's mother repeatedly failed to take him to the eye doctor, the child protective services (CPS) hotline was notified because failure to address the retinopathy could result in blindness. Less than 3 weeks after discharge from the NICU, Raymond was removed from his mother's care and placed in foster care with the John Smith and James Conner family.

The foster parents were informed of Raymond's need to be seen by the eye doctor, and Raymond received laser surgery to treat the retinopathy of prematurity. After 5 months in their home, Raymond's foster parents were concerned about his slow development, limited eye contact, and his tiny size. On their own initiative, they located the Starting Young (SY) program, a pediatric, interdisciplinary diagnostic and referral service exclusively for infants and toddlers who are involved with the child welfare system.

When evaluated by the SY team at 7 months of age, Raymond presented as a happy and active infant. Raymond's birth mother was invited to the evaluation, but she did not attend. During the evaluation, it was noted that Raymond exhibited amblyopia (sometimes called "lazy eye") in one eye. The foster parents reported that Raymond's feeding at home was going well.

The assessment of Raymond's cognitive, speech-language, and gross-motor development indicated significant delays in each of these domains, even when his prematurity was taken into account. The team recommended early intervention (EI) services (under Part C of the Individuals with Disabilities Education Act [IDEA] of 1997 [PL 105-17]) to address delayed early communication and gross motor skills. Due to his language delay, he was referred to a pediatric audiologist for a hearing evaluation.

The SY team also addressed the foster parents' concern about Raymond's tendency to avert his gaze and his limited eye contact. They informed the foster parents that gaze aversion can be a normal means of self-regulation for infants, and that Raymond tended to turn his eyes away when he needed a break from social interactions. The team also explained how Raymond's limited eye contact was a function of his "lazy eye," which made it difficult for him to focus directly on others. The foster parents were reassured by these explanations.

The pediatric assessment indicated that although Raymond's growth was appropriate when compared with the national norms for babies with very low birth weights, it still was on the low side and required monitoring by his pediatrician. Recommendations for hepatitis B screening and HIV testing were made due to maternal risk factors. It was also recommended that Raymond return to the ophthalmologist for evaluation of his amblyopia. The evaluation team encouraged a reevaluation with the SY clinic in 6 months to continue to monitor Raymond's health and development.

The foster parents followed through on many of the recommendations from the first evaluation. Raymond underwent corrective surgery for his amblyopia; he had his hearing evaluated, which indicated a mild hearing disability; and he took hepatitis B and HIV tests, which were negative. Raymond also began receiving EI services from a physical therapist to address his motor development and from a teacher who focused on communication skills.

Raymond returned with the foster parents for a reevaluation with the SY program when he was nearly 17 months old. Once again, his mother was invited to the session, agreed to attend, but did not show up. Throughout the evaluation, Raymond smiled and maintained good eye contact with the evaluators. He was attentive and turned his head toward speakers' voices. The reevaluation indicated that Raymond excelled at verbal tasks. He performed at his age level on a variety of language-based measures, in contrast to his performance 10 months previously when he was found to have a 50% delay in communication skills. Raymond's gross motor skills also had improved significantly and currently were at age level.

Despite these excellent advances, Raymond had significant difficulty with both fine and visual motor skills, which required use of his hands, as well as eye–hand coordination. The SY team recommended that Raymond receive an evaluation by a pediatric occupational therapist through EI services and receive intervention, if warranted, to improve his ability with fine and visual motor activities. Reevaluation with the SY team was recommended in 6 months to continue to monitor his development.

Raymond returned for a reevaluation when he was 25 months old. As in all previous evaluations, Raymond's birth mother was invited, but she did not attend. She had not attended any medical, early intervention, or other appointments. After his previous evaluation, he began to receive occupational therapy through EI. The SY reevaluation indicted that Raymond was benefiting from this intervention because his visual and motor skills progressed from a 47% delay at age 17 months to a 22% delay at 25 months of age. Speech-language skills continued to be age appropriate.

Soon after the reevaluation, the foster parents began pressing the department of human services to change Raymond's goal to adoption. After almost a year, a permanency hearing was held in Philadelphia Family Court with a major focus on the goal change. Raymond's birth mother contested this new goal, wanting to assume custody of Raymond. At the hearing, the director of the SY program testified that given Raymond's complex medical and developmental needs, he required a parent who would take him to all primary health care and medical specialty appointments, participate in EI treatment, take him for any therapeutic visits, adhere to treatment recommendations, observe his development over time, and advocate for health and special education services throughout his childhood. The court ordered Raymond's goal to be changed to adoption. Thereafter, his birth mother's parental rights were terminated, and Raymond was adopted.

PHILADELPHIA EARLY INTERVENTION CASE STUDY

The EI program is the richest entitlement that exists for our nation's most vulnerable children—very young children involved in the child welfare system. The research has demonstrated that children ages birth to 3 who have been maltreated are more likely to have fragile health and developmental disabilities and delays than any other group of American children. Yet, ensuring that these most vulnerable children are referred, screened, evaluated, and in receipt of the rich array of services for EI has been a Herculean task. This chapter traces the efforts of professionals working in the health care, EI, and child welfare systems to make EI screening universal and EI services available to children associated with child welfare. After a decade-long struggle, positive steps have been made toward achieving this goal. Today, all identified children under age 5 in Philadelphia with open cases served by the child welfare system—children in foster care, children with substantiated cases of maltreatment living at home receiving services, and even children whose reports were unsubstantiated—are eligible for the Child Welfare Early Intervention Initiative (CWEII) developmental surveillance program. This program, developed after many refinements, provides developmental screening to all children known to the Philadelphia Department of Human Services (DHS), referral to EI for children with any suspicion of delay, and rescreening every 6 months of children under the age of 3 who are found ineligible as a way to track and monitor development to identify delays that emerged over time. This program's breadth is consistent with the recommendations of the Institute of Medicine and National Research Council's definitive guide to the research on early childhood, *From Neurons to Neighborhoods: The Science of Early Childhood Development* (Shonkoff & Phillips, 2000), and is far more encompassing than even the federal law provisions in the Child Abuse Prevention and Treatment Act (CAPTA) of 2003 (PL 93-247) and the Individuals with Disabilities Education Improvement Act (IDEA) 2004 (PL 108-446), which only target children involved in substantiated cases.

Yet, the genesis of the Philadelphia CWEII can be traced long before national attention formulated the new federal EI referral provisions. It began in the early 1990s as a concern of EI and health care professionals anxious to connect children in the child welfare system to important EI services. This is the story of that effort and the effective partnerships forged to make connection to EI a reality for Philadelphia's most vulnerable very young children.

STARTING YOUNG

The Starting Young (SY) program was founded and developed by Dr. Judith Silver after she had been working for years as a psychologist in neonatal follow-up programs in Chicago and Philadelphia (J. Silver, personal communication, April 10, 2007; May 8, 2007). While working in a hospital-based neurodevelopmental evaluation clinic in Philadelphia, Silver noticed that a large number of children in foster care were referred due to concerns about behavior problems and developmental delays. The majority of these children were 4 or 5 years old, and evaluations confirmed that development was delayed. Many had been prenatally exposed to crack and/or cocaine and most had entered foster care placement in the first 2 years of life. Yet, their caseworkers did not flag problems until the children were 4 or 5 years old, and the EI system, with its required Child Find resources, did not reach out to the county children and youth agency or to private child welfare provider agencies to encourage referrals to EI for this group of children.

Silver was concerned that infants in foster care were not accessing their entitlement to EI, despite their evident need. She believed that if these foster children could be reached in the first years of life through interdisciplinary evaluation, they could be evaluated and connected to important EI services that could address or ameliorate their delays. She seized the chance to establish such a program in response to a request for proposals (RFPs) from the Pew Charitable Trusts, and, therefore, wrote a proposal to establish SY.

SY was funded and opened its doors in 1992. It is a multidisciplinary, developmental diagnostic and referral service, which was created exclusively for infants and toddlers who receive services from the Philadelphia DHS, including foster care, kinship care, family preservation, or in-home child welfare services (Silver, 2002; Silver, Amster, & Haecker, 1999). The program's goal is to connect DHS-involved children who have delayed development with EI so that they can receive needed developmental, family support, and other services. The SY interdisciplinary assessment team is composed of a pediatrician, as well as a child psychologist, speech-language pathologist, physical therapist, and an intake worker from Child Link, the EI coordination agency of Philadelphia (Silver, 2002). The presence of the EI worker is a critical innovation of SY because his or her attendance smoothes enrollment into the EI program and also provides a link for the children's caregivers. The actual intake interview is conducted by a pediatric social worker who also arranges referrals.

After completion of the interdisciplinary, comprehensive evaluation by the SY team, the entire team, including the EI worker, reviews the results and makes recommendations regarding the child's need for medical care, social services, and EI eligibility. The team's recommendations are discussed with the child's caregivers (biological parents and/or foster parents) and the child welfare worker prior to their departure from the clinic. Within a few weeks, the evaluation report and recommendations are sent to the child's biological and/or foster parents, child welfare worker, pediatrician, and, if necessary, the child's attorney. The program's caseworker follows up with the foster or biological parents within 8–12 weeks to encourage adherence to recommendations. Children are reevaluated every 6 months until they are 30 months old.

SY data underscores the importance of its service. Many of the children did not have adequate contact with their primary health care providers, with 22% needing immunizations and 20% presenting with growth delay. More than 40% of the children had health problems warranting referral to medical specialists. Approximately half of the children (49%) needed EI services due to developmental delays (Silver, Amster & Haecker, 1999).

The ability to produce a high-quality, multidisciplinary evaluation that is acceptable to EI in conjunction with the participation of an EI worker on the team facilitates the connection of children to this vital service. In addition to providing clinical evaluations, the SY team annually provides at least three full-day workshops for child welfare professionals on identifying the health and developmental needs of infants in foster care and how to obtain community-based services (including EI).

In the mid-1990s, as those involved with the child welfare system began to see the merit of the SY approach, not only did referrals increase but also team members were invited to participate on various initiatives focused on children in foster care. Requests for information and assistance came from senior administrators and provided an opportunity for the SY team to educate child welfare professionals about the health and developmental needs of children involved with DHS, which resulted in requests for training of public and private child welfare agency staff and also helped Silver and her colleagues become connected to the wider world of child welfare in their region.

These new contacts led to invitations for the SY team to write about this issue (Silver, Amster, et al., 1999). Indeed, finding a dearth of written materials about the health and developmental needs of young children in the child welfare system, Silver accepted an offer to edit and shepherd the first book published on young children in the child welfare system that provides an interdisciplinary pediatric and developmental perspective. Published in 1999, Silver, Amster, and Haecker edited a volume titled *Young Children and Foster Care: A Guide for Professionals* that is a sourcebook for professionals on a range of clinical issues confronting young children in foster care. The book also became a connection tool for Silver and her colleagues. They not only wrote various chapters but also they were able to invite new colleagues from the academic, clinical, public, and private sectors to write chapters. This collaboration contributed to the creation of diverse partnerships in the Philadelphia region, as well as state and nationwide. *Young Children and Foster Care* remains the seminal text in this field.

EARLY ADVOCACY EFFORTS

The expertise and the contacts that Silver and her team were acquiring about young children in foster care inevitably led them to be invited to present at policy-focused forums and serve on city task forces. Perhaps the most significant invitation occurred only a year after SY opened its doors, when Trude Haecker, SY's team pediatrician, and Silver were asked to serve on a community task force created by the Pennsylvania Department of Public Welfare and Philadelphia DHS to shape the implementation of the Annie E. Casey Foundation's Family to Family Initiative in Philadelphia (Silver, 2002; J. Silver, personal communication, May 8, 2007). This participation made SY visible to an important group of child welfare leaders in the city, raising awareness that EI and health care services for infants and toddlers were seriously underutilized. It also enabled them to forge important connections and to establish SY's reputation as a key partner in the child welfare system. For Silver, developing working relationships with committed inside players in the field of child welfare was a significant outcome of her participation on the task force.

One of these connections led to Silver's participation in a key policy initiative concerning children in foster care. A DHS official requested her assistance in writing a grant to establish a step-down practice aimed at moving children with complex medical needs out of nursing homes and into less-restrictive settings. A large number of these children were very young, and many were placed directly from hospital NICUs. In helping to fashion the proposal, Silver urged the adoption of a case review system as the cornerstone of the project. She hoped that a multidisciplinary committee (including pediatricians, psychologists, and social workers) could work with DHS administrators and review the cases of every child in DHS placed in a nursing home and provide consultation on how to better meet their health, developmental, academic, and social-emotional needs, ideally in family foster care (J. Silver, personal communication, May 8, 2007).

The 3-year federal grant from CAPTA funds was awarded to Philadelphia DHS in 1993 and became one of the nation's first efforts to use a multidisciplinary review committee to address the needs of medically complex children in the child welfare system. Dr. Joseph Kuna, an administrator at DHS, chaired the task force known as the Medically Complex Multidisciplinary Review Team (MRT). Julie Alexander, a psychologist at DHS, also participated and eventually chaired the task force. Silver became a central player on this task force, which reviewed the cases of all DHS children with complex medical needs placed in nursing homes and made recommendations regarding improving the children's access to health care, awarding educational and disability entitlements, and stepping down to less restrictive settings—notably for family medical foster care. It was here that Silver, Alexander, and Kuna developed a good working relationship. Alexander says that it was here, too, that she learned from Silver about the needs of the youngest children in foster care. Alexander noted that Silver was a "central figure" in the MRT who conveyed the "urgency" of these young children's plights in a nonconfrontational way (J. Alexander, personal communication, May 7, 2007). Perhaps the greatest tangible policy achievement of this collaboration happened without anyone really noticing it and without any formal written policy. Philadelphia DHS ended the practice, which still goes on in other jurisdictions, of placing medically complex babies directly from NICUs into nursing homes.

SUBCOMMITTEE ON THE HEALTH CARE OF CHILDREN IN SUBSTITUTE CARE

In the mid-1990s, Haecker and Silver moved to the Children's Hospital of Philadelphia (CHOP). This provided SY a more visible and prestigious setting for its groundbreaking work and helped elevate the program in the eyes of the health care community (Silver, 2002). At CHOP, Haecker supervised pediatric residents, many of whom treated children in foster care. Heather Forkey, M.D., then chief resident (and who later would become the SY pediatrician), helped identify the medical residents' concerns about this population and conveyed them to Haecker.

Because of her prior experiences as the SY pediatrician, Haecker was able to help focus residents' frustration concerning a myriad of problems and group these problems into the three categories of 1) accessing medical records, 2) securing consent for treatment, and 3) confusion regarding confidentiality issues involving children in DHS's custody.

Haecker encouraged Forkey to contact Margaret Zukoski at the Children, Youth and Family Council (a consortium of private child welfare provider agencies), who was the former social worker at SY (H. Forkey, personal communication, December, 2007; M. Zukoski, personal communication, January 5, 2008). Zukoski then arranged for the residents to meet with a range of experts from lawyers to government officials to ask their questions and voice their concerns on these systemic issues. Frustrated, the residents began holding open meetings inviting all concerned with the well-being of children in out-of-home care to discuss these issues. This group became the Subcommittee on Children in Substitute Care, a part of the Pennsylvania Children's Health Care Coalition, a broad-based advocacy coalition (Silver, 2002). The Subcommittee included health care professionals, social workers from private child welfare provider agencies, a DHS administrator and nurse from its Health Management Unit, Philadelphia's director of EI services and children's mental retardation services, attorneys from the Juvenile Law Center (JLC), and a policy analyst from a consortium of private child welfare provider agencies. For the next decade, Silver played an active role as its sole staff member, booking speakers; taking critical meeting minutes; encouraging the production of publications, such as the *Health Policy Recommendations for Children in Substitute Care* (Subcommittee on Children in Substitute Care, 1999); recruiting new participants; and, most important, keeping the Subcommittee alive.

Moving from concern about individual cases to seeing the problems as systemic took a set course. First, the residents and the other participants on the Subcommittee discussed their own clinical work, heard from child welfare providers and legal advocates, examined SY data, and began seeing threads of common themes. Those threads identified that children in substitute care often were not even receiving basic health care or EI services as guaranteed by the federal early and periodic screening, diagnosis, and treatment (EPSDT) and EI laws. They were not receiving health care consistent with the standards of the American Academy of Pediatrics (AAP) and the Child Welfare League of America (CWLA). They discovered that health information was not being uniformly reported or gathered in an organized fashion in DHS files, and that DHS claims that information could not be shared with the doctors due to confidentiality were often erroneous, based on a long-standing practice but not law. Armed with this learning, the Subcommittee was determined to find a way to help child welfare professionals easily gather basic information about children entering substitute care. The members developed five basic questions for all involved with children in substitute care to ask.

1. Did the child's mother have any health issues during pregnancy?

2. Has the child ever been hospitalized?

3. Does the child have any medical diagnoses?

4. Does the child have any allergies?

5. Are there any medical problems that run in the family? (Silver, 2002, p. 49)

 During the course of numerous meetings, the Subcommittee discussed how the questions could be integrated into the work of DHS investigators and case-workers. DHS agreed to add these five simple questions to an intake form and have this form placed in each child's DHS file and the foster care agency file as a starting point for health care information. Lourdes Rosado and her attorney colleagues from the JLC were key players in this effort as they researched consent and confidentiality issues for children in substitute care in Pennsylvania so that the effort could be instituted. Despite this early paper victory, the Subcommittee learned an important lesson—implementation is hard. Although the forms were vetted and available at DHS, the section related to the five questions was not being completed by DHS workers. DHS later issued written policy in 2001 that required that all of the forms be filled out and filed in DHS and agency files. Adherence, however, remained inconsistent.

 Recognizing the difficulty of accomplishing one small task to better the health care of Philadelphia's children in substitute care only served to galvanize the Subcommittee. Instead of giving up, they expanded their mission. Convinced now that piecemeal remedies would not suffice, they decided to aim higher to reform the entire system. They formed a committee to draft a document that would contain concrete broad-based proposals for improving health care for children in substitute care. Forkey wrote the first draft of the document and then it was refined extensively by Rosado and her JLC colleagues. Because of the years of meetings, DHS was on board since the director of the medical unit played a key role in shaping the recommendations and gaining DHS support. It was published in November 1999 as the *Health Policy Recommendations for Children in Substitute Care in Philadelphia* (Subcommittee on Children in Substitute Care, 1999). It enumerated health care changes into three discrete categories to aid implementation: 1) laws, policy, and regulation; 2) child welfare practice; and 3) juvenile court procedures. For each problem, the recommendations listed the applicable solutions according to those three implementation categories.

 The major recommendations included

1. Prompt, convenient access to physicians and other health care providers

2. Comprehensive physical health assessments and developmental and mental health evaluations for children on entering substitute care

3. Ongoing well-child and preventive health care that meets the EPSDT guidelines, including appropriate linkages to mental health, EI, and special education services

4. A records system to ensure that essential health information is collected, maintained, shared with appropriate parties, and transferred when children change placements, change health care providers, and/or leave substitute care (Subcommittee on Children in Substitute Care, 1999, p. 5)

In order to raise awareness of the issues, the draft of the *Recommendations* was distributed for endorsement to a range of private provider agencies, pediatric practices, and legal advocacy organizations. The published version includes endorsements by the broad-based membership of the Subcommittee, including not only CHOP and SY professionals but also child welfare, health care, and EI providers; legal advocates; and members of the Pennsylvania State Foster Parents Association. Indeed, the final *Health Policy Recommendations for Children in Substitute Care in Philadelphia* were unveiled at an event that included city officials and judges (L. Rosado, personal communication, January 11, 2008). This effort heightened awareness of the health needs of children in foster care and dovetailed with the related policy issues of the move to Medicaid Managed Care for foster children (M. Zukoski, personal communication, January 5, 2008).

The *Health Policy Recommendations* were published and widely distributed across the city and state to health care providers, child welfare professionals, judges, lawyers, and city and state policy makers. This document served as a springboard for discussion about reform with this array of stakeholders and helped to frame the Subcommittee's future work. It chose to focus its energies on three projects that directly flowed from the *Health Policy Recommendations*:

1. Development and adoption of a health passport for all children in substitute care

2. Creation and use of consent forms and mirror court orders (orders that reflect the components of the consent forms in the event the forms are not signed) in the juvenile court for consents, sharing of medical information, and obtaining EI evaluations

3. Establishment of policy and practice to connect all DHS-involved children to EI

During the next several years, the Subcommittee work would focus on these three initiatives. Each followed an unpredictable course.

Health Passport

The proposal for creation of a health care passport was a logical end product of the effort to develop a simple, accessible mechanism to gather and keep medical records on children in substitute care. It was one of the major proposals of the

Health Policy Recommendations. For health care professionals, access to this information was vital for quality care. Other jurisdictions were trying to develop health care passports as well, and the Subcommittee effort involved studying and gleaning learnings from those efforts (McCarthy, 2002).

The Subcommittee effort kindled an awareness of the need for a passport by DHS, who worked closely with members to create a draft passport that was unveiled at the Subcommittee meeting in December 2000 (Subcommittee on Children in Substitute Care, 2000). The new system, however, depended on the presence of public health nurses to gather and document health care information. When DHS failed to obtain funding for those public health nurses, the initiative faltered. Forkey notes that,

> At that time the computerized medical record was becoming the new standard, and further efforts on a paper passport seemed anachronistic.... [They] had (at that time) hoped to link the DHS computer record with the computerized medical record, but tabled that right away as security and interface concerns were too great, and [they] hoped that technology advances in the near future would allow such an integration. (H. Forkey, personal communication, January 14, 2008)

An electronic passport still does not exist, but the issue of health information remains a central focus of the Subcommittee.

Court Forms Initiative

The effort to implement consent forms and uniform mirror court orders in juvenile court seemed like a doable task to the Subcommittee. That, too, naturally flowed from the *Health Policy Recommendations* to provide comprehensive health care, assessments, and records for all children in substitute care. Led by Rosado, the Subcommittee drafted consent forms for parents to sign granting release of medical, mental health, EI, and other records to DHS, including AIDS and HIV test results, as well as authorization for EI and mental health evaluations. These consent forms were matched with mirror court orders enabling the juvenile court to authorize quickly the release of information or evaluations in instances of parental refusal. During the next year, Rosado and her colleagues shared drafts of these forms with judges, city solicitors who represent DHS on these cases in court, the child advocacy attorneys who represent the children, and lawyers for parents. Painstakingly taking into account all of the various comments and objections, Lourdes produced a final set of forms ratified by the Subcommittee.

Throughout this process, Subcommittee members met with the judge of family court (also called juvenile court) who was developing a model court under the federal Court Improvement Project (CIP). A centerpiece of the model court for dependency cases (so named in Philadelphia for abuse and neglect cases) was the institution of prehearing conferences on all new cases. All the parties—parents, lawyers, DHS child welfare caseworkers—would be present at the prehearing conference where they could discuss the case at the outset. This discussion would include gathering information about the circumstances of the case and the needs of the parents and child. It would also formulate early agreements on placement, services, and the allegations of abuse and neglect as well as develop a discovery plan for the case's future. In other words, agreed-upon issues could be identified early, and contested issues could be flagged at the outset.

Rosado realized that these prehearing conferences could serve as a place to secure parental consent on the new forms. The prehearing sessions occurred in the courthouse, but outside of the courtroom and could be a uniform, non-threatening, accessible site led by a facilitator for explaining and filling out these important forms. Once these forms were finalized, Rosado, Haecker, Silver, and Bob Schwartz, Executive Director of the Juvenile Law Center of Philadelphia and a national leader in juvenile law, met with the administrative judge to obtain the judge's assent. She gave them her approval and instructed them to work with the judge who presided over the model court.

After lengthy discussion and review by the CIP committee, an agreement was obtained to pilot the forms in the prehearing conference setting. By April 2001, the forms were finalized, and by July, they were available in the prehearing conference room. Yet, gaining agreement, even from a key inside player such as the judge or the committee, did not guarantee success (L. Rosado, personal communication, January 11, 2008). Someone needed to be responsible for the forms and court orders. Someone needed to explain the forms to parents, request their signatures, and flag refusals so the court could follow up and, if needed, enter court orders. The facilitators who presided over the prehearing conferences voiced concerns that the forms added one more task to their already full plate and declined to facilitate the signing of the forms. The city solicitor reluctantly agreed to play this role, but the task was often overlooked in time pressed, prehearing conferences, so the information was not gathered. Without a responsible party, the initiative fell apart with ongoing, periodic efforts to resurrect it.

Connecting Children to Early Intervention

The third project of the Subcommittee—connecting young children in substitute care to EI—seemed the least promising venture in 1999. In fact, the court forms initiative was seen as the most promising path to connection with EI because lack of consent was viewed as the major barrier for these children. Although the *Healthy Policy Recommendations* specifically targeted linkage to EI (including recommendations about gaining consent from parents, educating caseworkers about developmental needs, and developing DHS policy for linkage), the other projects—the health care passport and court forms—were elaborated in greater detail in the *Health Policy Recommendations,* and a path for Subcommittee work and implementation seemed to be more readily apparent. EI seemed far more intractable; however, Silver and her colleagues began to explore this issue, too.

In 1999, Silver and her colleagues invited Denise Taylor Patterson, who directs Philadelphia Early Intervention Services, to join the Subcommittee (D. Patterson, personal communication, January 15, 2008). Patterson was a useful addition because she had worked in child welfare for more than 20 years, as well as heading the local EI program and being awarded a Pew Foundation Grant to provide outreach services to at-risk children. (Her Pew Grant was part of a series of grants in the 1990s that included SY.)

To underscore the issue as well as tap Patterson's position, it became important that every Subcommittee meeting contain a discussion of some facet of EI. Many of those early meetings focused on the consent hurdles—parents refusing consent for evaluation or services—and the need for surrogate parents to consent for children whose parents were unknown or unavailable. At that time, Pennsylvania, in contrast to other states, was barring foster parents from serving as surrogate parents for EI and special education. This was not just an intellectual issue, but also a real barrier to services. Since EI requires parental consent at every juncture in the eligibility and service delivery process, failure to obtain consent can close a case. Furthermore, if no surrogate parent could be identified to give the required consent, the likelihood of a child in substitute care ever securing needed EI services was nonexistent. Fortunately, during the summer of 2001, a breakthrough occurred. After years of advocacy, Pennsylvania, in line with other states, determined that foster parents could serve as surrogate parents and verbally advised the city of this change (Rosado & Siddique, 2001).

The new policy required Silver and other members of the Subcommittee to become involved with issues of training foster parents to become surrogate parents and working with EI on this endeavor. These discussions also brought Julie Alexander of DHS and Patterson and her colleagues at EI together to talk about the range of EI problems (Siddique, 2002). Those discussions between Alexander and Patterson and their colleagues recognized that—although anecdotes underscored that children were not getting connected to EI—real data was needed. Indeed, at this juncture, Patterson had begun outreach efforts to other required Pennsylvania children considered at risk for developmental delays (such as homeless children) by providing training to staff in homeless shelters. She also knew from her own experience as an assistant director of a child welfare agency before coming to EI that many children involved with child welfare had developmental delays and would therefore be eligible for EI services (D. Patterson, personal communication, January 15, 2008).

The EI and DHS government officials agreed to shepherd a data request through both systems. When matched, comparing children in DHS custody with children enrolled in EI from December 1993 to June 2001 supported the prevailing view that these children were not getting connected to services. Only 14% of the children matched (Siddique, 2002); thus, only 14% of children in foster care in Philadelphia were receiving EI services, far less than the almost half of children with developmental delays found by the SY data (Silver, Amster, et al., 1999).

Children were simply not getting into the front door of EI, which underscored the need for a more systemic focus.

The data highlighted the importance of the *Healthy Policy Recommendations* proposal for the Department of Public Welfare (DPW) to revise its regulations to require the referral of all children entering substitute care under age 5 for multi-disciplinary developmental evaluation for EI services (Subcommittee on Children in Substitute Care, 1999). This proposal was written a year before the compa-rable recommendation in *From Neurons to Neighborhoods: The Science of Early Childhood Development* (Shonkoff & Phillips, 2000). During the next several years, the Subcommittee would continue to facilitate interagency dialogue and make suggestions, often trying to shape the smaller issues—consent and surrogate parent training—while advocating for the larger policy effort to refer *all* children for evaluation (Siddique, 2002).

CHANGES AT DHS

Although the Subcommittee meetings involved discussion of specific EI prob-lems, there were glimmers that something larger was occurring in Philadelphia. On December 21, 2001, the DHS Commissioner announced the creation of the Behavioral Health Services Support Center (BHSSC) within DHS (A. Martinez, staff memo, December 21, 2001). Only a few weeks later, Kuna, who would direct the new unit with Alexander as his deputy, would make a formal presenta-tion to the Subcommittee (Siddique, 2002). As part of a larger reorganization effort combining access to mental health and intellectual disabilities services, as well as drug treatment for DHS-involved children and families, four support centers were created to help child welfare and operational staff and to provide consultation and connection to services for children. Although the discussion focused on older children, Alexander noted that they hoped to develop an early intervention unit to evaluate and offer services to children from 30 days to 5 years old. She also alluded to an attempt to work out a tool for universal behavioral health screening for children (Siddique, 2002).

Beginning in the mid-1990s, Kuna, Silver, and Alexander discussed the health and developmental needs of young children in the child welfare system. Kuna reports that his role has been to listen, learn, and try to champion those ideas within the bureaucracy (J. Kuna, personal communication, July 26, 2007). Those ongoing conversations influenced the planning stages for the new BHSSC unit. In the spring of 2001, Kuna asked Silver to draft a proposal for universal developmental screening for all infants and toddlers in foster care (Silver, Gerdes, & Haecker, 2001). The draft proposal acknowledged the importance of ensuring EI identification and intervention while warning that, without such an effort, children with unidentified developmental delays are at risk for placement disrup-tions and impaired school readiness. It also bemoaned the lack of screening resources in Philadelphia.

To address these concerns, the proposal called for screenings and linkages to evaluations for young children who are involved with DHS. The proposal underscored the importance of early screening because children are entering care with unidentified delays and disorders, which could place stress on the children and their families; contribute to placement failures; and also magnify children's developmental, emotional, and medical problems. The proposal urged a developmental screening program for all children entering foster care from birth to age 3. It suggested hiring infant development specialists, also called *early childhood developmental specialists,* who would be colocated at DHS and work closely with caseworkers. These new specialists would provide on-site screenings that would triage cases by helping to identify red flags for EI eligibility, such as growth delay, muscle tone abnormalities, NICU history, eye conditions, and poor hearing. These specialists would also provide guidance to families, referrals, and training, as well as technical assistance and consultation to DHS.

Silver and her colleagues proposed that each child should be screened within 45 days of entry into care through an hour-long, interactive process, which would include questions about the child's health and skills as well as an observation of the child playing, but would also allow time for counseling about the child's needs and for providing anticipatory guidance to the parent or foster parent. The proposal also contained an anticipatory guidance packet to be given to all foster parents, including a list of developmental milestones and red flags, handouts, and even toys. According to the proposal, all children would be screened, and if a given child failed the screen or evidenced a suspected delay, the child would be referred to EI for evaluation. The DHS would monitor the referral and evaluation services process, participate in the shaping of the service plan, add the results of the screen to the child's DHS plan and case file, and keep data on all referred children. Training for foster parents and caseworkers on infant development and the EI entitlement, as well as meeting young children's health care needs, would be a central role for the new unit.

The proposal raised the knotty question of the screening tool, suggesting that existing tools, such as the *Ages & Stages Questionnaires® (ASQ): A Parent-Completed, Child-Monitoring System* (Bricker & Squires, 1999), might be used with some modification. The proposal had blanks and questions directed to Kuna. Yet, after hurrying to produce the draft proposal, Silver never heard of it again. By the time Silver delivered the draft in May 2001, Kuna realized that the timing to advance the universal screening proposal within the bureaucracy was premature, so he waited for a more opportune time (J. Kuna, personal communication, July 26, 2007). Silver respected Kuna's political instincts and stopped pressing for the proposal. Indeed, at the time she didn't even know why the proposal was deferred, but she saw it as an exercise comparable to her trainings and the writings, similar to "planting a seed" (J. Silver, personal communication, July 27, 2007).

In the ensuing years, Silver would continue to raise the importance of EI for children in foster care in various forums. She received a 2005 federal grant to create the Child Welfare Early Childhood Initiative at CHOP where she spearheaded an educational series for supervisors at DHS and its contract agencies, judges, attorneys, and court-appointed special advocates (CASAs). Every session emphasized the vulnerability of the youngest children in the child welfare system and their need for connection to vital services, with an emphasis on EI. She also continued to pepper Kuna and Alexander on the bigger issue—connecting children to EI—by keeping them up to date on legislative developments that would eventually become the Keeping Children and Families Safe Act (CAPTA) of 2003 (PL 108-36) and IDEA 2004 (PL 108-446) referral requirements (J. Silver, personal communication, July 25, 2008).

The Child Welfare Early Intervention Initiative

From 2001 to 2003, the new DHS unit, BHSSC, worked to become a strong citywide entity. Kuna wrestled with integrating county mental retardation services (MRS) with DHS. This integration with MRS was critical because it was the lead city agency for EI. Yet, the timing for the universal screen for DHS children still was not right. Only after the mantle of integration was completed and the federal mandates of the CAPTA 2003 and IDEA 2004 were passed could Kuna begin to move this issue (J. Kuna, personal communication, July 26, 2007). Indeed, the new laws "represented efforts to drive policy and program development to reduce risks of poor developmental outcomes among infants and toddlers in the child welfare system" (Alexander, 2004, p. 4), underscoring the Adoption and Safe Families Act (ASFA) of 1997 (PL 105-89) and its well-being requirements (Alexander, 2004).

As a result of years of internal and external work, a groundbreaking policy was issued in 2004: Philadelphia would be one of only a few jurisdictions nationwide to refer all children in the child welfare system to EI (Child Information Welfare Gateway, 2007). The 2004 directive established the CWEII to be headed by Alexander. This directive was created by many factors—mandate of federal law, integration of the systems, and an increasing awareness of the prevalence of developmental delays and disabilities among DHS-involved children. It required all providers of in-home services to "work with parents, guardians and custodians to facilitate referral for developmental screening of all children birth to age 5 years" (Alexander, 2004, p. 6). This broad response to facilitate universal referrals recognized that the first 5 years of life presented an excellent opportunity to help mold, educate, and support a caregiver's ability to augment their child's development. It would also diminish the chances of future behavior and/or health problems, an underlying and cost-saving goal of the new agency. Thus, EI was a set of interventions that could add support for parents, sensitize caregivers, and reduce the risk of poor outcomes, thereby promoting permanency and well-being. The key referral source would be the private providers of child welfare services rather than child protective service workers, intake workers, or others employed by the city.

This was a practice meant to comply with the union mandate against more paper-work (D. Patterson, personal communication, January 15, 2008).

To implement this broad mandate, Alexander undertook several initiatives. She would develop a help unit specifically geared toward responding to problems with referrals from the field (Cohen, 2005). She further devised an elaborate data system that included a tickler system to track referrals and contact EI to follow progress and ameliorate problems. Training for both DHS providers and staff would ensure knowledge about the EI system. Thus, the universal referral policy furthered DHS's agenda and compliance with ASFA, as well as the other federal laws. By the summer of 2004, more than 600 referrals had resulted in completed IFSPs (J. Alexander, personal communication, July 26, 2007).

Despite the early glimmers of success of the broad mandate and the elaborate implementation strategies, referrals faltered. The system ran into unantici-pated problems. Since all children were treated alike, children with the most urgent problems were no more likely to be referred than those without delays. Furthermore, DHS providers found making EI referrals difficult. Parents too seemed wary and unclear about EI. Despite the changes, foster parents were often still not permitted to sign consent forms, resulting in delays and EI case closures before evaluations could even occur. The data being reported were incomplete, so it was unclear how the system was working. In essence, the task of referring thou-sands of Philadelphia's children under age 5 involved in the child welfare system—there were 6,000 children in 2006—was trapped in a logjam (J. Alexander, personal communication, July 26, 2007).

Alexander and her colleagues determined that reform was needed, and in 2007, working very closely with Patterson and the EI staff, they began imple-menting the Developmental Surveillance project (Evans, 2006). The new policy required developmental surveillance for all children under age 5 known to DHS, a far broader category than the federal law requirement of children birth to 3 involved in substantiated cases of abuse and neglect. It would facilitate the use of the ASQ (Bricker & Squires, 1999) screening tool for all children under age 3 and, if no delays, again every 6 months. The broader purview for the screens was justified in the directive citing the high risk factors of those children and the importance of ensuring that all children who may have potential developmental delays are identified and receive EI. Trained DHS or provider agency staff would screen all children under 4.9 years of age in their home or foster home using the ASQ. Children in foster care would be screened within 60–90 days of placement. If the screen results flag one or more areas of potential delay, children would be referred to EI. In the event that no suspected delay is identified, the parent must be informed of the right to request an evaluation—a right embodied in federal EI law and critical for these children. DHS also requires documentation of all screen-ings and referrals.

To further open the logjam, full implementation of the provisions permit-ting foster parents to give consent to evaluation and services and to serve as surrogate parents if needed would occur. The legal staff at DHS developed a procedure for securing court authorization, now permitted by IDEA 2004 in cases of refusal of consent where medical necessity dictated immediate connection to EI (J. Alexander, personal communication, July 26, 2007).

Most significantly, the developmental surveillance program would establish a triage system ensuring that the most urgent cases were referred to and served by EI. The new in-home use of the ASQ is designed to facilitate parental under-standing of their child's delays. Asking specific developmental questions of the parent or foster parent and then together watching the child's performance has opened discussion of the child's real needs, rendering parents more receptive to the EI program and more willing to sign consents. In essence, they can witness the delays because the family is really administering the ASQ in concert with the caseworker (J. Alexander, personal communication, July 26, 2007).

An intensive training program has been presented to child welfare supervi-sors jointly by DHS and EI. It has focused on the urgency of addressing the needs of these children, but its most important component has been instructions on the use of the screening tool—a concrete topic that leads to enhanced skills to better understand the EI program. All supervisors were trained and, in turn, required to train their staffs. This enhanced professional development is an interesting side benefit of using the ASQ. For example, as child welfare caseworkers administer the ASQ with children's caregivers, they themselves will be learning more about early child development and have a means of better focusing on infants' and toddlers' functioning.

To further implement the policy, DHS and EI have executed an elaborate interagency agreement (DHS EI Interagency Agreement, 2006). EI is responsible for Child Find activities that include outreach to DHS. Upon referral, EI will per-form intake as well as assign a service coordinator to the case. In turn, DHS, through its contractual agencies, will perform the developmental screens for all children and refer any child where "developmental concerns are identified" with-in 2 working days (DHS EI Interagency Agreement, 2006). The process for refer-rals was delineated and included faxed referrals by DHS to EI. EI will then contact the family within 48 hours or, if there is no phone, DHS will facilitate a joint home visit. If contact with the family is lost, EI will contact DHS, and EI will keep DHS apprised of the process and advise DHS once the evaluation is complete. Parents will be asked to sign a release permitting DHS to participate in the IFSP meeting. Most significantly, for the future, DHS and EI agree to provide joint training and share each other's mailing lists and notices. Monthly troubleshooter meetings are led by Alexander and attended by Patterson. The initial results have been promising despite problems in the training, consistent use of the ASQ, and hurdles at the referral site (M. Zukoski, personal communication, January 5, 2008). In the first year of operation, more than 1,000 children with open DHS cases have been found eligible and actually enrolled and were receiv-ing EI services. More tinkering is needed to increase the number of well-documented referrals. Underscoring the importance of the Philadelphia universal screening policy, the state of Pennsylvania has now adopted a similar directive requiring developmental screens for children under age 3 (Gold, 2008).

The idea of universal screening for all children touched by DHS was, of course, the brainchild of the Subcommittee as early as 1999. Silver's 2001 proposal informed the design of the CWEII, even suggesting use of the ASQ and the idea of rescreens every 6 months. Indeed, the seeds of a court-ordered mechanism to override refusal of consent were planted by the Subcommittee's court forms initiative. According to Alexander, the universal developmental surveillance program is the result of both "top down and grassroots" efforts. It needed not only the many seeds planted by Silver and her colleagues but also the political will and managerial expertise at DHS and EI to make the proposal a reality.

SCANDAL AND CALLS FOR REFORM

The backdrop of the child welfare system since the 1800s has been the interplay between scandal and reform. Most scandals have been precipitated by the death of a child, followed by blue ribbon commissions, expert panels urging change, and litigation. Since the mid-1980s, Philadelphia has seen several cycles of this pattern. The latest scandals surfaced in the fall of 2006 when the *Philadelphia Inquirer* began a series of articles focusing on deaths of children known to DHS. In response, the mayor followed a set course; he appointed an expert panel called the Philadelphia Child Welfare Review Panel. The panel, composed of national and local experts and a battery of staff, met for several months to conduct case reviews and interviews with DHS officials and focus groups of parents, caseworkers, and other system players. They also held a series of town hall meetings with parents, officials, and experts, including the Subcommittee, who all presented testimony.

On May 31, 2007, the panel released its report, titled *Protecting Philadelphia's Children: The Call to Action* (Spigner et al., 2007), calling for major reform at DHS. Although it highlighted the importance of leadership and development of a mission statement, its core recommendations were for an overhaul of child protection investigations and follow-up to protect the safety of Philadelphia's children. It emphasized a fact highlighted by this book—that virtually all of the child fatalities involved children under age 5, and two thirds involved children under age 1. Indeed, it found that of the 52 children who died from 2001–2006, 36 were under 1 year of age and 13 were just under 3 months of age. Yet, the majority of the families were known to DHS and more than half received child welfare preventive services.

The report emphasized that "infants were the most likely to die" (Spigner et al., 2007, p. 8), in part because of the inability of workers to flag medical problems and because of a lack of understanding both of medical information and of the need for health information about the infants. To respond to this dire situation, the panel recommended a new protective services focus on children under age 5, including a face-to-face immediate interview within 2 hours of receiving a report of suspected child abuse or neglect involving a child under age 5 and a monthly face-to-face contact with a child under age 5 of any founded report. These face-to-face contacts are required to observe the "condition, safety, and behavior" (Spigner et al., 2007, p. v) of any child under age 5.

Yet, the report makes no recommendations about the content of those face-to-face contacts, the training required for staff, or even the requirement that experts in infancy and toddlerhood be involved in shaping the safety assessment instruments, training, or consultation. Ironically, although focusing on children under age 5, it neither mentions the DHS CWEII to screen all children under age 5 with open DHS cases or even the EI program. The mayor appointed a Community Oversight Board to report periodically on the recommendations. Those reports have also failed to mention EI or the CWEII (Community Oversight Board, 2007).

Paradoxically, EI could provide the richest array of services to those who were the focus of the report. This disconnect between meeting the real needs of these children and understanding ways to address these concerns continues to haunt the child welfare system as evidenced by the panel's report. For example, the panel did not even learn about an internal report from DHS showing that children in long-term foster care displayed developmental delays in the early years (Elfman, 2007), and it ignored an ongoing effort, the CWEII, which could be deployed to promote the healthy development of Philadelphia's most vulnerable children—its youngest children in the child welfare system.

LESSONS LEARNED

Despite the turmoil in child welfare in Philadelphia, the CWEII survived the change in administration in 2007. Indeed, Kuna now directs the Support Center for Family and Child Well Being that combines health and behavioral services for all children with open DHS cases, further addressing the Subcommittee Health Policy recommendations of 1999 (J. Silver, personal communication, November 10, 2008). The CWEII's survival seems axiomatic given its deep DHS staff commitment and support from outside advocates, including Silver and the Subcommittee. Moreover, it has enhanced the involvement of unionized staff due to the union involvement in every step of the development of the CWEII. This is significant because the union is a central power in Philadelphia.

Interestingly, as the spotlight remained on the panel's recommendation, Silver continued doing her training and education work. Under her federal grant for the Child Welfare Early Childhood Initiative at CHOP, she trained child welfare supervisors, lawyers, and judges, thereby laying the groundwork for implementation of reforms. This effort reopened the court forms initiative and now new judges are working with Rosado and Silver and the SY team to use those court forms in child abuse and neglect proceedings. In addition, Kuna's new expanded role is bringing renewed interest to the Subcommittee's recommendations on health care records. Thus, the interconnection of all of these efforts is critical and underscores recognition of change as a long-term process.

The effort to get the Philadelphia child welfare system to focus on young children and connect those children to the vital two-generation entitlement of EI was shaped by a myriad of factors. First and foremost was the long-term commitment of Silver and her colleagues to this issue. They never wavered in making the needs of young children paramount. They never changed their focus to adolescents or children leaving care or children needing adoptions—all laudatory goals—but steadfastly concentrated on addressing the needs of the youngest children. Prolonged activity is at the heart of this success.

In addition to a decade-long commitment to reform, Silver and her colleagues inside and outside government never wavered in their proposed solution—the need to connect children to EI services. Again, they didn't invent a new remedy, but believed that EI provided the cornerstone for addressing young children's needs. Their efforts were multistrategic and seized every opportunity to create reform—proposing written recommendations for reform and court forms for consent; changing state policy to allow foster parents to consent to EI and also serve as surrogate parents; providing training to everyone who touches a child welfare case, including caseworkers and professionals in the fields of health care, early intervention and child care, judges, lawyers, and CASAs; writing articles and books; creating a new agency; drafting proposals for universal screening; and, finally, developing and refining a universal developmental surveillance program.

Each of these initiatives required commitment and skill from players inside and outside of government. Silver and her colleagues brought a wealth of professional expertise to the table, but without the managerial skill and dedication of Kuna and Alexander, their proposals would not have reached fruition. Indeed, Kuna and Alexander were informed by the draft proposal, but had to shape an initiative that would fit at DHS. Both inside and outside partners needed each other's expertise, political savvy, and perseverance. Only time will tell if the universal developmental surveillance system triumphs and truly identifies, refers, and connects children to vital EI services.

9

Unlocking a New Portal for Healthy Development

Early Childhood Education

MIRA'S STORY

Mira was born 2 weeks premature to a teenage mother whose breath smelled strongly of alcohol. The mother, Sally, admitted to using alcohol, as well as other drugs during her pregnancy. Following protocol, the hospital called child protective services (CPS). At their urging, Sally agreed to attend an alcohol and drug abuse day program, which provided child care for Mira. When Mira was 1 week old, she left the hospital.

After leaving the hospital, Sally and Mira moved into a homeless shelter for mothers and children. Sally had no relatives in the area as she had been banished from her home when her parents learned of her pregnancy. After several weeks of waiting, Sally was enrolled in a day treatment program. She brought Mira along with her every day, dropping her off at the child care program, which was little more than a babysitting facility. Mira was fed and changed and put in front of the television set for most of the day. During treatment program hours, Sally spent no time with Mira.

When Mira was 4 months old, a health worker came to the shelter, and Sally brought Mira for her first check-up. It was discovered that she was already behind in her immunizations. The physician conducted an examination, gave Mira immunizations, and advised Sally to bring her back for a visit next month. Sally did not bring her back for the next 3 months because she was having great difficulty going to the treatment program every day and caring for Mira at night. She was exhausted, had trouble remaining sober, and had no one to help her. When she did bring Mira to the doctor again, he was concerned about Mira's development. She seemed very withdrawn and had grown little since the visit 3 months before. The doctor felt compelled to call CPS.

CPS investigated and determined that Mira was not in danger, but that Sally should be enrolled in a parenting program. Almost immediately, the conflict between the parenting program and the treatment program became overwhelming to Sally. She rarely attended the parenting program, and they reported her absence to CPS. CPS again investigated and urged Mira to attend the two programs. CPS looked at Mira to determine if she was safe—if she had any bruises, but made no other assessment of her.

The overlapping programs and the challenge of carrying Mira everywhere and caring for her alone became overwhelming for 17-year-old Sally. She stopped going to both programs and began to drink and use drugs again. At some point, the shelter staff confronted Sally and threatened to discharge her from the shelter. Together, they agreed instead to call CPS. CPS arrived when Mira was 13 months old. She was withdrawn and didn't make a sound. She also wasn't crawling or walking, and she could barely sit with support. Alarmed by Mira's appearance and Sally's inability to care for her, CPS took Mira into emergency foster care. The next day's court hearing affirmed that decision and ordered Sally to attend a residential alcohol and drug treatment program and gave her biweekly, supervised visitation.

Mira went to a foster home with several young children. She was quiet, but she wasn't eating, which caused great frustration to the foster mother. She became animated only when Sally came to visit, at which time Mira would cling to her. After several months of difficulty, the foster mother requested that Mira be moved. When she was 17 months old, she was moved to a new foster home with a foster mother who had adopted two children from foster care. Georgia, the new foster mother, was concerned about Mira's developmental lags and began spending lots of time with her. She also called Head Start (HS), which she knew to do because a young child once in her care had attended Early Head Start (EHS). Georgia called several times and her persistence secured a place at the local EHS program for Mira. The program provided both center-based and at-home services.

The EHS staff immediately noticed that Mira had delays in several domains, including motor, cognitive, and social-emotional development. They called early intervention (EI) and were able to get her evaluated quickly. Within several weeks, EI began sending a physical therapist into the EHS center-based program. Eventually a speech therapist and an occupational therapist came to EHS. They taught Georgia how to do exercises to augment the therapies. At the same time, EHS staff focused intently on building a relationship between Georgia and Mira and assisting Mira in learning how to interact with the other children. They invited Sally to come to the EHS site as well to observe Mira and their modeled interactions with Mira. This, in turn, helped Sally build her relationship with Mira. At EHS, Sally also learned the EI exercises and soon was using EHS as a site for weekly and sometimes more frequent visits. Georgia, encouraged by EHS staff, starting inviting Sally to her home for visitation.

Meanwhile, Mira began to make progress. She was less withdrawn, having established caring relationships with Georgia, her EHS teachers, and Sally. She was walking and speaking a few words by her second birthday.

At the permanency hearing held when Mira was 27 months old, all reported progress and satisfaction with the situation. Sally had now been sober for almost a year. Mira continued to thrive at EHS, in Georgia's home, and through her frequent visits with her mother. The judge continued the placement for another year with the goal of reunification.

Several months later, all involved in Mira's care—Georgia, Sally, EHS, and EI—met to plan her transition from EHS. It was agreed that she would attend the HS program 5 days per week, but be referred for preschool special education to continue needed therapies. During the next year, Sally visited very often. She and Georgia became close—almost like a mother and daughter. At the next permanency hearing, the judge wanted to send Mira home to live with her mother, but Sally said she wasn't ready. During the next year, with the help of the HS family worker, Sally found an apartment and a job. Mira moved home before starting regular kindergarten, where she receives special education and related services. As a result of her immersion in early childhood education, Mira is ready for school and ready to learn. Georgia often watches Mira after school and over the weekend.

Mira's story illustrates the potential of early childhood education as a strong portal for services. Through the gateway of EHS, Mira was connected to EI, then at age 3 to HS and preschool special education. The EHS program provided a strong foundation for her education, health, and social-emotional development. Through daily contacts with EHS staff, along with parent activities, Georgia, her foster mother, learned to enhance Mira's development as well as receive needed respite from the stress of caring for a child with complex needs. These supports all combined to stabilize Mira's placement. They also made it possible to help build her relationship with Sally, her birth mother, by using EHS and later HS as a site for visits and for parent training and support. Through this gateway of early childhood education, Mira became ready for kindergarten and secured a foundation for strong caregiving relationships, which led to reunification with her birth mother supported by continued involvement of her foster mother.

Mira's experience echoes the positive findings of the evaluation of EHS first performed in 2001 by Mathematica in Princeton, New Jersey, and Columbia University's Center for Children and Families at Teachers College, in collaboration with the Early Head Start Research Consortium (U.S. Department of Health and Human Services [DHHS], Administration for Children & Families [ACF], 2001). That research found positive results after a year or more of EHS participation when compared with a randomly assigned control group. Not only were the 2-year-old children involved with EHS operating significantly better on a series of trials of cognitive, language, and social-emotional skills than their non-EHS cohorts, but also their parents were improving. The parents of EHS children were shown to score significantly higher on many of the measures than the control group parents, including maintaining a home environment, their personal parenting behavior, and knowledge of infant and toddler development. Other positive results included that EHS families were more likely to attend school or job training. At the same time, they were more likely to experience a lessening in both parental stress and internal family conflict. When looked at singularly, these impacts seem modest in size; while looking at them as part of the big picture, they show improvement across a range of areas that have proven to be important for children's well-being and future development (DHHS, ACF, 2001). These findings echo those of other studies concerning the beneficial effects of quality two-generation early childhood education programs for vulnerable children (Center on the Developing Child at Harvard University, 2007).

While half of young children in foster care or even the child welfare system may be eligible for the EI program, the remaining children are also at serious risk of poor outcomes. Moreover, as Mira's story illustrates, even children eligible for EI may need the additional stimulation, enrichment, and relationship-building efforts of EHS. As the research well documents, these children can reap substantial benefits from early childhood programs (Center on the Developing Child at Harvard University, 2007). High-quality early childhood programs provide more than simply respite and child care for caregivers. They can enable all children to be ready for school by promoting early learning skills, enhancing the well-being of children in foster care by linking them to vital health and entitlement programs, and creating a critical opportunity for these children to establish a stable relationship with a caring adult. Quality early childhood education can strengthen families by teaching parents about skills and resources, as well as providing models demonstrating ways to cope with the individual needs of each child. These programs also can promote safety by providing a second set of eyes to observe the child and a second hand to support permanency efforts by offering a neutral, supervised setting for visitation and other services.

Yet, all too often, children in foster care are not connected to these programs. Mira was only enrolled because of her foster mother's experience and persistence. Other children may be fortunate enough to have a child welfare caseworker with knowledge of EHS or HS. Although some programs have enrolled children who are in foster care because of the knowledge of a foster parent or even a caseworker, very few have developed targeted initiatives to identify and recruit these children. Indeed, the National Survey of Child and Adolescent Well-Being (NSCAW) found that less than 23% of young children involved in the child welfare system were enrolled in any early education program (Stahmer et al., 2005). Thus, unlike their peers who are not in child welfare, these children will be far less ready for school and behind at the start of kindergarten. The ramifications are clear—these children will continue to drop out of school, be involved in the juvenile and criminal justice system, and become teen parents at far higher rates than their peers. They will also be more likely to be placed in special education classes and to suffer grade retention and suspension (Center on the Developing Child at Harvard University, 2007).

To stem this tide, early childhood education must be placed on the radar screen of child welfare agencies nationwide. Indeed, the NSCAW also found little effort on the part of state child welfare agencies to collaborate with early childhood education, which is in stark contrast to formal efforts with agencies providing substance abuse or mental health services or even the courts (DHHS, ACF, 2001). Only a small number of states have begun to include these programs in case planning and case review. Yet, given the national emphasis on making all children ready to learn and the Improving Head Start for School Readiness Act of 2007 (PL 110-134), the reauthorization of Head Start, the time is ripe to insist that children in child welfare be enrolled automatically in early childhood programs. To do otherwise is to further compromise the fragile development of these children, making it even less likely that they will become successful, productive citizens. This gateway for services has seldom been tapped, so no systems have yet become worthy of the in-depth study available for the other portals for services—the court, health, and early intervention systems—profiled in this book. Instead, this chapter highlights the promise of those programs, with special emphasis on EHS.

HEAD START AND EARLY HEAD START

HS and EHS are federally funded, comprehensive, multidisciplinary national programs of educational, health, mental health, social, nutritional, and family support services designed to serve low-income children from birth to 5 years and their families. Unlike EI and health care, they are not entitlement programs, and, therefore, eligibility is limited by available funding. Unlike the child welfare and court systems, they are not required by law to target efforts to children involved in the child welfare system. EHS and HS are, however, child-focused programs with a strong parental component and have the overall goal of promoting healthy child development and school readiness for young children in low-income families. HS is operated by local programs under the aegis of the HS bureau within the Administration on Children, Youth and Families (ACYF), which is in the Administration for Children and Families (ACF) of the U.S. Department of Health and Human Services (DHHS).

The EHS program established in 1994 builds on the original HS program, which had been founded as a centerpiece of President Johnson's War on Poverty (Children's Defense Fund, 2005). Preschool HS serves children ages 3–5 years. EHS, established by the Head Start Reauthorization Act of 1994 (PL 103-252), with grants first awarded in 1995, serves pregnant women and families with children from birth to 3 (Early Head Start, Administration for Children & Families, n.d.). Since its inception in 1965, HS has served more than 22 million children (Children's Defense Fund, 2005). More than 741 EHS programs serve nearly

62,000 children under the age of 3 (Lombardi & Bogle 2004). Similar to EI, they are two-generation programs. HS regulations require programs to assess the "child's unique strengths and needs" [45 CFR 1304.3(a)(1)(i)] and the services appropriate to meet those needs as well as the "resources, priorities and concerns of the family and the supports and services necessary to enhance the family's capacity to meet the developmental needs of the child" [45 CFR 1304.3(a)(1)(ii)]. HS programs also must assist families in accessing continuous, accessible medical, dental, and mental health services as required under EPSDT and identify a child's developmental, sensory, and behavioral needs.

HS programs are required to serve children with special needs, including children with physical disabilities, intellectual disabilities, emotional disturbances, and developmental delays; at least 10% of the spaces in the HS program must be allocated to children with special needs. It is noteworthy that HS regulations require programs to establish ongoing, collaborative partnerships with family preservation and support services and child protective agencies.

Similar to the EI program, HS programs are premised on active parental involvement and require parental consent for evaluation and services. Under HS regulations, *parent* is defined broadly as a mother, father, or other family member who serves as the primary caregiver, foster parent, or guardian, or someone with whom the child has been placed for "purposes of adoption pending a final adoption decree." Thus, Mira's foster mother had no problem granting consent to admission and program services. Programs must work with parents to identify family goals, strengths, and needed services; access community resources; and assist parents in enhancing the development of their children. They must inform parents of the need for all health and developmental screenings and services, explain all procedures in advance, assist in securing needed services, and maintain written documentation of any refusal of consent. As Mira's case illustrates, EHS has particular promise for children in the child welfare system. Yet, little data exist on their participation in this critical program.

Early Head Start/Child Welfare Services Grants

There is an obvious fit between the needs of children in the child welfare system (CWS), such as Mira, and EHS. In 2002, dovetailing on an earlier 1998 Request for Proposals (RFP) that Joan Lombardi, then Deputy Assistant Secretary for Children and Families, DHHS, and I developed seeking proposals to serve this population, the HS bureau awarded 24 grants to establish EHS/CWS programs (DHHS, ACF, n.d.a). It was hoped that the EHS/CWS initiative would result in the creation of a new category of programs. To this end, the HS bureau, working in concert with the Children's Bureau, gave grantees freedom to design projects that targeted children involved with the child welfare system. This cluster of programs became so diverse that they included programs for children at risk of abuse and neglect, foster children, children living at home but involved with child welfare services, and other permutations. Little guidance was given to these programs and they were free to use any design—center-based, home-based, combination of both, or even development of an infant mental health program.

Thus, they were seeds thrown in the wind. Underscoring this open methodology was the freedom that programs were given for recruiting, training, and serving families. Not surprisingly, with little federal guidance and accountability, the total number of children served was less than 200 nationwide. Predictably, too, the evaluations have been disappointing, showing poor attendance, inadequate outreach, and problems in collaboration with child welfare; although some glimmers of hope were noted showing improved parental capacities through increased parental empathy and less use of punitive measures (James Bell Associates, 2006). Therefore, the learning has been minimal but the difficulties of serving this population were only highlighted by these projects. Indeed, this disappointing pilot serves to discourage other programs worried about the many challenges, such as outreach to a new population, high absenteeism, and the complications of court and child welfare system involvement (Early Head Start National Resource Center EHS, n.d). The disappointing results of the EHS/CWS projects stifled any further expansion or even continuation of these endeavors.

Head Start Reauthorization

The Improving Head Start for School Readiness Act of 2007 (PL 110-134) reauthorized and renewed the HS and EHS programs in December 2007. It preserves the comprehensive nature of the program and identifies its purpose "to promote the school readiness of low-income children by enhancing their cognitive, social and emotional development" through the provision of "health, education, nutritional, social and other services." The Act does not establish any new category of program, such as continuation or expansion of the EHS/CWS initiatives. It does, however, contain several references to children in the child welfare system that could be used to increase their participation in the programs. Specific language exists in the new law concerning the needs of "children in foster care" or children "referred by a child welfare agency," including funds for training, inclusion in program strategic plans and needs assessments, development of formal linkages with CAPTA agencies, promoting involvement of and providing family assessments to foster parents and kinship caregivers, considering the needs of these children in modification of program standards as well as program monitoring efforts, and developing research and demonstration projects to test how best to serve these children.

These new provisions in the Improving Head Start for School Readiness Act of 2007 (PL 110-134) could spur HS and EHS programs to place children in child welfare services on their radar screen. Ideally, as programs develop their needs assessments, they will note the low participation of these children and include them in strategic planning. This effort will be augmented for EHS because of the specific requirement of linkage with CAPTA agencies (agencies receiving federal funds for child protective and other child welfare services). This information, in turn, can lay the groundwork for increased outreach and enrollment of these children. In addition, the new funds targeted to training can enhance program capacity to address the unique needs of children in the child welfare system. Using these new provisions of the 2007 Head Start reauthorization act can stimulate greater enrollment of young children touched by the child welfare system in vital EHS and HS programs.

Ironically, although the new law has promise, it has far less potential than the earlier bills introduced in Congress to reauthorize HS and EHS. Indeed, in H.R. 2123, the proposed School Readiness Act of 2005, children in child welfare services were targeted for additional funding as a new underserved population. The House bill had specifically stated that those children should benefit from "quality improvement funds" that could have been used to ensure that programs have adequate numbers of qualified staff to increase program participation and to promote attendance and stability of "highly mobile children," including "children in foster care." Underscoring the importance of serving these children, the proposed legislation had a provision giving preference for designation as an EHS for agencies that "meet the needs" of children in foster care. This is important because there are far fewer EHS than HS programs nationwide, but the need is enormous, particularly for underserved children. To facilitate this expansion, Congress would have required HS agencies to coordinate and collaborate with local educational agencies to engage in community outreach to identify "underserved populations." Additional credentialed training would have been required for personnel providing services to "children determined to be abused or neglected" and to "children referred by or receiving child welfare services." Similarly, the Senate Bill, S. 1107, the Head Start Improvements for School Readiness Act, had parallel proposals targeting children in the child welfare system to benefit from various quality improvement goals and activities.

Yet, the broader provisions did not pass and the conference report only was adopted following years of wrangling between the White House and Congress. A review of the recommendations of proponents of reauthorization finds no group lobbying on behalf of retaining the specific targeted language in the House or Senate bills. Although, clearly House and Senate staff and members were aware of the EHS/CWS evaluations and sought to address these concerns and encourage serving this most vulnerable population, these children remained a low priority for several reasons. First, cost became a critical issue in the debate, and expanding programs in tight budget times is always difficult. Second, establishing a new category of program for children in the child welfare system or otherwise targeting funds to that group would have required hard evidence of effectiveness of the CWS/EHS grants. These programs were off the radar screen of advocates, as well as HS, and never even mentioned in advocacy reports or letters. Although the targeted funding approach failed, the orientation taken in the proposal bills can chart a path for the targeted growth of EHS and HS to serve children in the child welfare system. The reauthorization law, however, has promise. Its broad statutory approach may be a more realistic policy, as well as more consistent with the recommendation of early childhood policy experts (Center on the Developing Child at Harvard University, 2007).

STRATEGIES FOR UNLOCKING EARLY HEAD START

With the nation so focused on the importance of early childhood education, why are those involved in the child welfare system sitting on the abyss without any notice? Why are thousands of America's most vulnerable children on the precipice, ready to fall into the void of being unprepared to start school? Why are they ignored and not included in this national effort to make all children ready to learn? Is it race or poverty? Certainly those are components; however, the focus of the state and local school readiness initiatives are often targeted at poor, at-risk children.

It is actually something even deeper. These children, at some level, are frightening to our society. We are more comfortable with them off the radar screen, even though the cost to our society—in dollars, lives lost, and threats to public safety—are enormous. Even those who work daily with these children seem to ignore the reality that children in the child welfare system are not receiving the same early education opportunities as their age peers. It took more than a decade for efforts to begin to connect foster children to health care and early intervention services—programs that are entitlements. The clock has only begun to chime for early childhood education. Only fledging efforts are apparent, and more needs to be done.

A few states have begun initiatives to target children in the child welfare system to ensure that they are ready for school. Most noteworthy is the effort in Illinois that has made school mandatory for all children in foster care over the age of 3. The vast majority of Illinois children in foster care (known as *wards of the state* in Illinois) between ages 3 and 5 are now enrolled in HS, prekindergarten, or other early childhood programs. This mandate, known as the Illinois School Readiness Initiative, considers education an entitlement for all children who are the state's wards (Illinois Department of Children and Family Services, 2006). This mandate was built on a strong early childhood foundation in Illinois and was facilitated by agreements and trainings with HS and other providers. Child welfare caseworkers can no longer write "not applicable" next to education on any forms or case plans for children ages 3–5 because the policy specifically requires that education start at age 3. Extending this provision to children under age 3 has proven to be more challenging and is in its earliest phases (W. Goetz, personal communication, October 2007).

Yet, the Illinois mandate approach shows great promise and is far more hopeful than the wide open approach of the EHS/CWS programs. Indeed, targeting children who are actually served by child welfare, not just at risk, has greater prospects for identification, recruitment, and priority for enrollment. Several states in concert with existing early childhood initiatives are taking the first steps to try to create needed programs for this population. In Connecticut and several other states, efforts have convened collaboratives with HS and child welfare to begin planning a new system to ensure foster children's admission to HS. These multiagency efforts have focused on training, recruitment, and outreach (G. Whitney, personal communication, March 2008).

Finally, New York has taken another approach. New York's 2005 New Permanency Bill (Chapter 3 of the Laws of 2005) requires child welfare agencies to file permanency hearing reports that specifically list whether children attend early childhood education, EI, or prekindergarten programs. This report gives the judge an opportunity to inquire about early childhood education and, if necessary, order a referral (Laws of New York, 2005). To date, no data exist on the efficacy of these fledging strategies.

With the clarity of the research and the enormity of the need, unlocking early childhood education, particularly EHS, needs to be a priority for those involved in the child welfare and early childhood education systems. Obviously, creating a mandate for early childhood education for this most vulnerable group would be the best starting point. As the Illinois experience demonstrates, this is a laudable goal. While working toward that goal, gathering the data to analyze the dilemma is step one. Every community should be gathering data on these children's lack of participation. The data tell the story and underscore the truth—that not all children are prepared to learn.

Step two is finding champions who will make ensuring early childhood education for all children in the child welfare system a priority, including those in foster care. Those champions should be available from professionals who work in the child welfare and court systems—caseworkers, program administrators, judges, lawyers, and CASAs. By tying the research to the ASFA well-being requirements that include education, it should be readily apparent that early childhood education could help augment children's healthy development, bring a second set of eyes to ensure safety, help stabilize placements, and build permanent relationships. Indeed, early childhood education can serve as an extraordinary site for visitation—safe but observed through professional eyes. Thus, it is a strong weapon in the arsenal of ASFA compliance. Judges will order these referrals if requested, but the programs need to be open and prepared to embrace these most vulnerable children.

Step three, building collaborations with the broad early childhood education world, is essential. Just like in the EI efforts, child welfare and other professionals have to seize every opportunity to plant seeds. They must attend conferences, make presentations on the data and the need, construct partnerships, and build models. Judges can be tapped to serve as conveners for these collaborations (Townsend & Carroll, 2002). In many jurisdictions, collaborations already exist for early childhood education; now, child welfare and the courts need to be seated at those tables. That may take persistence on the part of those champions, but it is a doable task. This is an ignored issue, but there is no counter argument. There is no research showing that these children will not benefit from programs or that such programs are undermined by their presence. Yet, as in EI and health, they do bring additional issues (Dicker & Gordon, 2006).

Indeed, the new HS reauthorization requires HS and EHS to build collaborations with child welfare. For those collaborations to be meaningful, they will have to address issues of outreach, identification, eligibility, and services, even if the law does not specify those central concerns. Fortunately, the first three are relatively easy tasks. Child welfare can identify all children of the relevant ages. It knows where they are and with whom they live. Child welfare caseworkers can be trained to understand the importance of EHS and HS and how to make referrals. Eligibility, too, is easy—all children involved in the foster care system are income eligible for EHS and HS, and children who have been abused and neglected are a priority category in most programs.

The service issues bring new challenges. Program adaptations will be needed to best serve this group of children in large numbers. As with EI, what are needed are not new models but additional permutations on those models (Dicker & Gordon, 2006). Early childhood educators will need professional development and support by child welfare to navigate those new hurdles. They will need to understand the child welfare and court systems, and particularly how they affect the lives of these children and how they can share information with decision makers that could enhance those children's lives. They also will need help in understanding the roles of the additional players, such as judges, child welfare caseworkers, foster parents, attorneys, and CASAs. Most important, they will need ongoing support to deal effectively with biological and foster parents. Yet, as evident in Mira's case, those EHS and HS educators can be the key to understanding and augmenting the caregiving capacity of parents. Thus, unlocking the portal of early childhood education, particularly EHS, for the youngest children in the child welfare system, is necessary to promote their healthy development. If EHS and other programs remain locked, the ramifications for these children are bleak.

IV

Conclusion

10

Putting the Pieces Together

One Jurisdiction at One Point in Time

THE LANS CHILDREN

Alexandra Lans, a 6-year-old girl, was placed in foster care in January 2004, along with her 3-year-old brother, Ben, and her 1-year-old brother, Mike, after Alexandra's school called the child abuse hotline concerning bruises on her body. The Department of Social Services (DSS) went to the school and, after observing the bruises, brought Alexandra to the hospital. DSS called the mother who admitted to hitting Alexandra. When DSS went to the home to investigate, it found 13 people crammed into a small, dirty, dark house, and the two youngest children unattended, wearing soiled clothes, smelling foul, and crying. These children also were taken to the hospital. In addition to the bruises, Alexandra was found with pubic lice and soiled underwear, and the two youngest children had severe diaper rash, later found to be a fungus. The child abuse report was found to be indicated (or substantiated) and the children were removed to emergency foster care because it was after court hours. The mother was arrested and subsequently spent several months in jail. The father, a recovering drug addict, was also jailed for a parole violation. After the arrest, the mother was found to be a victim of domestic violence.

The next morning, a hearing was held in Westchester County Family Court. Judge Joan Cooney presided in the specialized Permanency Part that hears only abuse and neglect cases. She found that the children were in imminent risk of harm and placed them in emergency foster care. She ordered a hearing to be held in 3 days that required the presence of the parents. She also ordered counsel for the parents and a law guardian for the children.

At the next hearing, Judge Cooney ordered a court-appointed special advocate (CASA) to be involved with the three children and to report back to the court in 1 month about their health, education, and other needs. This would include a referral to early intervention (EI) for the youngest child. She further ordered that the parents undergo an assessment, along with the children, after they were released from prison.

At the next hearing a few weeks later, again with all counsel present, Judge Cooney spoke directly to the parents. She reviewed the petition's allegations and accepted the parents' admission of neglect. After the admission, all counsel agreed to expedite the case and hold the dispositional hearing at that time. Judge Cooney focused most of her attention during this hearing at the parents. She looked right at the parents and said, "This case is very important. Do you understand that your children are in foster care and will stay in foster care because of these allegations?" The parents replied that they understood. She then said, "There are steps you can take to get your children back, and if you do them, then it's likely that you will get your children back because that's what's best. But if you do not, I will not hesitate to terminate your parental rights. This is about your children, please understand that. In fact, I will do everything in my power to help you—order services, make sure you're getting services, make sure you have transportation or child care, or whatever—to get your children back. I will order services you need, not things that will waste your time, but things that you need to do to get your children back. But, time is of the essence under the federal law known as the Adoption and Safe Families Act (ASFA)—you have only a total of 15 months to do this and it's your responsibility. If there are problems, you must tell your lawyer who will advise me so I can help you."

Judge Cooney then instructed the parents that the court would do all it could to help them get their children back, but that they must cooperate. She ordered the parents to attend all medical appointments, therapy sessions, and school conferences, explaining that she was giving them the chance to do what all parents do for their children. She further ordered DSS to bring the children to the prison for biweekly visitation with the parents and to facilitate weekly sibling visits.

The children originally were placed in two separate foster homes— Alexandra alone in one and the boys together in another. Following DSS protocol, the Westchester Institute for Human Development (WIHD) performed an assessment of the foster homes within a few days of placement. Although they bemoaned the children's separation, they found the homes adequate at that time. The children all had a comprehensive physical exam at the county DSS pediatric clinic within a few weeks of entering care. They also all received a psychological assessment at WIHD.

After these exams, DSS referred the youngest child, Mike, to EI, and he was found eligible for the program. He began receiving daily services at a children's rehabilitation hospital, including physical, occupational, and speech therapy services. He was given braces for his legs for stability. Ben, who was 3 years old, was enrolled in a Head Start program and referred to the committee on preschool special education for additional services. The education advocate at CASA became very involved in securing school-based services for Alexandra at the elementary school near her foster home. This included discussions with the school psychologist and guidance counselor to address not only her academic progress but also her social interaction with teachers and students, her personal hygiene, and her self-mutilating behavior.

When the parents were released from prison, they received an assessment at WIHD that included observing the parents' interaction with the children. WIHD recommended family therapy, as well as parenting skills training for the parents. The parents were eager to cooperate with DSS and WIHD. They understood Judge Cooney's admonition that they would be given a chance and had to show that they could be good parents. With the help of DSS, they moved to a new apartment just for their family. At the WIHD parenting skills program, they had weekly opportunities to interact with their children under the guidance of professional staff. Indeed, when the issue of hygiene was raised by WIHD, the parents were open to learning how to address these concerns. Learning not to use excessive corporal discipline with the children—particularly with Alexandra—took more time.

The court received CASA reports and updates every month. By the summer, Judge Cooney ordered more visitations so that the family could have more opportunities to practice their parenting skills and demonstrate progress. She also inquired about the children's progress, pressing for services. After a few months, the youngest boys were doing well in their educational placements, but the foster homes were problematic. Alexandra and Ben had to be moved to several different foster homes. In less than a year, the children had been in four different homes. By the fall, foster home placement improved for all of the children, as did their interactions with their parents. Supervised visitation reported positive interactions with the youngest boys and improvements with Alexandra. At this juncture, reunification was on track, and the judge ordered increased visits, including overnight stays, and further ordered Alexandra to return to her home school. At the judge's insistence, CASA began working very closely with the school social work and special education staff concerning Alexandra. The mother began meeting with school staff to support her daughter. Subsequent hearings reported progress during visitation, with the parents showing appropriate interaction and affection with all the children.

At the permanency hearing held in March 2005, all agreed that the family was ready for trial reunification or a trial discharge for the children. CASA was ordered to continue monitoring the family. DSS agreed to visit the family three times a week to ensure continuing progress and assist with all of the various therapies and other appointments. Problems still persist for Alexandra in school, but the youngest boys are faring well. Court supervision will continue.

The Lans family story is about hope. It is the story of how one jurisdiction was able to put all of the pieces together—use all the portals for healthy development—for a period of time to achieve healthy development and permanency for three vulnerable children in a fragile family in the child welfare system. The collaboration among the court, DSS, CASA, EI, medical, mental health, and educational service providers demonstrates that using the law and the research can not only improve children's healthy development, but also will enhance their prospects for the permanency of a family. All of these pieces not only need to be in place, but, most importantly, they need to be coordinated.

For several years in Westchester County, New York, the court acted as the central decision maker and coordinator, ensuring that every available portal for services was used to improve children's lives. The reunification of the Lans family and their revitalization in every domain—enhanced parenting skills, special services for the children, and new housing—was only possible because all of the pieces were put together over a prolonged period of time.

In 1999, Judge Cooney, Supervising Judge of the Westchester Family Court and all Family Courts in the 9th judicial district (which includes five counties in New York State north of New York City—Westchester, Rockland, Putnam, Orange, and Dutchess) opened the Permanency Part (or special court) in the White Plains Family Court (New York State Permanent Judicial Commission on Justice for Children, 2006). In this court, she would hear the majority of all abuse and neglect cases filed in Westchester County outside of Yonkers (Westchester has three courthouses—Yonkers, White Plains, and New Rochelle). The aim was to create a model court where one judge, backed by a small team, would hear every abuse and neglect case from intake to permanency. Over the next 7 years, Judge Cooney turned this Permanency Part into a laboratory where the necessary pieces could be tinkered with through extensive collaboration with DSS, engagement of a diverse and active stakeholders group, utilization of the resources of CASA and a variety of early childhood providers, access to additional oversight assistance of a court attorney referee, and use of the materials and resources available from the Permanent Judicial Commission on Justice for Children (referred to as *Commission* in this chapter). Significantly, the court and its partner, DSS, also would expand the available medical, developmental, and mental health services provided by EI and WIHD, the unique national center for excellence in developmental disabilities that is affiliated with New York Medical College.

THE COURT

Judge Cooney was elected to the Westchester Family Court and took office in January 1993 after a career as a lawyer for children and families. Westchester is a suburban county north of New York City with just under 1 million residents and approximately 850 children in foster care (Georgetown University Child Development Center, 2000; Kids Well-Being Indicators Clearinghouse 2008). Although from the Midwest, she began her career as a law guardian representing children in New York City for the Legal Aid Society. Before her judicial election, she was legal director of Student Advocacy, an educational advocacy organization representing parents in efforts to obtain educational services for their children. It was through this work that Judge Cooney recognized the centrality of education for all children, believing that schooling was the work of childhood. From the beginning of her judicial tenure, whether hearing juvenile delinquency, custody, visitation, or abuse and neglect cases, she would always inquire about a child's education (J. Cooney, personal communication, April 24, 2007; January 3, 2008).

For the first few years of her tenure, Judge Cooney sat in a variety of cases honing her judicial skills. Sitting in juvenile delinquency cases, she came to believe that these adolescents' lives could have been improved if intervention had occurred during the first years of life. She had established a reputation as a highly effective judge when, in 1999, she was appointed to be the Supervising Judge of Westchester Family Court and the 9th judicial district. Now, privy to the entire court system, she found abuse and neglect cases particularly undervalued, further reinforcing her feeling that opportunities to intervene early had been forsaken. Indeed, in prior years, so few children had been adopted from foster care in Westchester—Judge Cooney even found adoption petitions in locked drawers—that DSS rarely filed petitions for Termination of Parental Rights (TPR) or adoption (J. Cooney, personal communication, April 24, 2007). Oversight of cases was scant, with judges often rubberstamping removals or reunification of children. Judge Cooney was cognizant that the law had changed—ASFA had just been passed, and the children involved in the cases were now the focus of proceedings, with permanency as the goal. She was also aware of the model courts developed by the Commission in Buffalo and New York City that showed promise in moving cases more expeditiously to permanency. Thus, she decided to develop her own Permanency Part.

Two things happened that year that shaped her efforts. First, knowing of her interest, her talent as a judge, and her new leadership role, Chief Judge Judith Kaye appointed Judge Cooney to the Commission. She would later be appointed to the court system's rules committee and chair its child welfare committee. Second, a new administration in Westchester brought a committed new face to DSS—Nancy Travers, First Deputy Commissioner—to oversee the child welfare system. These developments enabled Judge Cooney to begin her Permanency Part.

Judge Cooney quickly became an active member of the Commission, tapping its expertise and learning from Commission meetings that her gut feeling about the importance of intervening early in the lives of young children was supported by the scientific research. She fully utilized consultation from Commission colleagues and staff to learn more about the early childhood research and its importance for the youngest children in foster care. She also was able to secure additional resources and use the fortuitous location of the Commission offices, across the street from her courthouse, to tap the staff's expertise and assistance.

Indeed, two Commission staff members—Elysa Gordon and Rob Conlon—would provide ongoing support to Judge Cooney over the years. Her court's location made it a logical repository for Commission projects. Her court became the locus for the healthy development initiative beginning in 1999 that tested the use of CASAs to ask the questions from the Permanent Judicial Commission on Justice for Children's Healthy Development Checklist (Dicker & Gordon, 2004b) for all children under age 5 (see Chapter 6). Her uniform appointment of CASAs to ask those key questions set the standard statewide and laid the groundwork for other well-being projects. Indeed, her vision that education was central to children's lives enabled her to secure Commission funding for a part-time educational consultant available through CASA. Also, she secured the assistance of a court attorney referee, based on the Commission's model court experience, which is a nonjudge court official who can hear cases postdisposition, thereby increasing oversight of cases.

Judge Cooney recognized that collaboration with DSS would be vital for progress. She inherited a court paralyzed by its relationship with DSS, resulting in little movement on cases, including the never granted adoptions. The relationship between the court and DSS was quite poor, with caseworkers and attorneys routinely unprepared and scolded in open court. Yet, things were changing at DSS. Just a few months before, Nancy Travers, an administrator with years of experience in Albany and New York City, came to Westchester to oversee child welfare. Having worked with other agencies in Albany, principally developing homeless services, Travers was used to working collaboratively. Almost immediately, Judge Cooney began calling Travers with questions regarding systemic problems, such as transportation or visitation. These calls were never acrimonious and occurred almost daily for the first year, even though Judge Cooney and Travers had never met. They finally did meet after a year of phone calls and then became close professional colleagues and eventually friends (N. Travers, personal communication, December 26, 2007).

To implement the goals of ASFA, the Westchester County Family Court established a Permanency Planning Part (a specialized court), located in the White Plains Family Court, to hear all neglect and abuse cases involving children from Westchester County (except Yonkers). The Part was presided over by Judge Cooney and focused on achieving prompt resolutions of abuse and neglect cases and making permanent plans for foster children within time frames set by ASFA. The many hearings held on these cases established a permanency plan for each child, including a wealth of upfront services for the child and the parents, as well as set a specific time within which the plan must be accomplished. To effectively resolve these cases, the court utilized the help of a variety of resources. The court's full-time court attorney referee held permanency hearings for each child who had been in foster care for 1 year and, after changes in the law, those children who had been in for 8 months, and 6 months thereafter. In cases in which close monitoring was necessary, the court attorney referee held postdispositional conferences to monitor compliance with court orders. The Commission brought several critical resources to the Westchester Family Court. The Commission used federal Court Improvement Program (CIP) funds to hire a part-time educational consultant based at CASA to assist Judge Cooney in reviewing records, evaluating children, and providing recommendations as to the appropriateness of school placements. The education consultant helped to identify barriers to permanency and compliance with service plans, and she facilitated solutions involving children with special education and general education problems by negotiating with school systems. In addition, the court assigned a CASA volunteer to each foster child under age 5 to monitor the child's health and developmental needs. The CASAs used the Commission's Healthy Development Checklist (Dicker & Gordon, 2004c) to identify health needs of young foster children and gaps in services. The court incorporated the information gathered by the CASAs in court orders for specific health and developmental screenings to be obtained for individual children (National Child Welfare Resource Center on Legal Aid and Judicial Issues, n.d.).

One of the goals of the Westchester Permanency Part was to identify and remove both individual and systematic barriers to permanency. To achieve this goal, Judge Cooney convened bimonthly meetings of a multidisciplinary advisory council, later called *the stakeholders group.* Judge Cooney asked Nancy Travers to co-chair the stakeholders group. Travers agreed, as this gave evidence of the collaboration between the court and DSS. The stakeholders group included representatives from the court; DSS; CASA; the Commission; the county attorney's office; parents' attorneys and law guardians; WIHD; and other service providers. Others were added later as the stakeholders' projects increased. Although the group met bimonthly in Judge Cooney's chambers, the real work was done in committees that worked on training, visitation, education, and other issues. It never discussed individual cases. Perhaps most important, the stakeholders group did more than provide opportunities to work more efficiently to improve the court process. For most, it was the first time they were provided a picture of the puzzle as a whole. Every member was encouraged to bring their ideas to the table, work across disciplines, and share in the success or failure of the system.

The presence of the stakeholders group as a sounding board for Judge Cooney proved very useful. One of her first tasks was to reform the adoption process. Judge Cooney and her staff, along with members of the stakeholders group, reviewed every case with adoption as a goal to understand problems, identify hurdles, and solve and expedite the cases. This resulted in a spike in adoption from 2003 to 2007. By 2003, the total number of adoptions had doubled since 2001. In fact, the number of adoptions involving young children under age 5 has remained high, with an average (mean) of 23 adoptions per year from 2002 to 2007. This is in contrast to just nine adoptions for children under 5 in 2001, and only one of those involved a child under age 2 (Westchester Department of Social Services, 2001–2007). Thus, before the adoption project began to analyze, reform, and spearhead adoptions of young children, few were occurring in the county. This became one of the first tangible successes of the Permanency Part.

CHANGES AT DEPARTMENT OF SOCIAL SERVICES

Without an effective DSS, the Permanency Part could not make the changes Judge Cooney planned. Indeed, Nancy Travers found a demoralized and disorganized DSS upon her appointment in 1998. At that time, the court's antagonistic relationship toward DSS stifled any innovation, and, because of the lack of adoptions, the lowest performing staff members were assigned to that division. The new County Executive, Andrew Spano, however, promised to better fund DSS, and Travers reported a "real advantage working in Westchester," where requests for innovation and new funding were seldom denied (N. Travers, personal communication, December 24, 2007). This enabled her to expand a program unit to develop new initiatives; hire top-level managers, as well as more caseworkers; and upgrade the quality of casework, including bringing in the Child Welfare League of America's (CWLA) certification process to do a thorough review of the department's operations and make recommendations for improving practice.

One of Travers's efforts that advanced the court's collaboration was to develop good assessments as the backbone for decision making. Early in her tenure, she discovered that DSS had its own pediatric clinic right in the main DSS office building in White Plains. Unlike the Lans family, for which hospitalization was indicated, in most cases, the pediatrician and nurses (then all county employees) would conduct the initial intake exam and often the required comprehensive examinations. This procedure had already gone on for decades. Thereafter, the WIHD would conduct psychological assessments on the children, an undertaking begun almost a decade earlier. Despite the presence of these physical, developmental, and psychological assessments, none were fit together for case planning or shared with the court and often did not even appear in children's court or social services records. There also were few patterns found regarding which children received which type of assessment. Travers was determined to change this.

She first enlisted WIHD to do assessments on all children entering care and designed a system that would notify WIHD of placements and replacements. Using WIHD was innovative because it was a National Center for Excellence for Developmental Disabilities and affiliated with the New York Medical College. Forging collaboration with an entity steeped in developmental disabilities was an early recognition of the needs of the children DSS served. However, Travers realized that good assessments were only part of what was needed for decision making. Something needed to happen even earlier than the assessments. Since making effective early placement decisions was vital, she secured WIHD's assistance in conducting preliminary foster care visits shortly after children were in care to make sure the homes were adequate (Georgetown University Child Development

Center, 2000). While at the homes, WIHD staff would review not only for safety but also for issues related to the capacity of the home to meet the children's needs. Thus, WIHD's review would include whether the foster home could promote parent involvement with the children; provide stimulation, structure, and play opportunities; promote active venues for language and cognitive development; and make recommendations for improvements. Most significantly, they also performed screenings in order to refer children who needed immediate assistance to EI, early childhood education, or other services.

In the following years, WIHD would be tapped to do parental assessments for the vast majority of families slated for reunification. These assessments became 3-hour sessions that included intake by a social worker, psychological testing of children and parents separately, and parent–child observation. These thorough parent and child assessments would be shared with all involved in the case and placed in case records (Georgetown University Child Development Center, 2000). For example, the Lans family had the three-part assessment after the parents were released from prison, and WIHD then recommended family therapy for the parents and Alexandra, as well as participation in a parenting skills training program involving all the children. These programs, in contrast to most parent training nationwide, include the children in every session and are tailored to teach parents to care for their own children.

Eventually, WIHD would develop an electronic records system accessible to everyone involved in a case. This unique web-based, electronic record far exceeds the expectations for a health care passport (CureMD, 2007). Developed with DSS funding though a contract with CureMD, it is a specially tailored, easily accessible system developed to capture key information concerning children in the child welfare system. It captures demographic information; all health, developmental, and mental health assessments; all services received prior to and during placement; any disability classification or other diagnosis; the ingredients of the individualized education program (IEP) or the individualized family service plan (IFSP); immunization records; school attendance; and any other medical records (W. Breitner, personal communication, May 10, 2008). The system is so sophisticated that it fills out the required New York Permanency Hearing report filed with the court.

Thus, in a few short years, Travers had developed a strong assessment process that could underpin all planning and follow-up concerning children and families. The assessments would be provided to the court soon after the initial hearing, and its recommendations would shape court orders for services. At this juncture, another advantage of working at that time in Westchester would be tapped as DSS participated in a countywide early childhood workgroup that enhanced access to all programs for young court-involved children, such as Mike and Ben (N. Travers, personal communication, December 24, 2007).

As the court began routinely referring children under age 3 to EI, the WIHD/DSS collaboration could be built on to facilitate eligibility. Often the WIHD assessments resulted in immediate acceptance of young children into EI.

Furthermore, negotiations between the EI program and WIHD resulted in EI accepting the initial screens performed at the WIHD initial foster care placement reviews as sufficient for referral, and the full WIHD assessments would qualify as EI multidisciplinary assessments. Virtually all children found by WIHD to have significant delays were enrolled in EI, which resulted in more than two thirds of all children under age 3 in Westchester's foster care system in EI. This collaboration not only smoothed the enrollment process, it also harnessed scarce resources by using DSS funds for the assessment and EI funds for actual provision of EI services (W. Breitner, personal communication, December 28, 2007).

To create a seamless assessment process, Travers proposed to move the pediatric clinic to WIHD. She planned this at what seemed an opportune time—the retirement of the long-serving pediatrician. A firestorm ensued when the proposal was made public, and the nurses who would retain their positions but no longer be county employees went to the media. This stifled the proposal to move the clinic, rendering the medical and all other assessments still unrelated. Efforts to coordinate the medical and all other assessments into the electronic records continue.

Travers found another route to secure the needed health services while retaining the DSS pediatric clinic. A contract was entered into between the county and River Valley Health Care in 2006 for $198,966 that would increase in 2008 to $254,444 for medical services for foster children in Westchester County (River Valley Health Care/DSS, n.d.). Under the contract, the medical treatment is required to meet the stringent practice standards of the New York AAP and New York State law (AAP District II, 2001), including detailed requirements on intake and discharge, the capacity of comprehensive health assessments, periodic preventive health care, immunization tracking, and developmental follow-up care for children who have experienced abuse or neglect. Not only does the pediatric clinic provide one full-time equivalent of a pediatrician, there are also the equivalent of three full-time nurses and one administrative support person (all those other than the pediatrician are county employees) on duty when the clinic is open. The clinic remains open 5 days a week, 2 evenings a month, and, worth noting, also provides on-call services for emergency situations, including an on-call pediatrician.

OPERATION OF THE PERMANENCY PART

As the Lans case illustrated, the court Permanency Part provided the oversight framework for child abuse and neglect cases. The court was the central decision maker in all cases and set the parameters for the case. Due to the high expectations set by Judge Cooney and reinforced by Travers, the assessments and services were provided at generally high standards, and caseworkers and attorneys understood that preparation and adhering to court orders was mandatory. At the intake hearing, Judge Cooney focused on the child. She made initial findings, including whether the children were at imminent risk of harm, whether they needed foster care placement, and whether reasonable efforts to prevent placement had been made. She ordered the assessments—medical, developmental, and psychological—for the children and the parents, and she ordered referrals to EI for children under age 3. She also secured educational records for school-age children. These assessments were generally performed by the DSS pediatric clinic and WIHD. She assigned CASAs for cases involving children under age 5 to provide a report to the court answering the healthy development and, later, the infant questions, to address the status of referrals, particularly EI; to document compliance with court orders; and to provide additional relevant information to aid decision making. She also ordered counsel for all children and parents. The courtroom was a calm and organized place with all parties—attorneys, caseworkers, and parents—treated with respect.

At the next hearing held within a few weeks, the legal focus was on the allegations of the petition because the court was required to make a finding of whether abuse or neglect had occurred. As in the Lans case, this elicited a fraction of the court's attention, with the hearing focusing on the assessments and the court's face-to-face discussion with the parents. Unprepared caseworkers or attorneys were not tolerated, and Judge Cooney often ordered them to return in the next few days with the needed information or evidence of the ordered action. Parents, such as the Lans, had an opportunity to talk with the judge and understand the nature of their case and the importance of cooperation with court orders and services. At the conclusion of this hearing, the judge often added services and new provisions for visiting to the court order. Thereafter, particularly in cases involving very young children, the court held frequent hearings to review progress and to resolve problems.

After passage of the 2005 New Permanency Bill (Laws of New York, 2005) that Judge Cooney helped draft and pass, permanency hearings were held after children were in care for no more than 8 months, followed by every 6 months if needed (Office of Children & Family Services, n.d.). These hearings were scheduled at the intake hearing to ensure that all parties received adequate prior notice and adjournments or postponements would become unnecessary. At the permanency hearings, either Judge Cooney or her court attorney referee would review the required permanency hearing report that must contain information about the child's physical, developmental, and mental health; education; and receipt of health and education services, including preschool and EI services. In this court, the interconnection between children's healthy development and permanency was recognized and addressed. This helped to expedite permanency for many young children. Indeed, in 2006, Commission staff reviewed all of Judge Cooney's abuse and neglect cases for children under age 5 who had entered foster care in 2004. Just under 80% of the children had found permanency by 2006, far in excess of the state or national average (personal memorandum, A. Sherman & T. Borra, December 11, 2006).

The stakeholders group would often be given the task of resolving systemic issues identified by the court. Conlon from the Commission and Breitner from WIHD, along with Jackie Boissonnault from CASA, formed the core of the committees that tackled these issues, including education and visitation. They would devise a system for gathering educational records within days of placement, allowing the court to resolve problems and ensure that placement decisions furthered children's educational needs. They would make recommendations for the scope and services for an RFP for a visitation center. The visitation center funded by DSS is a real house on a street that enables parents and children to visit in a home-like setting and practice cooking meals, having dinner, doing laundry, or participating in other family tasks in a comfortable setting, as well as facilitating more frequent visits for mothers with young children. The visitation center furthers Judge Cooney's vision that parents should have the opportunity to practice and demonstrate their ability to care for their children (J. Cooney, personal communication, January 3, 2008). In addition, the visitation center's location in the community allows staff to assist families in establishing and maintaining ongoing support from community programs.

LESSONS LEARNED

In November 2006, Judge Cooney retired, and in January 2008, Travers resigned. The loss of Judge Cooney had an immediate impact. In December 2006 alone, two adoption hearings were postponed. During 2007, the stakeholders group only met one time, and CASAs had not been routinely appointed to cases involving young children. Despite a spike in child abuse reports in 2007, Travers was able to shore up the scaffolding of assessments and services. She continued to support and expand the collaboration with WIHD, resulting in quality, multidisciplinary assessments of children and parents and high enrollments in EI, EHS, and other early childhood and parenting programs. While the pediatric clinic was still providing health care for foster children, Travers worked to connect it to WIHD and the electronic records system. Without Travers's watchful eye, the future remains uncertain.

Travers said, "You can set the policy but you have to clone the people" for reform to continue to prosper (N. Travers, personal communication, December 24, 2007). The Westchester experience does seem to underscore that statement. Yet, the core of quality services remains in place, and the oversight framework provided by Cooney and Travers can be replicated. Leadership is critical, and new champions must be found to recreate the structure. New champions are currently trying to rebuild some of that scaffolding.

CASAs are again being trained to use the Commission's Healthy Development and Infant Checklists (J. Bouissant, personal communication, June 11, 2008). WIHD is continuing its efforts to gather the medical information from the pediatric clinic and place it into the electronic data system as well as provide a host of assessments and services (W. Breitner, personal communication, December 27, 2007).

This reinvention process only proves that reform requires persistence and reexamination on a regular basis. The Westchester story does demonstrate that at one point in time, in one county, in one state, all of the pieces were put together and all of the portals tapped to ensure the healthy development of children in the child welfare system, thus proving that this is a doable task.

Epilogue

This book began with Jenny's story in the introduction and it ends with the stories of Jason, John, Raymond, Mira, Alexandra, and Mike in the case studies. Although Jenny and Mike, for example, were born only a few miles apart and both were subjected to neglect, drugs, and violence, their lives have been quite distinct. This difference is not due to the decade between their births; rather, it is due to the different approaches in their cases. For years, Jenny remained off the radar screen of everyone in her life—her family, caseworkers, judges, and lawyers. In contrast, from Mike's first encounter with child welfare services, many professionals—caseworkers, a judge, evaluators, pediatricians, and early interventionists—focused on his healthy development and helped his mother learn to address his needs. Through the keen oversight of a concerned and committed judge in partnership with a strong child welfare system, Mike received a wealth of targeted early intervention (EI) and other services and direct parent–child training that not only led to reunification, but also to enhanced healthy development. His health and developmental needs were interconnected with his need to grow up in a healthy, reunited family. In addition, Jason, John, Raymond, and Mira, also profiled in this book, had their prospects for healthy development or well-being augmented through intense child-focused interventions that supported their needs for permanency. Yet, sadly, many young children involved in the child welfare system nationwide have life experiences that are more reflective of the course of Jenny's life.

In essence, this book is about ensuring that the positive outcomes of children profiled here become the life trajectory of *all* infants and toddlers who enter the child welfare system. The data and history stack the deck against this positive outcome. A large cohort of infants and toddlers entering care—one third of all children—will spend large chunks of their childhood in the limbo of foster care and, thus, compromise their healthy development. In addition, the pendulum of history swings in response to scandal, often resulting only in safety reforms and ignoring the interconnections of safety, permanency, well-being, or healthy development.

Yet, as emphasized in this book, the research and the law provide a path to reverse this grim prognosis. That path is paved by a few evidence-based stepping stones—the presence of an available, stable, and loving family; the delivery of basic and consistent health care; the provision of two-generation EI services to ameliorate any developmental delays or disabilities; and the enrollment in a comprehensive early childhood education program. However, the existence of disparate, unconnected interventions does not ensure the healthy development of these most vulnerable children. Both pillars of child welfare decision making—the court and the child welfare system—must fulfill their mandated roles. Child welfare must develop and implement effective case plans to put together all of the necessary service and support pieces, and the court must keep a tight rein on the case by ordering early evaluations, reviewing the adequacy of case plans, and overseeing compliance against a backdrop of expedited decision making.

At its heart, this is an advocacy book. It sounds an alarm about the enormous needs of thousands of very young children. It also tries to blaze a trail shaped by the research and the law to ensure their healthy development. By identifying portals for healthy development or entry points that can open a host of services, this book shines a spotlight on a critical task. Three case studies focus on a portal for healthy development—the courts, the health care system, and the EI system. One additional case study contains a plea for development of a new and emergent portal—early childhood education. Finally, the last chapter highlights how one jurisdiction at one point in time was able to put all four portals—the courts, health care, EI, and early childhood education—together in concert with child welfare to begin to improve the life prospects of young children such as Mike. By putting together the pieces, Mike not only received needed interventions, but his family was stabilized and strengthened, which improved the odds that he will have a bright future.

The case studies demonstrate that creating portals for healthy development is a doable task. This task takes years of persistence by many committed people working inside and outside of government. At the outset, it requires a champion—sometimes only one person—who understands the problem as well as the research and the law. That person can galvanize new colleagues and together they can forge solutions. To highlight the problem and spotlight the solutions, they can use a multistrategic approach—studies, articles, presentations, administrative and legislative lobbying, media work, and litigation.

Yet, even after attaining paper victories, implementation is not achieved until a partner working inside the child welfare or court systems embraces the reform. These victories are fragile, too, and can be overwhelmed by the historic swings of scandal and reform, which often focus only on safety rather than its interconnection to healthy development. They can also be plagued by the predictable change in key players inside government. Thus, persistence is the hallmark of successful advocacy and is, perhaps, the most enduring requirement of all. In some ways, only through a lifetime of commitment by a changing group of people can we ensure young children's prospects to grow up healthy in a strong and stable family. This is critical because only through a concerted, targeted effort can we reverse the odds and ensure the healthy development of America's most vulnerable children—young children in the child welfare system.

Postscript

As this book went to press, President Bush signed into law the Fostering Connections to Success and Increasing Adoptions Act of 2008 (PL 110-351). This Act is the first major child welfare legislation enacted since the Adoption and Safe Families Act (ASFA) of 1997 (PL 105-89). Since its provisions provide important new tools to improve outcomes for children in the child welfare system, it is necessary to briefly summarize its key provisions.

The new Act grants states more flexibility in the use of federal funds, including options to develop kinship guardianship assistance programs and to expand foster care for American children age 18 to age 21 who are in school, working, or cannot so participate due to a medical condition. It also increases access to federal funds for American Indian children, allows states to use federal funds for expanded training of child welfare personnel, kinship relatives, and court staff, and improves access to special needs adoptions. The Act further contains provisions to promote educational stability for school-age children by enabling them to remain in their original school (school at time of placement) and allows federal funds to be used for transportation to that school. In addition, it requires states to develop health oversight and coordination plans and to exercise reasonable efforts to place siblings together. A new, modest program for family connection grants is also established. While many of the provisions of this new law focus on older children, some of the new Act's components add new tools to enhance the healthy development of young children in the child welfare system.

KINSHIP GUARDIANSHIP ASSISTANCE

Affording states the option to develop kinship guardianship assistance programs is the central provision of the new Act. States will be able to tap federal funds for such programs at the same rate as foster care. This provision is supported by new research findings of increased placement stability and decreased behavior problems for children living with relatives (Rubin et al., 2008). By establishing a kinship guardianship assistance program, Congress enables children across the nation to access this permanency option. Several states have enacted kinship guardianship programs either through federal waivers or through the use of state funds (Rubin 2008). This law ensures the availability of this option to all children in foster care across the country. Since kinship guardianship assistance cannot exceed foster care payments, this provision is revenue neutral. Indeed, it will most likely result in considerable fiscal savings since legal guardianship ends oversight by the court and child welfare staff.

This provision will permit states to use federal child welfare funds for payment for children eligible for foster care who have been raised by relative caretakers for 6 consecutive months. To be eligible for kinship guardianship assistance, a permanent return home and adoption must be ruled out as options. Most significantly, a child must demonstrate a strong attachment to the relative caregiver and that prospective kinship guardian must have a strong commitment to caring permanently for the child. A kinship guardian must pass a criminal records check but states may waive on a case-by-case basis non–safety deviations from strict licensing standards, such as the number of rooms in the house. Kinship guardians will be eligible for up to $2,000 for expenses associated with obtaining guardianship (presumably for legal fees and costs). Child stability will further be strengthened by the requirement that states notify relatives within 30 days of a child's placement into foster care about the options of foster care, kinship guardianship, and adoption assistance.

Although this provision contains ingredients for improving the lives of young children in foster care by enhancing their prospects for growing up in a stable home, it does contain some hidden problems. First, the long-term physical and emotional capacity of relatives has always been a concern hovering behind kinship placements. Second, by creating this new option, children may inadvertently lose important supports and services such as health care requirements and oversight, new educational stability rights, and access to legal counsel. The oversight of the court to ensure receipt of crucial early intervention, health, and educational services also will be eliminated. This result can be mitigated by ensuring that young children are enrolled in the vital services highlighted in this book—ongoing and continuous health care, early intervention, and early childhood education—prior to finalization of guardianship, and that kinship guardianship agreements and court orders are carefully crafted to provide mechanisms to continue those services. The interconnection between young children's healthy development and permanency is a key lesson of this book, and without those necessary services it will be far more difficult for families to stay together and for young children to grow up healthy in permanent homes.

OVERSIGHT OF HEALTH CARE

The new Act provides an additional tool to ensure the provision of health care to children in foster care. While all children in foster care are eligible for Medicaid and Early Periodic Screening Diagnosis and Treatment's (EPSDT's) comprehensive assessment, screenings, and follow-up care, many children are not receiving these services. In fact, health care for children in foster care resembles a nationwide checkerboard, with few states fully implementing the law and only a few jurisdictions providing high-quality care (Blatt et al., 1997; Georgetown University Child Development Center, 2000). The problem as discussed in this book is not the lack of legal requirements or standards for medical practice but rather the ineffective implementation of those requirements (American Academy of Pediatrics, 2000; Child Welfare League of America 1988, 2007).

The new act requires states to develop a plan in consultation with pediatricians and other experts for oversight and coordination of health care for children in foster care. The plan must describe how health needs will be identified and addressed; how medical information will be shared and updated, including the use of electronic records; the steps to ensure continuity of care including the possible development of medical homes; and a method for oversight of medication.

Requiring that states develop a plan for oversight and coordination of health care compels states to address this central but often ignored problem. As in the case of CAPTA and IDEA that mandated state plans for referral to EI (see Chapter 5), requiring a state plan for health care implementation also can provide an important hook to ensure compliance. It provides a vehicle for child advocates, pediatricians, parents, and child policy makers to compel state attention to health care by mandating the convening of stakeholders and the development and implemention of the federally required state plan. This plan will function as a blueprint for monitoring by facilitating implementation, observation, and data collection as well as the flagging and resolution of problems. Shining a spotlight on health care will improve outcomes for the youngest children in foster care.

OTHER IMPORTANT PROVISIONS FOR YOUNG CHILDREN

The new act strengthens young children's access for special needs adoption subsidies by ensuring the automatic eligibility of children who met the disability standards for Supplemental Security Income (SSI; Title XIX of the Social Security Act). While this latter provision will help the children with the most severe disabilities, other children with physical, medical, or emotional disabilities will also be eligible for the program if they could not be adopted without this assistance. These requirements will be of great importance to children under the age of 3 since a majority have serious medical conditions or developmental disabilities and better access to special needs adoption assistance will enhance their prospects for permanency.

Two other provisions have the potential to promote the healthy development of young children in the child welfare system. First, federal funds can be used to provide short-term training, not only for child welfare personnel but also for kinship guardians, court personnel, attorneys, and court appointed special advocates (CASAs). This is important because training can introduce these players to the important issues of infant health and development that are crucial to the lives of young children in the child welfare system. States can now develop training programs that target the youngest children and provide valuable information about the interconnection of their health, development and permanency. Second, a new federal program for family connection grants has one provision aimed at young children. It would allow states to develop residential programs for mothers and children that can include substance abuse treatment, early intervention, health care, and early childhood education programs. This two-generation approach holds great promise for advancing the healthy development of babies in the child welfare system.

Accordingly, the new law provides readers of this book some important new tools to improve outcomes for babies in the child welfare system. Utilizing these new strategies will advance the health care of the youngest children adrift in the child welfare system. Understanding the new funding flexibility given to states will facilitate the development of kinship guardianship, improve special needs adoption assistance, create infant-targeted training programs and new residential options for mothers and children, and will thereby spotlight the needs of young children in the child welfare system.

References

Abandoned Babies Increasing in City: 74 Brought into Foundling Hospital This Year. (1943, December 23). *The New York Times.* Retrieved February 14, 2008, from http://libmma.org/portal/new-york-times-historical-newspapers-from-proquest-1851-2003/

An Abandoned Pair of Twins. (1877, September 5). *The New York Times* (1857–Current file), p. 5. Retrieved March 5, 2008, from http://libmma.org/portal/new-york-times-historical-newspapers-from-proquest-1851-2003/

Administration on Children, Youth, and Families, Commissioner's Office of Research and Evaluation and the Head Start Bureau. (2001a). *Building their futures: How early Head Start programs are enhancing the lives of infants and toddlers in low-income families: Summary report.* Washington, DC: U.S. Department of Health and Human Services. Retrieved January 20, 2008, from http://www.eric.ed.gov/ERICDocs/data/ericdocs2sql/content_storage_01/0000019b/80/16/c6/28.pdf

Administration on Children, Youth, and Families, Commissioner's Office of Research and Evaluation and the Head Start Bureau. (2001b). *Head start family and child experiences survey. Third progress report.* Washington, DC: U.S. Department of Health and Human Services. Retrieved January 15, 2008, from http://www.acf.hhs.gov/programs/opre/hs/faces/reports/perform_3rd_rpt/meas_99_title.html

Adoption and Safe Families Act (ASFA) of 1997, PL 105-89. 2115 Stat. 111. Retrieved January 29, 2009, from GPO Access Online.

Adoption Assistance and Child Welfare Act of 1980, PL 96-272. 94 Stat. 500. Retrieved January 29, 2009, from http://www.ssa.gov/OP_Home/comp2/F096-272.html

Alcott, L.M. (1942). *Little men* (Rev. ed.). London: Little, Brown.

Alexander, J. (2004). *Child welfare early intervention initiative.* Philadelphia: DHS Behavioral Health & Wellness Center.

American Academy of Pediatrics (AAP). (2000). Health care of young children in foster care. *Pediatrics, 109*(3), 536–539.

American Academy of Pediatrics (AAP), Committee on Early Childhood, Adoption and Dependent Care. (2000). Developmental issues for young children in foster care (policy statement). *Pediatrics, 106*(5), 1145–1150.

American Academy of Pediatrics (AAP), Committee on Early Childhood, Adoption and Dependent Care. (2002). Health care of young children in foster care. *Pediatrics, 109*(3), 536–541. Retrieved May 12, 2008, from http://aappolicy.aappublications.org/cgi/reprint/pediatrics;109/3/536.pdf

American Academy of Pediatrics (AAP), District II Task Force on Health Care for Children in Foster Care. (2001). *Fostering health: Health care for children in foster care— A resource manual.* Lake Success, NY: AAP District II.

Angela R. v. Clinton, LR-C-91-415 (E.D. Ark., July 3, 1991).

Appleyard, K., & Berlin, L.J. (2007). Supporting healthy relationships between young children and their parents: Lessons from attachment theory. *Brown University Child and Adolescent Behavior Letter, 23*(5), 1, 4–6.

Arkansas Advocates for Children & Families. (1979). *Arkansas children have problems.* Little Rock, AR: Author.

Arkansas Child Welfare Compliance and Oversight Committee. (1994). *Annual report.* Little Rock, AR: Author.

Arkansas Department of Human Services (DHS). (1995). *DHS professional/consultant services contract with UAMS.* Little Rock, AR: Author.

Baker, H. (1910). Procedure of the Boston Juvenile Court. In C. Henderson, E. Smith, & H.H. Hart (Eds), *Correction and Prevention* (pp. 318–327). Philadelphia: Wm. F. Fell.

Baker, S. (2000). Boarder babies: A second chance for a new beginning. *Emory Medicine.* Retrieved February 12, 2008, from http://whsc.emory.edu/_pubs/em/2000fall/boarder.html

Barth, R.P., Landswerk, J., Chamberlain, P., Reid, J.B., Rolls, J.A., Hurlburt, M.S., et al. (2005). Parent-training programs in child welfare services: Planning for a more evidence-based approach to serving biological parents. *Research on Social Work Practice, 15*, 353. Retrieved January 8, 2008, from http://rsw.sagepub.com/cgi/content/abstract/15/5/353

Bartholet, E. (1999). *Nobody's children: Abuse and neglect, foster drift and the adoption alternative.* Boston: Beacon Press.

Bernstein, N. (2001). *The lost children of Wilder: The epic struggle to change foster care.* New York: Pantheon Books.

Beyer, M. (1999). Parent–child visits as opportunities for change. *National Resource Center for Family-Centered Practice, Prevention Report, 1,* 2–13. Retrieved November 19, 2008, from http://www.uiowa.edu/~nrcfcp/publications/documents/spring1999.pdf

Beyer, M. (2008). Visit coaching: Building on family strengths to meet children's needs. *Juvenile & Family Court Journal, 59*(1), 47–60.

Black, T. (Producer), & Washington, D. (Director). (2002). *Antwone Fisher* [Motion picture]. United States: Fox Searchlight Pictures & Mundy Lane Entertainment.

Blatt, S.D., Saletsky, R.D., Meguid, V., Church, C.C., O'Hara, M.T., Haller-Peck, S.M., et al. (1997). A comprehensive, multidisciplinary approach to providing health care for children in out-of-home care. *Child Welfare, 76*(2), 331–347. Retrieved December 6, 2008, from http://www.proquest.com/en-US/catalogs/databases/detail/pq_career_tech_ed.shtml

Blatt, S.D., & Simms, M. (1997). Foster care: Special children, special needs. *Contemporary Pediatrics, 14*(4), 109–129.

Bradbury, D.E., & Eliot, M.M. (1956). *Four decades of action for children: A short history of the Children's Bureau.* Retrieved February 28, 2008, from http://www.ssa.gov/history/pdf/child1.pdf

Bremner, R.H. (Ed.). (1970–1974). *Children and youth in America: A documentary history* (Vols. 1–3). Cambridge, MA: Harvard University Press.

Bricker, D., & Squires, J. (with Mounts, L., Potter, L., Nickel, R., Twombly, E., & Farrell, J.). (1999). *Ages & Stages Questionnaires® (ASQ): A parent-completed, child-monitoring system* (2nd ed.). Baltimore: Paul H. Brookes Publishing Co.

Bronte, C. (2003). *Jane Eyre* (Rev. ed.). New York: Dover Publications.

Burley, M., & Halpern, M. (2001). *Educational attainment of foster youth: Achievement and graduation outcomes for children in state care.* Retrieved December 14, 2008, from http://www.wsipp.wa.gov/rptfiles/FCEDReport.pdf

Center for the Study of Social Policy. (1998). *1997 assessment of the progress of the Arkansas department of human services (DHS) division of child and family services (DCFS) in meeting the requirements of the Angela R. settlement agreement decree at 16,20.*

Center on the Developing Child at Harvard University. (2007). *A science-based framework for early childhood policy: Using evidence to improve outcomes in learning, behavior, and health for vulnerable children.* Retrieved January 10, 2008, from http://www.developingchild.harvard.edu

Chahine, Z. (2006). *Factors for consideration in selecting a recruited foster/adoptive home for an infant meeting Babies Can't Wait criteria.* New York: Administration for Children Services.

Chernoff, R., Combs-Orme, T., Risley-Curtiss, C., & Heisler, A. (1994). Assessing the health status of children entering foster care. *Pediatrics, 93*(4), 594.

Child Abuse Prevention and Treatment Act (CAPTA), PL 93-247 42 U.S.C § 5101 (1974), sec 3. Retrieved November 19, 2008 from http://thomas.loc.gov/cgi-bin/bdquery/z?d093:SN01191:TOM:/bss/d093query.html

Child Welfare Information Gateway. (2006). *Child abuse and neglect fatalities: Statistics and intervention.* Retrieved November 11, 2007, from http://www.childwelfare.gov/pubs/factsheets/fatality.cfm

Child Welfare Information Gateway. (2007a). *Addressing the needs of young children in child welfare: Part C–Early intervention services.* Washington, DC: U.S. Department of Health and Human Services.

Child Welfare Information Gateway. (2007b). *Infant safe haven laws.* Retrieved November 13, 2008, from http://www.childwelfare.gov/systemwide/laws_policies/statutes/safehaven.cfm

Child Welfare Information Gateway. (2008a). *Types.* Retrieved November 13, 2008, from http://www.childwelfare.gov/can/types/

Child Welfare Information Gateway. (2008b). *Child abuse and neglect fatalities: Statistics and intervention.* Retrieved November 19, 2008, from http://www.childwelfare.gov/pubs/factsheets/fatality.cfm

Child Welfare League of America. (1988). *Standards for health care service for children in out-of-home care.* Washington, DC: Author.

Child Welfare League of America. (2007). *Standards for health care for children in out-of-home care.* Washington, DC: Author.

Children's Bureau, Child and Family Services Review. (2007). *Fact sheet.* Silver Spring, MD: Child Welfare Review Projects. Retrieved on March 11, 2008, from http://www.acf.hhs.gov/programs/cb/cwmonitoring/recruit/cfsrfactsheet.htm

Children's Bureau, Child and Family Services Review. (n.d). *Fact sheet for governors.* Retrieved March 11, 2008, from http://ncsacw.samhsa.gov/files/Governors%20Fact%20Sheet.pdf

Children's Defense Fund. (2005). *Head start basics.* Retrieved March 25, 2008, from http://www.childrensdefense.org/site/DocServer/headstartbasics2005.pdf?docID=616

[The] City's way with its waifs: About 200 abandoned babies are cared for every year. (1936, April 19). *The New York Times.* Retrieved February 14, 2008, from http://libmma.org/portal/new-york-times-historical-newspapers-from-proquest-1851-2003/

Cohen, J. (2005). *Meeting minutes for January 27, 2005.* Philadelphia: Subcommittee on Children in Substitute Care of the Pennsylvania Children's Health Coalition.

Cohen, J., & Youcha, V. (2004). Zero to three: Critical issues for the juvenile and family court. *Juvenile & Family Court Journal, 55*(2), 15–27.

Collins, G. (2007, September 3). Glimpses of heartache, and stories of survival. *The New York Times.* Retrieved March 5, 2008, from http://www.nytimes.com/2007/09/03/nyregion/03foundling.html?_r=1&st=cse&sq=%22glimpses+of+heartache%22&scp=1&oref=slogin#

Community Oversight Board. (2007, December 31). *Assessment of progress made by Philadelphia Department of Human Services in implementing child welfare reforms.* Retrieved April 14, 2008, from http://dhs.phila.gov/dhsphilagovp.nsf/c29e6584de1 379954a2566d500000bf0/885457bc0513ca5285257426007bcbf9/$FILE/COB Report.pdf

Condry, S.M., & Lazar, I. (1982). American values and social policy for children. *Annals of the American Academy of Political and Social Science, 461,* 21–31.

Cook, B.W. (1993). *Eleanor Roosevelt (Vol. 1): 1884–1933.* New York: Penguin Books.

Courtney, M.E., Piliavin, I., Grogan-Kaylor, A., & Nesmith, A. (1998). *Foster youth transitions to adulthood: Outcomes 12 to 18 months after leaving out-of-home care.* Unpublished manuscript, Institute for Research on Poverty, University of Wisconsin-Madison.

CureMD. (2007, May 2). *WIHD partners with CureMD to co-develop integrated foster care EMR.* Retrieved May 22, 2008, from http://www.curemd.com/news2007May2.html

Daley, S. (1987, April 25). Group foster homes spark a debate. *The New York Times.* Retrieved March 5, 2008, from http://libmma.org/portal/new-york-times-historical-newspapers-from-proquest-1851-2003/

Daley, S. (1987, June 13). Foster babies' hospital stays limited: New York City must remove all of the healthy infants by Dec. 1. *The New York Times.* Retrieved March 5, 2008, from http://libmma.org/portal/new-york-times-historical-newspapers-from-proquest-1851-2003/

Department of Human Services/Early Intervention. (2006). *Interagency Agreement.* Author.

DHS to overhaul child welfare. (1991, August 28). *Arkansas Democrat-Gazette.* Retrieved May 13, 2008, from LexisNexis Academic.

Dickens, C. (1970). *Oliver Twist* (Rev. ed.). New York: Random House. (Original work published in serial form from 1837–1839)

Dicker, S. (1999). The promise of early intervention for foster children and their families. *Interdisciplinary report on at risk children and families.* Retrieved March 15, 2008, from http://www.courts.state.ny.us/ip/justiceforchildren/PDF/promiseearly intervention.pdf

Dicker, S., & Crary, D. (1990). *Reforming the Arkansas juvenile justice system. Stepping stones: Successful advocacy for children.* New York: Foundation for Child Development.

Dicker, S., & Gordon, E. (2000). Harnessing the hidden influences of the courts to enhance the healthy development of foster children. *Protecting children: Children birth to three in foster care, 16*(1). Retrieved March 31, 2008, from https://www.courts.state. ny.us/ip/justiceforchildren/PDF/harnessinghiddeninfluence.pdf

Dicker, S., & Gordon, E. (2004a). Opening the door to early intervention for abused and neglected children: A new CAPTA requirement. *Child Law Practice, 23*(4). Retrieved

March 31, 2008, from http://www.nycourts.gov/ip/justiceforchildren/PDF/CAPTA%20ABA%20Article.pdf

Dicker, S., & Gordon, E. (2004b). Building bridges for babies in foster care: The babies can't wait initiative. *Juvenile and Family Court Journal, 55*(2), 29–44. Retrieved March 31, 2008 from http://www.nationalcasa.org/download/Judges_Page/0510_building_bridges_for_babies_0036.pdf

Dicker, S., & Gordon, E. (2004c). *Ensuring the health development of infants in foster care: A guide for judges, advocates, and child welfare professionals.* Washington, DC: ZERO TO THREE Policy Center.

Dicker, S., & Gordon, E. (2006). Critical connections for children who are abused and neglected: Harnessing the new federal referral provisions for early intervention. *Infants & Young Children, 19*(3), 170–178.

Dicker, S., Gordon, E., & Knitzer, J. (2001). *Improving the odds for the healthy development of young children in foster care.* New York: National Center for Children in Poverty, Columbia University.

Dicker, S., & Schall, E. (1996). The courts' role beyond the courtroom: A case study of New York's permanent judicial commission for children and early intervention. *Children's Legal Rights Journal, 16*(4). Retrieved April 22, 2008, from http://www.nycourts.gov/ip/justiceforchildren/PDF/courtsrolebeyondcourtroom.pdf

Dozier, M., Dozier, D., & Manni, M. (2002). Recognizing the special needs of infants' and toddlers' foster parents: Development of a relational intervention. *Zero to Three Bulletin, 22,* 7–13. Early Head Start, Administration for Children & Families (ACF). (n.d.). *About us.* Retrieved May 6, 2008, from http://www.ehsnrc.org/AboutUs/ehs.htm

Dozier, M., & Lindhiem, O. (2006). This is my child: Differences among foster parents in commitment to their young children. *Child Maltreatment, 2*(4), 338–345.

Dozier, M., Stovall, K., Albus, K., & Bates, B. (2001). Attachment for infants in foster care: The role of caregiver state of mind. *Child Development, 72*(5), 1467–1477.

Early Head Start, Administration for Children & Families (ACF). (n.d.). *About us.* Retrieved May 6, 2008, from http://www.ehsnrc.org/AboutUs/ehs.htm

Early Head Start National Resource Center. (n.d.). *Child welfare services and early head start initiative Retrieved March 6, 2008, from* http://www.ehsnrc.org/highlights/child-welfare.htm

Education for All Handicapped Children Act of 1975, PL 94-142, 20 U.S.C. §§ 1400 *et seq.*

Education of the Handicapped Act Amendments of 1986, PL 99-457, 20 U.S.C. §§ 1400 *et seq.*

Elfman, M.S. (2007). *Qualitative review of extended stay clients in TFC* (internal report). Philadelphia Department of Human Services.

Evans, A. (2006). *Revised policy and procedure guide for accessing EI: Series for children under age 5.* Philadelphia, PA: Philadelphia Department of Human Services.

Evans, L.D., Scott, S.S., & Schultz, E.G. (2004). The need for education assessment of children entering foster care. *Child Welfare, 83*(6), 565.

Evans, O. (1987, April 1). Boarder babies find comfort in foster grandparents' arms. *The New York Times.* Retrieved March 5, 2008, from ProQuest Historical Newspapers *The New York Times* (1851–2004) database.

Faster track for the boarder babies. (1986, December 25). *The New York Times.* Retrieved March 5, 2008, from ProQuest Historical Newspapers *The New York Times* (1851–2004) database.

Felitti, V.J., Anda, R.F., Nordenberg, D., Williamson, D.F., Spitz, A.M., Edwards, V., et al. (1998). Relationship of childhood abuse and household dysfunction to many of the leading causes of death in adults: The adverse childhood experiences (ACE) study. *American Journal of Preventive Medicine, 14*(4), 245–258. Retrieved December 15, 2008, from http://www.csac.counties.org/images/public/Advocacy/hhs/ace_study.pdf

Fisher, A.Q. (2002). *Finding fish: A memoir.* New York: HarperCollins.

Folks, H. (1940). Four milestones of progress. *Annals of the American Academy of Political and Social Science, 212,* 12–17.

Folks, H. (1978). *The care of destitute, neglected and delinquent children.* New York: National Association of Social Workers.

Fostering Connections to Success and Increasing Adoptions Act of 2008 (PL 110-351).

Fox, S. (1996). The early history of the court. *The Future of Children, 6*(3), 29–39.

Georgetown University Child Development Center. (2000, November 29–30). *The family program: Westchester institute for human development.* Retrieved May 1, 2008, from http://gucchd.georgetown.edu/files/products_publications/fcsvwestchester.pdf

Goerge, R.M., Van Voorhis, J., Grant, S., Casey, K., & Robinson, M. (1992). Special-education experiences of foster children: An empirical study. *Child Welfare, 71*(5), 419. Retrieved March 6, 2008, from Career and Technical Education database.

Goerge, R., & Wulczyn, F. (1998). Placement experiences of the youngest foster care population: Findings from the multistate foster care data archive. *Zero to Three, 19*(3), 8–13.

Gold, R. (2008). Developmental evaluation and early intervention referral policy. *Office of Children, Youth and Families Bulletin.* Philadelphia: Pennsylvania Department of Public Welfare.

Gray, H. (2008). *Complete little orphan Annie* (Vol 1). San Diego: IDW Publishing.

Gross, J. (1985, July 1). AIDS: Children struggle with tragic legacy *The New York Times.* Retrieved March 5, 2008, from http://libmma.org/portal/new-york-times-historical-newspapers-from-proquest-1851-2003/

Gross, J. (1987, May 8). Babies to have AIDS center in Harlem: Center in Harlem established for 15 infant AIDS patients. *The New York Times.* Retrieved March 5, 2008, http://libmma.org/portal/new-york-times-historical-newspapers-from-proquest-1851-2003/

Guralnick, M., & Albertini, G. (2005). Early intervention in an international perspective. *Journal of Policy and Practice in Intellectual Disabilities, 3*(1), 1–2.

Guralnick, M.J. (2006). The system of early intervention for children with developmental disabilities. In J.W. Jacobson, J.A. Mulick, & J. Rojahn (Eds.), *Handbook of mental retardation and developmental disabilities* (pp. 465–480). New York: Plenum.

Hacsi, T. (1995). From indenture to family foster care: A brief history of child placing. *Child Welfare, 74*(1), 162. Retrieved March 5, 2008, from ProQuest Career and Technical Education database.

Halfon N., Mendonca, A., & Berkowitz, G. (1995). Health status of children in foster care. *Archives of Pediatrics and Adolescent Medicine, 149*(4), 386–392.

Harden, B.J. (2007). *Infants in the child welfare system: A developmental framework for policy and practice.* Washington, DC: ZERO TO THREE.

Hart, B., & Risley, T.R. (1995). *Meaningful differences in the everyday experience of young American children.* Baltimore: Paul H. Brookes Publishing Co.

Head Start Reauthorization Act of 1994, PL 103-252, 42 U.S.C. §§ 9831 *et seq.*

Heidt, J. (1995). *A profile of the foster care population of New York state and survey of key actors in the child welfare system.* New York: Permanent Judicial Commission on Justice for Children.

High/Scope. (2005). *High/Scope Perry Preschool study.* Retrieved May 20, 2008, from

Hinden, B., Biebel, K., Nicholson, J., Henry, A., & Stier, L. (2002). *Steps toward evidence-based practices for parents with mental illness and their families.* Rockville, MD: Center for Mental Health Services Substance Abuse and Mental Health Services Administration.

Hochstadt, N.J., Jaudes, P.K., Zimo, D.A., & Schachter, J. (1987). The medical and psychosocial needs of children entering foster care. *Child Abuse & Neglect, 11*, 53–62.

Horne, R.L. (1996). *The education of children and youth with special needs.* National Information Center for Children and Youth With Disabilities. Retrieved March 21, 2008, from http://www.nichcy.org/pubs/outprint/nd15txt.htm

Hudson, L., Klain, E., Smariga, M., & Youcha, V. (2007). *Healing the youngest children: Model court–community partnerships.* Washington, DC: ZERO TO THREE Policy Center.

Huttenlocher, J., Haight, W., Bryk, A., Seltzer, M., & Lyons, T. (1991). Early vocabulary growth: Relation to language input and gender. *Development Psychology 27*(2), 236–248.

Illinois Department of Children & Family Services. (2006). *Illinois school readiness initiative: Key strategies for young children in the child welfare system.* Retrieved November 14, 2008 from http://www.strengtheningfamiliesillinois.org/downloads/ISRI_Hand out1.pdf

Improving Head Start for School Readiness Act of 2007, PL 110-134, H.R. 1429, S. 556.

Individuals with Disabilities Education Act Amendments (IDEA) of 1997, PL 105-17, 20 U.S.C. §§ 1400 *et seq.*

Individuals with Disabilities Education Improvement Act (IDEA) of 2004, PL 108-446, 20 U.S.C. §§ 1400 *et seq.*

Iverem, E. (1987, May 31). Rise seen in boarder babies, but more are finding homes. *The New York Times.* Retrieved March 5, 2008, from http://libmma.org/portal/new-york-times-historical-newspapers-from-proquest-1851-2003/

Jaffe, N. (1965, January 17). Adoption agency cuts city's costs: Gets homes for 550 babies abandoned by parents. *The New York Times.* Retrieved March 5, 2008, from ProQuest Historical Newspapers *The New York Times* (1851–2004) database.

James Bell Associates. (2006). *Briefing on the early head start/child welfare services initiative.* Retrieved November 14, 2008 from http://www.jbassoc.com/reports/documents/slides %20acyf%20briefing%20ehs.pdf

Jaudes, P.K., & Shapiro, L.D. (1999). Child abuse and developmental disabilities. In J.A. Silver, B.J. Amster, & T. Haecker (Eds.), *Young children and foster care: A guide for professionals* (pp. 213–234). Baltimore: Paul H. Brookes Publishing Co.

Johnson, K., & Kaye, N. (2003). *Using Medicaid to support young children's healthy mental development.* Portland, ME: National Academy for State Health Policy.

Kahn, A. (1953). *The court for children: A study of New York City's children's court.* New York: Columbia University Press.

Katz, M. (1986). *In the shadow of the poorhouse: A social history of welfare in America.* New York: Basic Books.

Kaye, J., Schall, E., Dicker, S., Nadel, S., & Kennedy, P. (1996). *A good place for children: A guide to starting, building and operating children's centers for New York's courts.* New York: Permanent Judicial Commission on Justice for Children.

Keeping Children and Families Safe Act of 2003, PL 108-36. 25 June 2003. Retrieved November 19, 2008 from http://thomas.loc.gov/cgi-bin/bdquery/z?d108:SN00342: TOM:/bss/d108query.html

Keesee, S. (1991, March 15). Clinton rejects jump in child welfare fund. *Arkansas Democrat-Gazette*. Retrieved May 13, 2008 from LexisNexis Academic.

Kelley, T. (2008, March 5). Parents in crisis have many options for giving babies haven, officials say. *The New York Times*. November 19, 2008, from http://www.nytimes.com/ 2008/03/05/nyregion/05baby.html

Kempe, C., Silverman, F., Steelle, B., Droegemueller, W., & Silver, H. (1962). The battered-child syndrome. *JAMA, 181,* 17–24.

Kerr, P. (1986, August 25). Babies of crack users fill hospital nurseries: Crack users' babies crowding hospital nurseries. *The New York Times*. Retrieved March 5, 2008, from http://libmma.org/portal/new-york-times-historical-newspapers-from-proquest-1851-2003/

Kids Well-Being Indicators Clearinghouse. (2008). *Child welfare region profile: Westchester County*. Retrieved May 22, 2008, from http://www.nyskwic.org/access_data/region_ profile.cfm?countyID=36119&profileType=2&region2.x=4&region2.y=6&region2 =Submit

Kortenkamp, K., & Macomber, J.E. (2002, January 15). *The well-being of children involved with the child welfare system: A national overview.* Washington, DC: The Urban Institute. Retrieved November 15, 2008, from http://www.urban.org/url.cfm? ID=310413

Kramer, R. (1965, October 24). Retarded child: What to do. *The New York Times*. Retrieved March 5, 2008, from http://libmma.org/portal/new-york-times-historical-newspapers-from-proquest-1851-2003/

Laws of New York. (1962). *Chapter 428. Early intervention services for infants and toddlers with disabling conditions.*

Laws of New York. (1993). *Chapter 231. Early intervention services for infants and toddlers with disabling conditions.*

Laws of New York. (2005*). Chapter 3, Permanency Bill.* Retrieved May 12, 2008, from http://ocfs.state.ny.us/main/legal/legislation/permanency/Chapter3Permanency.pdf

Legal Services Corporation Act Amendments of 1977, PL 95-222. (1977) U.S.C. §2996 *et. seq.* Retrieved February 27, 2009, from https://www.oig.lsc.gov/legis/lscact.htm

Lieberman, A.F., Silverman, R., & Pawl, J.H. (2005). *Infant–parent psychotherapy: Core concepts and current approaches.* In C. Zeanah (Ed.), *Handbook of infant mental health* (2nd ed.). New York: Guilford Press.

Lombardi, J., & Bogle, M. (Eds.). (2004). *Beacon of hope: The promise of Early Head Start for America's youngest children.* Washington, DC: ZERO TO THREE.

Lowe, A. (2003). *Factors to consider in selecting a recruited pre-adoptive foster home in which to place an infant coming into care alone with no siblings already in care.* Unpublished manuscript.

Lyall, S. (1988, June 21). Agency's family court work faulted. *The New York Times*. Retrieved April 22, 2008, from http://libmma.org/portal/new-york-times-historical-newspapers-from-proquest-1851-2003/

Mallon, G., & Hess, P. (Eds.). (2005). *Child welfare for the 21st century: A handbook of practices, policies and programs.* New York: Columbia University Press.

Martin, N. (1993). Who is she? *Mother Jones, 18*(6), 34.

Matthews, M. (1992). Major victory for Arkansas children. *Youth Law News.*

McCarthy J. (2002). *Meeting the health care needs of children in the foster care system: Summary of state and community efforts: Key findings.* Washington, DC: Georgetown University Child Development Center. Retrieved November 17, 2008, from http://gucchd.georgetown.edu/files/products_publications/fcsummary.pdf

McDonald, M. (1997). *The role and responsibility of New York's children's court.* Unpublished paper for the Permanent Judicial Commission on Justice for Children.

Medicaid Early and Periodic Screening, Diagnosis and Treatment Act Amendments of 1989, Omnibus Budget Reconciliation Act of 1989, PL 101-239, 42 U.S.C. §§ 1396 *et seq.*

Morris, E. (1979). *The rise of Theodore Roosevelt.* New York: Ballantine Books.

Morris, S. (1991, August 29). Clinton cites legislature in the delay of child aid. *Arkansas Democrat-Gazette.* Retrieved May 13, 2008, from LexisNexis Academic.

Murray, K.O., & Gesiriech, S. (2004). *A brief legislative history of the child welfare system.* The Pew Comission on Children in Foster Care. Retrieved March 15, 2008, from http://pewfostercare.org/research/docs/Legislative.pdf

National Abandoned Infants Assistance Resource Center. (2005). *Boarder babies: Abandoned infants and discarded infants.* Retrieved February, 21, 2008, from http://aia.berkeley.edu/publications/fact_sheets/boader_defs.php

National Child Welfare Resource Center on Legal and Judicial Issues. (n.d.). *State summaries.* Retrieved May 22, 2008, from http://www.abanet.org/abanet/child/statesum/allstate.cfm?y=2004

National Conference of State Legislatures. (n.d.). *Database search results: Permanency hearings.* Retrieved March 11, 2008, from http://www.ncsl.org/statefed/cf/perm.cfm?stateselect='ALL.'

NECTAC. (2007). *NECTAC list of part C lead agencies.* The National Early Childhood Technical Assistance Center. Retrieved March 23, 2008, from http://www.nectac.org/partc/ptclead.asp

Nelson, C. (2007). A neurobiological perspective on early human deprivation. *Child Development Perspectives, 1*(1), 1, 3–18.

New York State Council on Children and Families and New York State Permanent Judicial Commission on Justice for Children. (2006). *The child in child welfare and the courts: New York State court and child welfare 2006 data book.* Albany. Retrieved March 25, 2008, from http://www.nycourts.gov/ip/justiceforchildren/PDF/FullChildWelfareBook.pdf

New York State Court and New York State Permanent Judicial Commission on Justice for Children. (2006). *The child in child welfare and the courts: New York State court and child welfare 2006 data book.* Albany. Retrieved March 25, 2008, from http://www.nycourts.gov/ip/justiceforchildren/PDF/FullChildWelfareBook.pdf

New York State Family Court Act of 1962. Retrieved November 19, 2008 from http://public.leginfo.state.ny.us/menugetf.cgi?COMMONQUERY=LAWS

New York State Office of Children and Family Services. (2005). *Governor's permanency bill.* Retrieved March 11, 2008, from http://www.ocfs.state.ny.us/main/legal/legislation/permanency/

New York State Senate. (1857, January 9). *Report of the select committee to visit charitable institutions supported by the state, and all city and county poor and work houses and jails.* In Senate, No. 8.

New York State Unified Court System. (2000, December 18). *NY launches nation's first court-based literacy program.* Retrieved April 20, 2008, from http://nycourts.gov/press/pr2000_31.shtml

Nores, M., Belfield, C., Barnett, W., & Schweinhart, L. (2005). Updating the economic impacts of the High/Scope Perry Preschool program. *Educational Evaluation & Policy Analysis, 27*(3), 245–261.

O'Connor, S. (2001). *Orphan trains: The story of Charles Loring Brace and the children he saved and failed.* New York: Houghton Mifflin.

O'Connor, T., Rutter, M., Beckett, C., Keaveney, L., Kreppner, J., & the English and Romanian Adoptees Study Team. (2000). The effects of global severe privation on cognitive competence: Extension and longitudinal follow-up. *Child Development, 71*(2), 376–390.

Office of Children & Family Services. (n.d.). *Chapter 3 of the laws of 2005 Governor's permanency bill.* Retrieved May 22, 2008, from http://www.ocfs.state.ny.us/main/legal/legislation/permanency/

Official Home Page of the Queens Borough President's Office. (n.d.). Retrieved May 1, 2008, from http://www.queensbp.org/

Olmstead, L. (1993, May 18). Courthouse death: One family's tragedy—A special report. When passion explodes into a deadly rage. *The New York Times.* Retrieved April 30, 2008, from ProQuest Historical Newspapers *The New York Times* (1851–2004) database.

Omnibus Budget Reconciliation Act (OBRA) of 1993, PL 103-66, 42 U.S.C. §§ 629 *et seq.*

Parks, G. (2000, October). The High/Scope Perry Preschool project. *Juvenile Justice Bulletin.* Retrieved May 20, 2008, from http://www.ncjrs.gov/html/ojjdp/2000_10_1/contents.html

Parrish, L. (2002, October 10). *Talking points for babies can't wait.* Meeting minutes.

Permanent Judicial Commission on Justice for Children. (1998). Report to the court of appeals on the new court improvement project. Retrieved November 18, 2008, from http://www.nycourts.gov/ip/justiceforchildren/PDF/courtofappealsfirstreport.pdf

Permanent Judicial Commission on Justice for Children. (2003). *Babies Can't Wait phase II proposal to the New York community trust.* Author.

Permanent Judicial Commission on Justice for Children. (2005). *Accomplishments: Fifteen year report.* Retrieved May 22, 2008, from http://www.nycourts.gov/ip/justiceforchildren/PDF/Final%20Booklet%20to%20Print.pdf

Permanent Judicial Commission on Justice for Children. (2006). Final report to the New York community trust: Babies Can't Wait phase II. Author.

Pew Commission on Children in Foster Care. (2004). *Fostering the future: Safety, permanence and well-being for children in foster care.* Retrieved September, 3, 2008,

Polier, J. (1987). *Juvenile justice in double jeopardy: The distanced community and vengeful retribution.* Mahwah, NJ: Lawrence Erlbaum Associates.

Pound, R. (1997). *Criminal justice in America* (Rev. ed.). Edison, NJ: Transaction Publishers.

Project for Child and Adolescent Evaluation (PACE). (2007). *Report to Arkansas Department of Human Services*, Little Rock, AR. Author.

Promoting Safe and Stable Families Act of 2001, PL 107-133. 13. Retrieved November 19, 2008, from http://thomas.loc.gov/cgi-bin/bdquery/z?d107:HR02873:TOM:/bss/d107query.html

Publication Development Committee, Victims of Child Abuse Project. (1995). *Resource guidelines: Improving court practice in child abuse & neglect cases.* National Council of Juvenile and Family Court Judges. Retrieved April 22, 2008, from http://www.ncjfcj. org/content/blogcategory/369/438/

Purnick, J. (1987, April 22). Arson damages disputed foster home in Queens. *The New York Times.* Retrieved March 5, 2008, from from http://libmma.org/portal/new-york-times-historical-newspapers-from-proquest-1851-2003/

Reynolds, A., Temple, J., Ou, S., Robertson, D., Mersky, J., Topitzes, J., et al. (2007). Effects of a school-based, early childhood intervention on adult health and well-being. *Archives of Pediatrics & Adolescent Medicine, 161*(8), 730–739.

Risley-Curtiss, C., & Stites, B. (2007). Improving healthcare for children entering foster care. *Child Welfare, 86*(4), 123–144. Retrieved May 12, 2008, from Career and Technical Education database.

River Valley Health Care/DSS. Westchester contract for 2006–2008. (n.d). *Program description.*

Robinson, C., & Rosenberg, S. (2004). Child welfare referrals to part C. *Journal of Early Intervention, 26*(4), 284–291. Retrieved March 23, 2008, from Research Library Database.

Rodham, H. (1973). Children under the law. *Harvard Educational Review, 43,* 487–514.

Rolnick, A., & Grunewald, R. (2003). Early childhood development: Economic development with a high public return. Retrieved November 19, 2008, from http://www. minneapolisfed.org/publications_papers/pub_display.cfm?id=3832

Rosado, L., & Siddique, N. (2001). *Meeting minutes for 20 September 2001.* Subcommittee on Children in Substitute Care of the Pennsylvania Children's Health Coalition.

Rosenbaum, S., Proser, M., Schneider, A., & Sonosky, C. (2001). *Room to grow: Promoting child development through medicaid and CHIP.* Washington, DC: The George Washington University Medical Center, School of Public Health and Health Services, Center for Health Services Research and Policy. Retrieved March 11, 2008, from http://www.commonwealthfund.org/usr_doc/rosenbaum_room_451.pdf?section= 4039

Rosenfeld A.A., Pilowsky D.J., Fine, P., Thorpe, M., Fein, E., Simms, M., et al. (1997). Children in family foster care: An update for child and adolescent psychiatrists. *Journal of the American Academy of Child and Adolescent Psychiatry, 36*(4), 448–457.

Rothman, S., & Rothman, D. (2005). *Willowbrook wars* (Rev. ed). Edison, NJ: Transaction Publishers.

Rubin, D., Downes, K., O'Reilly, A., Mekonnen, R., Luan, X., & Localio, R. (2008). Impact of kinship care on behavioral well-being for children in out-of-home care. *Archives of Pediatrics & Adolescent Medicine, 162*(6), 550–556.

Runyan, D., Wattam, C., Ikeda, R., Hassan, F., & Ramiro, L. (2002). Child abuse and neglect by parents and caregivers. In E. Krug, L. Dahlberg, J. Mercy, A. Zwi, & R. Lozano (Eds.), *World report on violence and health* (pp. 59–86). Geneva, Switzerland: World Health Organization.

Ruptier, N.M. (1997). Ensuring health care for foster children through Medicaid's EPSDT program. *American Journal of Public Health, 87*(2), 290–191.

Ryan, J.P., & Testa, M.F. (2004). *Child maltreatment and juvenile delinquency: Investigating the role of placement and placement instability.* Urbana: Children and Family Research Center, School of Social Work, University of Illinois.

Schneiderman, M., Connors, M.M., Fribourg, A., Gries, L., & Gonzales, M. (1998). Mental health services for children in out-of-home care. *Child Welfare, 77*(1), 29–40. Retrieved March 6, 2008, from ProQuest Career and Technical Education database.

Schulz, E.G., Evans, L.D., & Russell, S.S. (1999). Medical status of children in foster care. *Journal of Investigative Medicine, 47*, 106A.

Schweinhart, L.J. (2000). *Recent evidence on preschool programs.* (Report No. ED458046). Champaign, IL: ERIC Clearinghouse on Elementary and Early Childhood Education. Retrieved January 20, 2008, from http://www.ericdigests.org/2002-2/preschool.htm

Schweinhart, L. (2003, May 21). *Using preschool research to facilitate change.* Engaging Leaders: Building Bright Futures for Young Children Conference Presentation. Retrieved May 20, 2008, from http://www.highscope.org/file/Research/working_papers/Charlotte_2003.pdf

Sheppard-Towner Maternity and Infancy Protection Act of 1921, PL 67-97. 23 November 1921.

Shonkoff, J.P., & Meisels, S.J. (Eds.). (2000). *Handbook of early childhood intervention* (2nd ed.). New York: Cambridge University Press.

Shonkoff, J.P., & Phillips, D.A. (Eds). (2000). *From neurons to neighborhoods: The science of early childhood development.* Washington, DC: National Academies Press.

Shores, E.F. (1998). *Child protective services in Arkansas, 1974–1994: Struggling to meet the needs.* Little Rock: Arkansas Advocates for Children and Families.

Siddique, N. (2002). *Minute Meetings for 28 February 2002.* Subcommittee on Children in Substitute Care of the Pennsylvania Children's Health Coalition.

Silver J. (2002). The accidental advocate: Clinicians and systems change. *Zero to Three Bulletin, 22*, 45–51.

Silver, J.A., Amster, B.J., & Haecker, T. (Eds.). (1999). *Young children and foster care: A guide for professionals.* Baltimore: Paul H. Brookes Publishing Co.

Silver, J., DiLorenzo, P., Zukoski, M., Ross, P., Amster, B.J., & Schlegel, D. (1999). Starting young: Improving the health and developmental outcomes of infants and toddlers in the child welfare system. *Child Welfare, 78*(1), 148–165. Retrieved April 1, 2008, from ProQuest Career and Technical Education database.

Silver, J., Gerdes, M., & Haecker, T. (2001). *A proposal for universal developmental screening for infants and toddlers in foster care.* Philadelphia: Draft Proposal for the Philadelphia Department of Human Services.

Simms, M., Dubowitz, H., & Szilagi, M. (2000). Needs of children in the foster care system. *Journal of the Ambulatory Pediatrics Association in Pediatrics, 106* (Supplement), 909–918.

Smariga, M. (2007). *Visitation with infants and toddlers in foster care: What judges and attorneys need to know.* Washington, DC: ZERO TO THREE.

Smith, E.P. (1995). Bring back the orphanages? What policymakers of today can learn from the past. *Child Welfare, 74*(1), 115. Retrieved March 5, 2008, from ProQuest Career and Technical Education database.

Social Security Act of 1935, PL 74-271, 42 U.S.C. §§ 301 *et seq.*

Social Security Act Title IV. U.S.C §§601–687, IV, 7, 42. Retrieved November 19, 2008, from http://www.ssa.gov/OP_Home/ssact/title04/0400.htm

Social Security Act Title XX U.S.C §§1397-1397f, XX, 7, 42. Retrieved November 19, 2008, from http://www.ssa.gov/OP_Home/ssact/title20/2000.htm#ft1

Social Security Online. (2007). Supplemental security income. SSA Publication no. 05-11000. Retrieved November 17, 2008, from http://www.ssa.gov/pubs/11000.html

Special Committee on Families Meeting. (2000, May 2). *Meeting minutes.* Retrieved on May 22, 2008 from http://www.watpa.org/wcbol/comm/fa/2000/fa000502.htm

Spigner, C.W., Mills, J.W., Cervone, F., Cherna, M., Christian, C.W., Sanders, D., et al. (2007). *Protecting Philadelphia's children: The call to action.* The Child Welfare Review Panel. Retrieved November 17, 2008, from http://inquirer.philly.com/rss/News/dhsreport.pdf

Spiker, D., & Silver, J. (1999). Early intervention services for infants and preschoolers in foster care. In J.A. Silver, B.J. Amster, & T. Haecker (Eds), *Young children and foster care: A guide for professionals,* pp. 347–371. Baltimore: Paul H. Brookes Publishing Co.

Stahmer, A.C., Leslie, L.K., Hurlburt, M., Barth, R.P., Webb, M.B., Landsverk, J., & Zhang, J. (2005). Developmental and behavioral need and service use for young children in child welfare. *Pediatrics, 116.* 891–900.

Stone, S. (2007). Child maltreatment, out-of-home placement and academic vulnerability: A fifteen-year review of evidence and future directions. *Children and Youth Services Review, 29*(2), 139–161.

Subcommittee on Children in Substitute Care. (1999). Health policy recommendations for children in substitute care in Philadelphia. Philadelphia: Pennsylvania Children's Health Coalition.

Subcommittee on Children in Substitute Care. (2000). *Meeting minutes for December 14, 2000.* Author.

Swire, M., & Kavaler, F. (1977). The health status of foster children. *Child Welfare, 56*(10), 635–653.

Takayama, J., Wolfe, E., & Coulter, K. (1998). Relationship between reason for placement and medical findings among children in foster care. *Pediatrics, 101*(2), 201–207.

Townsend, S., & Carroll, K. (2002). System change through collaboration…eight steps for getting from there to here. *Juvenile and Family Court Journal, 53*(4), 19–30.

U.S. Department of Health and Human Services. (2001). *1998 National estimates of the number of boarder babies, abandoned infants, and discarded infants.* Washington, DC: U.S. Government Printing Office. Publication No. 21-10205.

U.S. Department of Health and Human Services, Administration for Children & Families. (2001). Building their futures: How Early Head Start programs are enhancing the lives of infants and toddlers in low-income families: Summary report. Retrieved May 5, 2008, from http://www.acf.hhs.gov/programs/opre/ehs/ehs_resrch/reports/building_summary/building_exesum.pdf

U.S. Department of Health and Human Services, Administration for Children & Families. (2008). *Child maltreatment 2006.* Washington, DC: U.S. Government Printing Office. Retrieved November 11, 2007, from http://www.acf.hhs.gov/programs/cb/pubs/cm06/index.htm

U.S. Department of Health and Human Services, Administration for Children & Families. (n.d.a). *EHS program highlights.* Washington, DC: Early Head Start National Research Center. Retrieved March 27, 2008, from http://www.ehsnrc.org/highlights/child welfare.htm

U.S. Department of Health and Human Services, Administration for Children & Families. (n.d.b). *Abuse, neglect, adoption & foster care research: National survey of child and adolescent well-being (NSCAW), 1997–2010.* Retrieved January 3, 2008, from http://www.acf.hhs.gov/programs/opre/abuse_neglect/nscaw/index.html

U.S. Department of Health and Human Services, Administration for Children & Families, Children's Bureau. (2006). *The AFCARS report: Preliminary FY 2005 estimates as of September 2006.* Retrieved November 12, 2007, from http://www.acf.hhs.gov/programs/cb/stats_research/afcars/tar/report13.htm

U.S. Department of Health and Human Services, Administration for Children & Families, Office of Planning, Research, & Evaluation. (2001). *National survery of child and adolescent well-being (NSCAW) state child welfare agency survey: Report.* Retrieved November 14, 2008 from http://www.acf.hhs.gov/programs/opre/abuse_neglect/nscaw/reports/wellbeing_state_child/wellbeing_state_toc.html

U.S. Department of Health and Human Services, Head Start Bureau. (2007). *Head Start program fact sheet.* Washington, DC: Author. Retrieved March 25, 2008, from http://www.acf.hhs.gov/programs/hsb/about/fy2007.html

U.S. Department of Health and Human Services, National Center on Child Abuse and Neglect. (1994). *Child maltreatment 1992: Reports from the states to the National Center on Child Abuse and Neglect.* Washington, DC: U.S. Government Printing Office.

U.S. General Accounting Office (GAO). (1995, May). *Foster care: Health needs of many young children are unknown and unmet.* Washington, DC: U.S. Government Printing Office. Retrieved May 12, 2008, from http://www.gao.gov/archive/1995/he95114.pdf

U.S. General Accounting Office (GAO). (2001, July). *Medicaid: Stronger efforts needed to ensure children's access to health screening services.* Washington, DC: U.S. General Accounting Office. Retrieved March 11, 2008, from http://www.gao.gov/new.items/d01749.pdf

University of Arkansas Medical School (UAMS) Department of Pediatrics. (1995). *Contract with DHS.*

University of North Carolina, FPG Child Development Institute. (2007, April). Poverty and early childhood intervention. *FPG Snapshot, 42.* Retrieved May 20, 2008, from http://www.fpg.unc.edu/~snapshots/snap42.pdf

Webster-Stratton, C., Reid, M., Stoolmilller, M. (2008). Preventing conduct problems and improving school readiness: Evaluation of the incredible years teacher and child training programs in high-risk schools. *Journal of Child Psychology & Psychiatry, 49*(5), 471–488.

Well babies' care burdens hospitals: Month's drive being made to find families to board 250 healthy infants. (1946, January 15). *The New York Times.* Retrieved March 5, 2008, from ProQuest Historical Newspapers *The New York Times* (1851–2004) database.

Westchester Department of Social Services. (2001-2007). *Discharge to adoption by age group.*

Who could have put it there? (1884, April 21). *The New York Times.* Retrieved March 5, 2008, from ProQuest Historical Newspapers *The New York Times* (1851–2004) database.

Widom, C., & Maxfield, M. (2001) *An update on the cycle of violence. Research in brief.* Washington, DC: U.S. Department of Justice, Office of Justice Programs, National Institute of Justice.

Wingert, P., & Brant, M. (2005, August 15). Reading your baby's mind: New research on infants finally begins to answer the question, What's going on in there? *Newsweek,* 32–35.

Winton, P., Buysse, V., & Hamrick, C. (Eds.). (2006). How FPG got its groove: The Abecedarian story. *Early Developments, 10*(1), 5–10. Retrieved May 20, 2008, from http://www.fpg.unc.edu/~NCEDL/PDFs/ED10_1.pdf

Work of Children's Bureau. (1912, September 29). *The New York Times.* Retrieved June 25, 2008 from http://query.nytimes.com/mem/archive-free/pdf?res=940DE6D 8113AE633A2575AC2A96F9C946396D6CF

Wright, L.E. (2001). *Toolbox no. 1: Using visitation to support permanency.* Washington, DC: CWLA Press.

Wulczyn, F., Barth, R., Yuan, Y., Harden, B., & Landsverk, J. (2005). *Beyond common sense: Child welfare, child well-being, and the evidence for policy reform.* Chicago: Chapin Hall Center for Children, University of Chicago.

Wulczyn, F., Harden, A., & George, R. (1997). *Foster care dynamics 1983–1994: An update from the multistate foster care data archive.* Chicago: Chapin Hall Center for Children, University of Chicago.

Wulczyn, F., & Hislop, K. (2002). Babies in foster care: The numbers call for attention. *Zero to Three Journal. 22*(5), 14–15.

Yardley, J. (1999, December 26). A flurry of baby abandonment leaves Houston wondering why. *The New York Times.* Retrieved March 5, 2008, from http://libmma.org/ portal/new-york-times-historical-newspapers-from-proquest-1851-2003/

Youcha, V. (2005). Ten key facts about the healthy development of infants and toddlers and recommendations to help young foster children thrive. *The Judges' Pages Newsletter.* National Zero to Three. Retrieved on January 2, 2008, from http://www.nationalcasa. org/download/Judges_Page/0510_child_development_and_parenting_issue_0036.pdf

Young victims of AIDS suffer its harsh stigma. (1984, June 17). *The New York Times.* Retrieved March 5, 2008, from from http://libmma.org/portal/new-york-times-historical-newspapers-from-proquest-1851-2003/

Zero to Three Technical Assistance Paper. (2005) *Supporting infants and toddlers in the child welfare system: The hope of early Head Start.* Washington DC: ZERO TO THREE. (Technical Assistance Paper No. 9). Retrieved March 8, 2008, from http://ehsnrc.org/ PDFfiles/TA9.pdf

Zimmer, M.H., & Panko, L.M. (2006). Developmental status and service use among children in the child welfare system: A national survey. *Archives of Pediatrics & Adolescent Medicine, 160*(2), 183–188. Retrieved March 6, 2008, from ProQuest Health Module database.

Index

Page numbers followed by *f* indicate figures.